ESSAYS IN MEDIEVAL PHILOSOPHY AND THEOLOGY IN MEMORY OF WALTER H. PRINCIPE, CSB

Walter H. Principe, CSB (1922-1996)

by permission of the General Archives of the Basilian Fathers in
Toronto

Essays in Medieval Philosophy and Theology in Memory of Walter H. Principe, CSB

Fortresses and Launching Pads

Edited by
JAMES R. GINTHER
St Louis University

and

CARL N. STILL
St Thomas More College

Routledge
Taylor & Francis Group
LONDON AND NEW YORK

First published 2005 by Ashgate Publishing

Reissued 2018 by Routledge
2 Park Square, Milton Park, Abingdon, Oxon OX14 4RN
711 Third Avenue, New York, NY 10017, USA

Routledge is an imprint of the Taylor & Francis Group, an informa business

First issued in paperback 2018

A Library of Congress record exists under LC control number: 2004007848

Notice:
Product or corporate names may be trademarks or registered trademarks, and are used only for identification and explanation without intent to infringe.

Publisher's Note
The publisher has gone to great lengths to ensure the quality of this reprint but points out that some imperfections in the original copies may be apparent.

Disclaimer
The publisher has made every effort to trace copyright holders and welcomes correspondence from those they have been unable to contact.

ISBN 13: 978-0-815-38885-2 (hbk)
ISBN 13: 978-1-138-61959-3 (pbk)
ISBN 13: 978-1-351-15888-6 (ebk)

Contents

List of Contributors

Romanus Cessario, *OP*, is Professor of Theology and Coordinator of the Master of Arts in Theology Program at St John's Seminary in Boston.

Lawrence Dewan, *OP*, is Professor of Medieval Philosophy and Metaphysics in the Department of Philosophy at the Collège Dominicain de Philosophie et Théologie in Ottawa.

James R. Ginther is Associate Professor of Medieval Theology in the Department of Theological Studies at St Louis University.

Mark Johnson is Associate Professor of Systematic Theology in the Department of Theology at Marquette University.

Joanne McWilliam is Professor Emerita at the University of Toronto and a Sessional Lecturer in the Faculty of Divinity at Trinity College of the University of Toronto.

Charles Principe, *CSB*, is Professor Emeritus in the Department of French at University of Toronto.

Pamela J. Reeve is Assistant Professor of Philosophy at St Augustine's Seminary in the Toronto School of Theology.

Philip Lyndon Reynolds is the Aquinas Professor of Catholic Theology in the Chandler School of Theology at Emory University.

Carl N. Still is Assistant Professor of Philosophy at St Thomas More College of the University of Saskatchewan.

Jean-Pierre Torrell, *OP*, is Professor Emeritus in the Faculty of Theology at the University of Fribourg.

Abigail Ann Young is a Research Fellow in the Records of Early English Drama at the University of Toronto.

Acknowledgements

From the beginning of this project we have counted on the generosity and good will of all who became involved with it. Our thanks are due first to all those who contributed their work to the volume. They took a leap of faith with us and have waited patiently to see their investment come to fruition. Among the contributors we doubly thank Fr Charles Principe, CSB, who responded to a special request to compose a recollection of his brother and then translated Jean-Pierre Torrell's essay from French. We are also grateful to his confrere, Armand Maurer, CSB, for expert advice on the translation. Fr James Farge, CSB, provided support and encouragement right from the project's inception, and we thank him for granting us permission to include an updated version of the bibliography listing Walter Principe's writings, which he prepared for *Mediaeval Studies*.

In the preparation of the volume, Joshua Benson and Ursula Acton provided expert and timely proofreading and re-editing of the text, while Robert Simpson offered valuable technical assistance. Despite the difficulties that typically attend the publication of *Festschriften* and memorial volumes, we were fortunate to find a receptive audience at Ashgate, thanks especially to Sarah Lloyd. She and her colleague Anne Keirby have also been helpful and gracious in responding to inquiries and requests from the editors. To all and each we acknowledge our debt and offer our thanks.

List of Abbreviations

CCL   *Corpus christianorum: series latina*

CCM   *Corpus christianorum: continuatio medievalis*

CSEL   *Corpus scriptorum ecclesiasticorum latinorum*

PL   *Patrologia latina*

SCG   Thomas Aquinas, *Summa contra gentiles*

ST   Thomas Aquinas, *Summa theologiae*

Introduction

James R. Ginther and Carl N. Still

In 1988, the Catholic Theological Society of America published a collection of essays whose intent was to 'begin a new conversation among scholars about the sources of Catholic theology'.[1] The Society had called upon its then Vice-President, Walter H. Principe, CSB, to reflect on the history of theology as a principal source for theological work. His essay invokes two metaphors to describe the role that historical study can play in theological argument: the history of theology can be a fortress or a launching pad. In Principe's view, the first metaphor points to both positive and negative activities. In a positive way, fortresses protect human lives and valuable possessions, and the history of theology does something similar when scholars ensure that historical sources do not disappear. More commonly, however, a fortress protects against unwanted attack, and in this mode the history of theology can help to protect a theological idea from receiving legitimate criticism. By contrast, the history of theology can function like a launching pad: it can propel scholars into new spheres of inquiry. The study of the past can be a means to engage the present, not just because scholars can then gain an understanding of the origins of current debates, but because they can also come to terms with how previous theologians responded to their own contemporaneous problems. In other words, the history of theology offers a rich context to reflect both on methodology and major themes of the discipline. The two metaphors, Principe concludes, need not exclude each other. Scholars who employ them both should be able to

> construct one of these launching pads within the courtyard of the fortress of the history of theology. Using the past as a launching pad for creative theologies in the present and future will prevent a stagnating fortress use of past theology and at the same time (to change the metaphor) provide a gravitational pull that will keep space-travelling theologians from floating off into the darkness of outer space.[2]

What made this research programme so credible was Principe's own experience. He had acted as an *ad hoc* advisor to the Canadian Conference of Catholic Bishops, had been a member of the Vatican's International Theological Commission (1980–1985) and in 1988 had just begun to serve on the Committee for Lutheran-Roman Catholic Dialogue. He knew the contours of contemporary theology and was attuned to both its pastoral and academic dimensions. Moreover, Principe was an internationally recognized historian of patristic and medieval theology. That very article was his sixtieth publication in that research field, in addition to the five monographs he had authored – and he would go on to write another forty pieces before his death in 1996.[3] Although he would never have said so, the call to a rigorous study of the past in order to make an impact on the present was, in effect, an invitation to walk in Principe's own footsteps.

This collection of essays, written by four of his colleagues and six of his former students, seeks to honour the memory of Walter Principe by exploring the ways in which these two metaphors can function in the history of medieval theology and philosophy. Both subjects have a place here, for Principe embraced both with equal enthusiasm. Indeed, it would be difficult to engage either discipline – at least in its medieval form – without encountering the other. It is one reason why Principe felt so at home with the interdisciplinary perspective that Etienne Gilson had initiated at the Pontifical Institute of Mediaeval Studies in Toronto.

The aim of these papers, however, is not to relativize the study of medieval theology and philosophy; that is, to establish the significance of a narrative or idea based only on how it can relate directly to a contemporary context. Principe was not so naïve, nor so functionalist in his own writing as to suggest that history become the handmaiden for modern theologians and philosophers. Rather, he saw the value of history itself: it was a laudable discipline and specifically the Early Church and the Medieval periods were worthy objects of study in and of themselves. But, as their content was so rich, historical findings could easily spill into the modern world: in other words, history could instruct. Some of the essays, then, directly address Principe's call to relate the historical record to contemporary ideas and problems, that is, using the past to launch into new territory. Other essays focus on the shape of the historical record and so attempt to preserve carefully the treasures of the past. Above all, each contributor adheres to Principe's overriding concern that the study of the past be rigorous. Within the discipline of theology, he distinguished between the *history of theology* and *historical theology*. It was a distinction that allowed scholars to proceed with rigorous and detailed historical research without always having to justify the application of their results to contemporary concerns.[4]

In many respects, Principe bequeathed to his students the same outlook he had gained while studying at the *École pratique des hautes études*, University of Paris, and *Le Saulchoir* in the 1950s. He had the opportunity to sit at the feet of the leading proponents of the *resourcement* movement, including Marie-Dominique Chenu, Henri de Lubac and Yves Congar. This new approach, which underpinned the *nouvelle théologie*, stood in stark contrast to the desiccated manualist theology that dominated Catholic thinkers of the late nineteenth and early twentieth centuries.[5] There was a certain irony that Catholic thought had regained its vigour not by looking outside itself, but rather by looking to its own past. These new methodologies captured Principe's imagination, and in his teaching he shared his vision of the potential power of such historical research.

As a Senior Fellow at the Pontifical Institute (1964-1994), one of Principe's responsibilities was to teach an introductory course on patristic and medieval theology. While some of the contributors to this collection came to Toronto after he had ceased to teach this course, they, nonetheless, benefited from his notes, which he published for student use.[6] Interspersed between the extensive, annotated bibliographies are pithy summaries of the major theological ideas of all the major thinkers. The technical aspects of the various Christologies, in particular, are broken down into their constituent parts and lucidly explained. At the very heart of this survey was a desire to treat each thinker within his or her own context. It may very well be true, for example, that Augustine was a foundational thinker for the Middle Ages, but Principe explicates his thought in terms of the intellectual setting of late antiquity, not what later authors would derive from Augustine's writings.

Such a contextualized approach to Augustine is well-reflected in the first essay of this collection. Joanne McWilliam explores the effect Augustine's controversy with the Manichees had on the development of his Trinitarian theology. In particular, McWilliam argues that anti-Manichaean concern may explain his emphasis on divine inviolability and omnipotence, Trinitarian unity and equality, the doctrine of creation *ex nihilo*, and the doctrine of the Incarnation. These developments in the works from the 380s and 390s in turn point the way to Augustine's major work on the subject, *De trinitate*.

Before Principe gained a reputation as a Thomist, he had made his mark in Medieval Studies by publishing research on lesser-known scholastics.[7] He proved that historians of medieval theology could make significant contributions by looking beyond the Thomistic horizon. The following three essays attempt to do just that. Abigail Ann Young compares Rupert of Deutz and Hildegard of Bingen and argues for a remarkable likeness in their visionary inspiration. Rupert reports visions not only of Christ but even of the Trinity in human form, and claims to have received a gift of scriptural interpretation. In her writings, Hildegard reports a vision from 1141 in which she received understanding of the biblical books and was commanded to speak and write what she saw and heard. Both can be understood as prophets according to Mosaic and Pauline models of prophecy, and both illustrate how inspiration may arise from unlikely sources.

James Ginther then challenges the standard account of medieval scholastic theology as a whole, which reflects more the theological concerns of the late nineteenth century than the historical record. This revision is based on the assumption that if dialogue between the past and present is a laudable goal, then the past must be allowed to speak for itself. Ginther argues that the shape of medieval theology, especially when placed in its pedagogical and literary contexts, was composed of a more robust relationship between exegesis and speculative analysis than past scholars have allowed. He argues that the presence of the Bible in medieval theology must be reconsidered, in that it was textually dispersed throughout the literary and pedagogical resources for theological education. More importantly, the exposition of the Scripture remained the final goal of theologians.

The next essay attends the most closely to Principe's own research. At the time of his death, Principe was completing an edition and study of the quodlibetal questions of the Dominican, Guerric of Saint-Quentin.[8] These questions were of great importance for a number of reasons, including the fact that they were one of the first attempts at a quodlibetal dispute at Paris. While the questions cover a broad range of subjects (as quodlibetal disputes were meant to do), Torrell focuses on the Christological aspects. These range from the motive for the Incarnation, to the nature of the hypostatic union, to the status of the soul of Jesus. They reveal an early Dominican theologian who was well read in patristic theology, yet also alert to some of the newer questions of his day. When responding to the question 'Would have there been the Incarnation, if man had not sinned?' Guerric is the first to answer in the negative – a response, so Torrell notes, that one finds echoed in Thomas Aquinas. Indeed, much of Guerric's Christology – at least in these questions – resonates in Aquinas. It may be possible, Torrell suggests, that Guerric was a source for Thomas's own theological system. As an expert in Aquinas himself,[9] Torrell presents the link between Guerric and Thomas as putative, but certainly worthy of more investigation.

Lyndon Reynolds' essay is another way of extending Principe's research on medieval Christology, and moves into the realm of Thomistic studies as well. In the same way that Thomas argues for the humanity of Christ as an instrumental cause in satisfaction, so too are the sacraments in salvation. As straightforward as this might appear, however, the underbrush of later Thomistic ideas must first be cleared away since it can obfuscate the theology of Thomas himself. Only then can one gain a precise view of Thomas's own position on sacramental causality – which comes into even sharper relief when compared to Bonaventure's treatment. Reynolds further suggests that Thomas's conclusion is problematic, but that a possible resolution is found in the application of one interpretive method to Thomas's theology – a method that has the added advantage of highlighting the (intended) unfinished nature of Thomas's theological enterprise.

Keeping with the Thomistic theme, Mark Johnson makes a case for the novelty of the *secunda pars* of Aquinas's second *summa* against the background of the Dominican tradition of penitential literature. There Aquinas transformed the manual for pastoral instruction into a treatise on moral theology organized around the principle, derived from John Damascene, that the human being is an image of God seeking its beatitude. Thus the *prima secundae* begins from the notion of beatitude and works towards its acquisition, while the *secunda secundae*'s order is based on the particular actualizations needed to fulfil our rational nature. Aquinas, therefore, based his treatment of morals on a consideration of human nature, a topic that Principe himself had broached on occasion.[10] This new point of departure meant that Aquinas was able to free himself from more extrinsic and accidental ordering principles used by his predecessors and to find a concrete link between morals and the rest of sacred theology. Johnson concludes that the structure of the work has as much to teach us as its content.

Drawing on the results of a dissertation directed by Walter Principe, Pamela J. Reeve considers how Aquinas explains cognitive elevations beyond the normal human mode. Despite the human soul's usual reliance on images in all its cognition, Aquinas finds a way to account for prophecy, spiritual dreams, and rapture as partial separations of the soul from the embodied state. In particular, rapture presents a challenge to Thomistic psychology, since in the biblical cases of Moses and Paul there seems to have been a temporary elevation to the vision of God. Though it is impossible to see God in this life through any created form, Aquinas allows that in view of the *per se* operation of the soul, it can be withdrawn from its senses and normal cognitive activity on occasion by means of divine influence. This possibility is realized more fully in the separated soul after death, and most fully in the permanent and beatifying vision of God. Reeve concludes by comparing Aquinas's thought to some recent suggestions in the philosophy of mysticism and finds Aquinas distinctive in his insistence that it is precisely our embodied human nature that must be withdrawn from if we are to have mystical experience.

In his essay, Carl N. Still asks how Aquinas might be engaged to help us produce an account of how faith may be epistemically justified. While many recent accounts of Aquinas on faith tend to neglect the role of grace, Still contends that Aquinas's understanding of faith requires grace not only for the initial assent but also for the completion of faith's intrinsic exigency for knowledge and experience of God. By building the gifts of knowledge and understanding into an account of faith as Aquinas does, one can address the powerful objection against faith that it gives the believer no subjective certainty. Because Aquinas's account of faith is ultimately completed in his teaching on charity perfected by the gift of wisdom, the faithful believer is promised not only a penetrating glimpse into the meaning of what is held on faith, but also a direct experience of the divine mysteries that lie behind the articles of faith.

The theme of the certainty of faith in Aquinas's teaching is carried forward in Romanus Cessario's contribution. Citing Capreolus as the inaugurator of Thomism as an intellectual tradition, Cessario reviews his disputation in the fifteenth century with Durandus on faith as a theological virtue. Where Durandus had effectively broken with Aquinas's perspective by accepting scientific knowledge as more certain than faith, Capreolus identified the key role of adherence to the authoritative word of another in achieving certain knowledge. Thus, the basis of faith is God's speaking through the testimony of the church. Yet since faith implies not only believing but also living, the theological virtue of faith attains certainty in the lived experience of the 'theologal life'.

Finally, Lawrence Dewan considers a recent explanation of the doctrine of the Trinity by Richard Swinburne. Swinburne asserts that if there is one God, it follows that there must be three (but only three) Gods, since in a being all-powerful and entirely good, a perfect sharing must take place that manifests itself in the production of other Gods. Dewan compares this perspective on the Trinity with Aquinas's teaching and finds it unsatisfying on two scores. First, Aquinas holds that no necessary reason can be given for positing a trinity of persons in God, despite some medieval suggestions to the contrary. Second, Aquinas carefully considers the divine simplicity and goodness before taking up the issue of divine volition. As a result, a theology of God emerges in which choice does not apply to the divine being itself. While God wills other things by choice, he wills his own goodness necessarily. By introducing choice at too primary a level in his understanding of God, Swinburne misconstrues the nature of God as Trinity as well as the relation of God to creatures.

It is appropriate that this collection end with a personal account of Principe, and there is no one more fitting for this task than his brother, Fr. Charles Principe, CSB. Charles lived in the same religious community and taught at the same university as

Walter. Charles watched his brother grow into a world-renowned scholar, but at the same time was a witness to the generosity and pastoral heart that endeared Walter to colleagues, students, and parishioners alike. Charles offers a strong reminder of why his brother became so influential in the lives of all whom he met. Not only was Walter a formidable scholar, he was equally a person committed to service to others. His intellectual life had an easy confluence with his own spirituality, which made every encounter with Walter meaningful.

It is our hope that this collection bears sufficient witness to the scholarship of this one man. We hope too that it would please him, since he found so much delight in the discoveries of others. However, we are aware that he would disapprove of one thing. In reviewing graduate essays, theses for the Licentiate in Mediaeval Studies and doctoral dissertations, Walter constantly repeated one phrase: 'There must be more Latin in the footnotes!' The statement was a reflection of his own commitment to intellectual honesty, for if the principal task is to interpret texts, then one has to show the reader those texts as much as possible. Unfortunately, the pressures on academic publications make it difficult for collections such as this to include expansive footnotes full of long Latin texts. Instead, we have made the decision to include Latin citation in the notes mainly in two cases: where it accompanies an English translation of the text in the essay, or where the Latin text is not available in published form. We trust that this editorial decision will not diminish the tribute we wish to offer to the memory of our teacher and friend.

Notes

1   John P. Boyle, 'Introduction', in *The Sources of Theology*, ed. J.P. Boyle, Current Issues in Theology, 3 (Washington, DC: Catholic Theological Society of America, 1988), vii.
2   Walter H. Principe, 'The History of Theology: Fortress or Launching Pad?' in *The Sources of Theology*, ed. J. P. Boyle, pp. 19-40, quotation from p. 39.
3   See the obituary by James K. Farge, 'Walter Henry Principe, CSB (1922-1996)', *Mediaeval Studies* 58 (1996), vii-xx. Farge also compiled a bibliography of Principe's writings (xi-xx).
4   Principe, 'The History of Theology: Fortress or Launching Pad?', p. 21; and idem, 'Catholic Theology and the Retrieval of its Intellectual Tradition: Problems and Possibilities (Presidential Address)', *Proceedings of the Catholic Theological Society of America* 1991 (46) 75-94. It is not unreasonable to apply the same distinction to medieval philosophy as well
5   The history of the *nouvelle théologie* movement has yet to be written, but see Raymond Winling, 'La théologie en France au XXe siècle', *Nouvelle revue théologique* 111 (1989) 537-55; Albert Raffelt, 'Nouvelle théologie', *Lexikon für Theologie und Kirche* 7 (1998) 935-7; and Jean-Pierre Wagner, *Henri de Lubac* (Paris: Cerf, 2001).
6   Walter Principe, *Introduction to Patristic and Medieval Theology*. Toronto: n.p., 1967; second edition, 1982.
7   In addition to his four volume work *The Theology of the Hypostatic Union in the Early Thirteenth Century*, Studies and Texts, 7, 12, 19 and 32 (Toronto: PIMS, 1963-1975), Principe published studies on a major collection of disputed questions from early

thirteenth-century Paris, the English Dominican, Richard Fishacre, and the Belgian Dominican, Guerric of Saint-Quentin. See the relevant items in the bibliography cited in note 3.

8 Guerric of Saint-Quentin, *Quaestiones de quolibet*, ed. W.H. Principe and J. Black, Studies and Texts, 143 (Toronto: PIMS, 2002). J.-P. Torrell wrote the introduction.

9 J.-P. Torrell, *Saint Thomas Aquinas: the Person and his Work*, trans. R. Royal (Washington, DC: Catholic University of America Press, 1996). The second volume, *Spiritual Master*, was published in Spring 2003.

10 See for example: Walter H. Principe, '"The Truth of Human Nature" according to Thomas Aquinas: Theology and Science in Interaction', in *Philosophy and the God of Abraham: Essays in Memory of James A. Weisheipl, OP*, ed. R.J. Long, Papers in Mediaeval Studies, 12 (Toronto: PIMS, 1991), pp. 161-77.

Chapter 1

Augustine's Early Trinitarian Thought

Joanne McWilliam

Olivier Du Roy's *L'intelligence de la foi en la Trinité selon saint Augustine: Genèse de sa théologie trinitaire jusqu'en 391*[1] was a landmark in Augustinian scholarship, notable for its meticulously detailed reading of the texts and its recognition that Augustine's early trinitarian theology evolved in many important ways. This developmental character is true of all Augustine's theology and is particularly evident in the writings of the 390s: his understanding of the work and person of Christ, his eucharistic theology, his views on free will, nature, and grace. Du Roy, to his credit, was among the first to acknowledge and illustrate this evolution. It has been pointed out more than once that Augustine's evolving theology is expressive of parallel shifts in his world-view.[2] Although Du Roy is aware of and mentions the Manichaean backdrop to all Augustine's writings of the 390s, he does not, in my opinion, do justice to the effect that context had on Augustine's trinitarian thought and language.

Du Roy argues that Augustine started his *intellectus fidei* by approaching the question of the Trinity in an anagogical context – the ascent of the soul to God (with some variations in his many descriptions of that ascent). In Du Roy's words, it is 'a discovery of the Trinity by a conversion and ascension when our enlightened spirit rises in the axis of the beam of light to the divine source of that light'.[3] This anagogical approach is also pedagogical as the soul learns that the divine light is also the creative Trinity. Du Roy argues that Augustine had trouble reconciling the two perspectives until he was able to bring them together under the concept of 'order'.[4] In exploring these two themes Du Roy finds many triads in the early writings and he notes, among other things, the change in terms and roles assigned to the Holy Spirit (for example, from 'Light of the Word' [*lumen verbi*] to Love [*caritas*]).[5]

Du Roy also claims, somewhat surprisingly, that after Augustine's ordination in 391 he either lost interest in, or at least chose not to display, his trinitarian *intellectus fidei* and that his statements on the Trinity tended to become only 'justifications for the formulas of faith'.[6] Certainly there is relatively little reference to the Trinity in the sermons of the 390s, nor is there the determined theological wrestling with the mystery of the Trinity that there is with the questions of original sin and operative grace,[7] which in turn affected his understanding of Christ's saving work.[8] But, if we accept James J. O'Donnell's contention that books 11, 12, and 13 of the *Confessions* are secondarily ordered (after the sequence of the creation narrative) by the trinitarian Three,[9] we must conclude that Augustine's search for a deeper understanding of the Trinity was still alive and well throughout the 390s.

To come from the general to the more particular: impressive as Du Roy's book is, his presentation of Augustine's early trinitarian thought is not entirely adequate in the one respect already mentioned, and it is that aspect I wish to address here. What follows are illustrations (by no means exhaustive, hardly more than soundings) of the effects on his trinitarian theology of his ongoing dissociation from and controversy with the Manichaeans.

There have been many attempts to describe the Manichaean Trinity, recently by Samuel Lieu.[10] While differing in detail, there is agreement that the Supreme God – the Father of Light and/or Greatness – was attacked by the powers of darkness. In danger of losing the battle, the Father of Light called forth a series of emanations beginning with the Mother of Life and the Primal Man. But they, too, were unable to overcome the hostile, material powers. The belief in an ongoing battle resulted in an elaborate Manichaean cosmogony and doctrine of salvation.

Against such a 'Supreme God' who could be thus attacked and defeated, Augustine necessarily had to affirm the inviolability and the omnipotence of God as understood by orthodox Christians. He had also to deny the existence of any other non-created being, and to assert creation *ex nihilo*. Thus, Augustine informed Fortunatus in 392 that he regarded it 'as the height of error to believe that Almighty God is in any part either violable, or contaminable, or corruptible'.[11] He told a gathering of bishops in 393 that

> certain persons have tried to argue that God is not almighty. They have not dared to say this [openly], but in their traditions they opine and believe this when they voice the riddle that there is a nature which God Almighty did not create.[12]

And to the readers of *On True Religion* (391) he insisted that

> [Scripture] is chiefly set against those who think that there are two natures or substances, each with its own principle, at war with each other. Some things they like and others they dislike, and they wish God be the author [only] of the things they like.[13]

Such dualism these 'certain persons' (the Manichaeans) extend to human persons.

> When they cannot overcome temptation and are snared in carnal traps, they think there are two souls in one body, one from God and sharing his nature, the other from the race of darkness.[14]

Augustine explained such errors by the worship of false gods, 'either a soul or a body of some phantasm of its own', but '[the soul] should have directed its regard to eternal things and worshipped the one God without whose changeless permanence no mutable thing could have any abiding existence'.[15]

Creation by divine emanation leads inevitably to the belief that at least all spiritual beings share to some degree in that divinity. Against this Manichaean tenet Augustine insisted that the created world, material and spiritual (including the human soul), is not divine and that those who do share the divine nature do not proceed from

God the Father by means of emanation or creation, but by birth. In human births, he pointed out that the father is at first greater than the son, but as the son matures and the father ages the son becomes greater than the father. But this is not so when 'begotten' and 'born' are used of God. In that case it is 'a birth which neither results in diminishment nor gives increase and so is perfect and results in equality'.[16] The Father in no sense antedates the Son and Holy Spirit. In 390 Augustine pointed out that the phrase 'forever born' does not mean 'forever being born' because a son cannot be called 'son' until fully born. The eternal Son is eternally and fully born.[17] And again, sometime between 388 and 391, he wrote,

> God is the cause of God's own wisdom and God is never without his wisdom, therefore the cause of his own eternal Wisdom is eternal as well and not prior to it.... It is God's very nature to be the eternal Father, therefore God never existed without the Son.[18]

Du Roy asserts that Augustine's earlier trinitarian writings are more concerned with the economic Trinity (the soul's ascent to the triune God and the work of creation) and less with the equality of the trinitarian Three.[19] This statement may well be true, but there is no doubt that Augustine was concerned about the trinitarian equality, as the texts just quoted illustrate. In an early sermon he was even more explicit: 'In that Trinity there is not one greater or less than another'.[20] Because God is both powerful and non-envious, '[the Father] has begotten the Son as his equal'.[21]

It has been argued (successfully, in my opinion) that, although Augustine did not often use the term *homoousios* (or its Latin equivalent) in this period of his life, his early trinitarian theology was in keeping with that of Nicaea.[22] Several writers on Manichaeism have pointed out that *homoousios* played a significant part in their theology, and Lieu remarks that the Manichaean doctrine of 'Jesus as an emanation of the Father of Greatness stood surprisingly close to the principle of consubstantiality'.[23] That was reason enough for Augustine to be leery of the term, but not the concept.

The trinitarian equality is brought about by participation in deity. In a well-known simile of 388 Augustine argued that just as one is chaste by participation in chastity and wise by participation in wisdom, so one is like by likeness itself. 'Therefore, it is understood that the likeness (*similem*) of the Father is thus by similitude, so that the Likeness shares the nature of the Father fully and perfectly'.[24]

The first quotation of a scriptural text in Augustine's writings was 1 Corinthians 1:24,[25] and it continued to be a favourite way of describing the second Person of the Trinity in contexts both of intra-trinitarian relationships and of the incarnation. So, in 391 he wrote,

> And so, he created everything from nothing; he did not create anything from himself, but he begot that which was equal to himself, whom we call the only Son of God and whom we endeavour to describe more fully when we call him the Power and Wisdom of God.[26]

This fuller designation is in accord with the book of Wisdom in the Hebrew scriptures, Augustine argued in 388 in *On the Morals of the Catholic Church and of the Manichaeans.*[27] He had heard 1 Corinthians 1:24 much cited in his Manichaean days, but with a particularly Manichaean understanding which we hear Faustus profess:

> We believe ... that the Father properly dwells in the highest or principal light ... and the Son in his second or visible light. And as the Son is himself twofold, according to the Apostle who speaks of Christ as the Power of God and the Wisdom of God, we believe that his Power dwells in the sun and his Wisdom in the moon.[28]

Augustine would have none of this. He ridiculed the Manichaeans' view of the work of the sun and the moon, and said that by assigning the Father, Son, and Holy Spirit to three places – highest light, secondary light, and 'the whole circle of the atmosphere' – they were positing God as material and divisible rather than 'an inseparable triune existence'.[29]

This division and diffusion of the Manichaean Trinity may explain Augustine's strong emphasis on trinitarian unity (for which he has been so strongly reprimanded recently[30]). There is no doubt that he insisted upon that unity and in his early years displayed that insistence by his use of the singular forms of verbs and pronouns relating to the Trinity. Thus, in another writing of 388 he argues that Paul, in writing 'to *him* be glory forever' (Rom. 11:36, emphasis added), is affirming the unity of the Trinity.[31] Again, in 392 in a homily on Psalm 5, he wrote that the Psalm says 'attend thou' because faith does not teach two or three gods, but 'the very Trinity, one God'.[32] Augustine would later think this emphasis on the singular unfortunate. A more nuanced expression came in 396 when, criticizing the Manichaean *Fundamental Letter*, Augustine said that the Trinity is not one person, but one existence, and he realizes that this existence is best depicted by a plural verb.[33] *Trinitas* is a singular noun, but it embraces a plurality of persons.

Augustine's insistence on the unity of the Trinity overflowed into his teaching on creation. In a letter to Nebridius he described the common work of the Trinity:

> There proceeds from the Father himself, as from a single principle from which are all things, understanding through the Son and a certain interior and ineffable sweetness and delight abiding in that understanding ... which gift and favour is rightly ascribed to the Holy Spirit.[34]

Augustine went on to explain that the lack of understanding which prompted Nebridius's question is the result of creation's fall. Therefore, although all these [works] occur with the most complete unity and inseparability, they nevertheless had to be proved separately, by reason of our weakness by which we have fallen from unity into multiplicity.[35]

A God who is one need not be a monistic God. Augustine frequently argued, on the contrary, that every created thing *needs* a threefold cause, not a monistic cause or three causes. In 389 he told Nebridius that this is because every substance has three characteristics: being, specificity, and a certain permanence. These three characteristics reflect the threefold creativity of God – bringing into being, giving form, and giving continuance. But since being, specificity, and duration cannot exist separately, this shows that none of the Trinity acts alone. In *On Eighty-three Disputed Questions* we find the same reasoning – a triad of necessary characteristics in anything reflects a triadic cause.[36] Again in *On True Religion*, written in 391, he concluded that the creative Trinity acts together, that 'together it made all things and each individual thing'.[37] The understanding of the Word as creative Form arises out of a development in Augustine's understanding of the Trinity found in this work. Here, the description of the relation of the Three is developed from the acknowledged power of the human mind to choose good or evil. Choice implies judgement, judgement a standard.

> The Measure of order itself lives in perpetual Truth.... The Son is rightly said to be from [*ex ipso*] that Measure of order; other creatures through [*per ipsum*] the Son. The Form [Son] precedes all things, completing the unity from which [that Form] is, so that all other things which exist, to the degree that they resemble the One, came into being through that Form.[38]

As early as 388 in *On the Morals of the Catholic Church and of the Manichaeans* the divinity of the Spirit is made explicit. Augustine wrote,

> It is by love then that we become conformed to God.... Moreover, this is done by the Holy Spirit.... But we could not possibly be restored to perfection by the Holy Spirit unless It itself continued always perfect and immutable. And this plainly could not be unless It were of the nature and very substance of God.[39]

Not only did the Holy Spirit bring gifts, but 'Gift' is one of the more frequent names Augustine gave to It.[40]

This conclusion that the Trinity acts as one poses particular problems for the doctrine of the Incarnation. In 389 Nebridius questioned Augustine why, since faith teaches that all the actions of the Trinity are in common, 'is the incarnation celebrated as if attributed to the Son?'[41] Augustine answered that it is appropriate to do so, asserting that 'the plan and form of God by which all things are made is called the Son'.[42] In a slightly earlier letter he had explained that ontological order is paralleled by moral order.

> [Since] it has been brought about by the assumption of a man that a certain method of living and example of precept has been conveyed to us under the majesty and clarity of his teaching, it is not without reason that this whole operation is rightly ascribed to the Son.[43]

Instruction of the man, Christ, is paralleled as well by the interior illumination of the Divine Teacher. Four years later, in 393, Augustine would say that the Son came as man to indicate a pattern of living, and the Holy Spirit as a dove 'to indicate the gift which virtuous living attains'.[44]

Du Roy sees in question 23 of the *Eighty-three Disputed Questions* (dated before 391) a hint of intra-trinitarian relations, that is, resemblance as a relation.[45] In question 69 of the same work (dated 394–95) there is a much more explicit presentation of this topic. Augustine was explaining what it is proper to predicate of Christ as human and as divine. He continued that 'many things are also said of the Son which concern that which is proper to the [divine] Person', for example, 'begotten' and 'image'. 'Proper to' indicates more than nominal identification, and it may be that here Augustine was suggesting that Father, Son, and Holy Spirit are indeed constituted by their relationships.[46]

Several times in his writings of the 390s Augustine asserted that a right understanding of the Trinity is the key to all knowledge and right conduct and, therefore, 'to understand the Trinity soberly and piously occupies the watchful care of all Christians and is the goal of every advance'.[47] But it is in the earlier *On True Religion* that the reason why knowledge of the Trinity is the primary goal was spelled out.[48] First, when the trinitarian character of creation is known as far as it can be known in this life, the right relationship between Creator and creature becomes apparent. Knowledge of this relationship leads secondly to knowledge of the moral law: '[I]t will be as clear as it can be...that all things are subject by necessary, indefeasible and just laws to their Lord God'. There are other things which, first accepted by faith, will be understood or at least seen as possible and fitting. These are the mysteries of the divine plan of salvation, from the incarnation to the last judgement. This will happen only 'when the eternity of the Trinity and the mutability of creation are known and no longer accepted by faith alone'.[49]

Augustine's discussions of the Trinity frequently (although not in this particular case) included references to the mercy of God, and he equally often moved from a presentation of the divine Word to the incarnation. In noting this, I come back to Du Roy's point, mentioned earlier, that in his earlier writings Augustine was more concerned with the economic than the immanent Trinity. While I think Du Roy did not do justice to Augustine's insistence on the equality of the trinitarian Three during these years, the passage cited above from *On True Religion* gives some support to his point. Augustine could not readily think of the Trinity apart from the economy of salvation or of the Word apart from the incarnation (*The Teacher* is the nearest to doing so).

One of the most interesting themes explored by Du Roy is Augustine's shift in his *intellectus fidei* of the Trinity from a philosophical approach to a scriptural one. It culminates in this trinitarian acknowledgement in the *Confessions*.

And now where the name of God occurs, I have come to see the Father who made these things; where the 'Beginning' is mentioned, I see the Son by whom he made these things. Believing that my God is a Trinity, in accordance with my belief I searched in God's holy oracles and found your Spirit to be borne above the waters. There is the Trinity, My God – Father and Son and Holy Spirit, Creator of the entire creation.[50]

At the beginning of book 13 of the *Confessions* Augustine issued an invitation to God to enter into his soul, which had been prepared to receive it by the longing that very God had inspired in it.[51] And very soon after the confession of the Trinity just quoted we receive an intimation of some unfinished business and of things to come.

> I wish that humans would know the triad within their own selves.... The triad I mean is that of being, knowing, willing.... Who can easily know whether because of this triad God is Trinity, or whether the three are in each [Person] so that the three belong to each?[52]

Soon after the *Confessions* were finished, Augustine began his deep and lengthy reflections upon these and other trinitarian mysteries. The result, of course, was *On the Trinity*.

Notes

1 Paris: Études Augustiniennes, 1966.
2 For example, see Douglas Mosher, *The Eighty-three Disputed Questions* (Westminster, MD: Catholic University of America Press, 1962), Introduction.
3 Du Roy, *L'intelligence de la foi*, pp. 266-7: 'Cependant l'anagogie qui était d'abord une découverte de la Trinité par une conversion et une ascension où notre esprit illuminé remontait dans l'axe du rayonnement jusqu'à la source de cette lumière'.
4 Ibid., 279-97.
5 Ibid., 219.
6 Ibid., 434.
7 See J. Patout Burns, *The Development of Augustine's Doctrine of Operative Grace* (Paris: Études Augustiniennes, 1980).
8 See Joanne McWilliam, 'Augustine's developing understanding of the cross', *Augustinian Studies* 17 (1986) 15-33.
9 James J. O'Donnell, *Augustine's Confessions* (Oxford: Clarendon Press, 1992), III.350f.
10 S.N.C. Lieu, *Manichaeism in the later Roman Empire and Medieval China: A Historical Survey* (Manchester: Manchester University Press, 1985).
11 *Contra Fortunatum Manichaeum* 1 (PL 42.81-112): 'In primis summum errorem puto, omnipotentem deum ex aliqua parte violabilem, aut coinquinabilem, aut corruptibilem credere'.
12 *De fide et symbolo* 2.2 (CSEL 41, ed. Joseph Zycha [1900] 4): 'Conati sunt enim quidem persuadere deum patrem non esse omnipotentem: non quia hoc dicere ausi sunt, sed in suis traditionibus hoc sentire et credere convincuntur cum enim dicunt esse naturam quam deus omnipotens non creaverit'.
13 *De vera religione* 9.16 (CCL 32, ed. Joseph Martin [1962] 198): '[Scriptura] contra eos tamen potissimum est instituta, qui duas naturas vel substantias singulis principiis adversus invicem rebelles esse arbitrantur. Offensi enim quibusdam rebus et rursus quibusdam delectati non earum quibus offenduntur, sed earum quibus delectantur volunt esse auctorem deum'.
14 Ibid.: '[C]um consuetudinem suam vincere nequeunt iam carnalibus laqueis irretiti, duas animas esse in uno corpore existimant, unam de deo, quae naturaliter hoc sit quod ipse, alteram de gente tenebrarum'.

15 Ibid., 10.18 (199): '...nullum errorem in religione esse potuisse, si anima pro deo suo non coleret animam aut corpus aut phantasmata sua.... [C]ongruens aeterna meditaretur unum deum colens, qui nisi permaneret incommutabilis, nulla mutabilis natura remaneret'.

16 *Sermo Ad Catechumenos De Symbolo* 2.5 (CCL 46, ed. R. Vander Plaetse [1969] 188): 'Perfectus quidem natus, si non crescit, et minor non remansit, aequalis est'.

17 *De diversis quaestionibus 83* 37 (CCL 44A, ed. Almut Mutzenbecher [1975] 59): 'Melior est semper natus quam qui semper nascitur, quia qui semper nascitur nondum est natus, et numquam natus est aut natus erit, si semper nascitur. Aliud est enim nasci aliud natum esse. Ac per hoc numquam filius, si numquam natus. Filius autem quia natus, et semper filius; semper igitur natus'.

18 Ibid., 16 (21): '...etiam sapientiae suae causa est; nec umquam deus sine sapientia. Suae igitur sempiternae sapientiae causa est sempiterna; nec tempore prior est quam sapientia. Deinde si patrem esse sempiternum inest deo nec fuit aliquando non pater, numquam sine filio fuit'.

19 Du Roy, *L'intelligence de la foi*, 439.

20 *Sermo* 214.10 (ed. P. Verbraken, in *Revue Benedictine* 72 (1962) 14-21 (esp. 20): 'In hac trinitate non est aliud alio maius aut minus, nulla operum separatio, nulla dissimilitudo substantiae'.

21 *De diversis quaestionibus 83* 50 (77): 'Si enim voluit [generare] et non potuit, infirmus est; si potuit et noluit, invidus est. Ex quo conficitur aequalem genuisse filium'.

22 Basil Studer, 'La foi de Nicée selon saint Augustin', *Revue des Études Augustiniennes* 19 (1984) 133-54.

23 Lieu, *Manichaeism*, 96.

24 *De Genesi ad litteram imperfectus liber* 16.58 (PL 34.242): 'Unde intelligitur ita patri esse similem similitudinem suam, ut eius naturam plenissime perfectissimeque impleat'. See also *De divers. quaest. 83* 23.

25 *Contra Academicos* 2.1.1 (CCL 29, ed. W. M. Green [1970] 18).

26 *De libero arbitrio* 1.2.5 (CCL 29, ed. W. M. Green [1970] 213): 'Ex quo fit ut de nihilo creaverit omnia, de se autem non crearit, sed genuerit quod sibi par esset, quem filium dei unicum dicimus; quem cum planius enuntiare conamur. dei virtutem et dei sapientiam nominamus'.

27 *De moribus ecclesiae Catholicae et de moribus manichaeorum libri duo* 1.16.27 (CSEL 90, ed. John B. Bauer [1992] 31-33).

28 *Contra Faustum manichaeum* 20.2 (PL 34.370): '[S]ed Patrem quidem ipsum lucem incolere credimus summam ac principalem.... Filium vero in hac secunda ac visibili luce consistere; qui quoniam sit et ipse geminus, ut cum Apostolus novit, Christum dicens esse Dei virtutem et Dei sapientiam; virtutem quidem ejus in sole habitare credimus, sapientiam vero in luna'.

29 Ibid., 20.7 (PL 34.375, 374): '[A]eris hunc omnem ambitum. Itaque lumen illud Trinitas inseparabilis, unus deus est'.

30 See, among many, Catherine LaCugna, *God for Us* (San Francisco: Harper, 1991); Thomas Marsh, *The Triune God* (Mystic, CT: Twenty-third Publications, 1994); Colin Gunton, *The Promise of Trinitarian Theology* (Edinburgh: T. and T. Clark, 1991); Jurgen Moltmann, *The Trinity and the Kingdom* (Minneapolis: Fortress, 1980).

31 *De moribus* 1.16.29 (34): 'Ostendit Paulus trinitatem istam unum deum esse, cum dicit, *ipsi gloria*'. See also *De moribus* 14.12; and J. Kevin Coyle, *Augustine's 'De moribus ecclesiae catholicae'* (Fribourg: the University Press, 1978), 245f.

32 *Enarrationes in Psalmos* 5.3 (CCL 28, ed. D. Eligius Dekkers and Johannes Fraipont [1966] 20): 'Non enim duos aut tres deos fides catholica praedicat, sed ipsam trinitatem unum deum'.

33 *Ep. Fund.* 6.7.

34 *Epistola* 11.4 (CSEL 34, ed. A. Goldbacher [1795] 28): '…et ipsius patris, id est unius principii, ex quo sunt omnia, cognitio per filium et quaedam interior et ineffabilis suavitas atque dulcedo in ista cognitione permanendi … quod donum et munus proprie spititui sancto tribuitur'.

35 Ibid.: 'Ergo cum agantur omnia summa communione et inseparabilitate, tamen distincte demonstranda erant propter imbecillitatem nostram, qui ab unitate in varietatem lapsi sumus'.

36 *De diversis quaestionibus 83* 18 (23).

37 *De vera religione* 7.13 (196): '[I]d est unum ipsum deum patrem et filium et spiritum sanctum, qua trinitate…. Non ut aliam partem totius creaturae fecisse intellegatur pater et aliam filius et aliam spiritus sanctus, sed et simul omnia et unamquamque naturam patrem fecisse per filum in dono spiritus sancti'.

38 Ibid., 43.81 (241): 'Ipse autem ordinis modus vivit in veritate perpetua…. Filius recte dicitur ex ipso, cetera per ipsum. Praecessit enim forma omnium summe implens unum de quo est, ut cetera quae sunt, in quantum sunt uni similia, per eam formam fierent'.

39 *De moribus* 1.13.23 (27): 'Fiet ergo per caritatem ut conformemur deo…. Fit autem hoc per spiritum sanctum…. Nullo modo autem redintegrari per spiritum sanctum possemus, nisi et ipse semper et integer et incommutabilis permaneret. Quod profecto non posset, nisi dei naturae esset ac ipsius substantiae'.

40 For example, *De vera relig.* 55.113 (260): 'Quare ipsum donum dei cum patre et filio aeque incommutabile colere et tenere nos convenit … donum benignitatis eius'.

41 *Ep.* 11.2 (26): '…quicquid ab ea [trinitate] fit, simul fieri sit existimandum et a patre et a filio et ab spiritu sancto…. Ex quo videtur esse consequens, ut hominem trinitas tota susceperit'.

42 *Ep.* 12 (29): 'Disciplina ipsa et forma dei, per quam facta sunt omnia quae facta sunt, filius nuncupatur'.

43 *Ep.* 11.4 (27): 'Itaque quoniam per illam susceptionem hominis id actum est, ut quaedam nobis disciplina vivendi et exemplum praecepti sub quarundam sententiarum maiestate ac perspicuitate insinuaretur, non sine ratione hoc totum filio tribuitur'.

44 *De diversis quaestionibus 83, 43.* (64).

45 Du Roy, *L'intelligence de la foi*, 340f.

46 *De diversis quaestionibus 83* 69: 'Sed quoniam multa etiam secundum proprietatem personae, excepto quod attinet ad susceptionem hominis' (185).

47 *De libero arbitrio* 3.21.60 (310): 'Cui trinitati pie sobrieque intellegendae omnis excubat vigilantia christiana et omnis eius provectus intenditur'. *De libero arbitrio* was written in 395.

48 *De vera religione* 8.14 (197): 'Quo cognito, satis apparebit quantum homo assequi potest, quam necessariis et invictis et iustis legibus, deo et domino suo cuncta subecta sint'.

49 Ibid.: '[E]x quo illa omnia, quae primo credidimus nihil nisi auctoritatem secuti, partim sic intelliguntur, ut videamus esse certissima, partim sic, ut videamus fieri posse atque ita fieri oportuisse…. [C]ognita aeternitate trinitatis et mutabilitate creaturae creduntur tantum' (197).

50 *Confessiones* 13.5.6 (CCL 27, ed. Lucas Verheijen [1981] 244): 'Et tenebam iam patrem in dei nomine, qui fecit haec, et filium in principii nomine, in quo fecit haec, et trinitatem credens deum meum, sicut credebam, quaerebam in eloquiis sanctis eius, et ecce spiritus

tuus superferebatur super aquas. Ecce trinitas deus meus, pater et filius et spiritus sanctus, creator universae creaturae'.

51 *Conf.* 13.1.1.
52 *Conf.* 13.11.12 (247-8): 'Vellem ut haec tria cogitarent homines in se ipsis.... Dico autem haec tria: esse, nosse, velle.... [E]t utrum propter tria haec et ibi trinitas, an in singulis haec tria, ut terna singulorum sint, an utrumque miris modis simpliciter et multipliciter infinito in se sibi fine'.

Chapter 2

Mission and Message: Two Prophetic Voices in the Twelfth Century

Abigail Ann Young

Rupert of Deutz (c. 1075–1129/30) and Hildegard of Bingen (1098–1179) stand among the dominant figures in the landscape of the twelfth century, at least from our late twentieth-century perspective. They share other common bonds as well: both traditional Benedictines, both heads of religious houses, both passionate defenders of clerical reform. And they share an even more fundamental bond, their common sense of having been commissioned by God in visions, an experience that shows affinities with the calls of biblical prophets. In Rupert's case, his commissioning vision was one of a series of eight, experienced at a crucial period in his early life and culminating in his ordination as a priest and the beginning of his life's work of scriptural exposition. For Hildegard, her commissioning vision was one among a countless number of visions that began in childhood and continued all her life and whose explication informed much of her writing. But in both cases, neither their inner nor their outer lives were the same after that visionary experience.

Rupert of Deutz

It was in the mid-1120s that the Walloon writer and teacher, Rupert of Deutz, offered two personal accounts in works written at around the same time, of the visions in which he believed that he had been commissioned as an exegete. Attention to Rupert has tended to dwell on his controversial side and these visions are less well known than those of his younger contemporary, Hildegard of Bingen, so I shall deal with them here in detail. The first account is in Book I of his commentary on the Benedictine Rule, addressed to his friend and patron, Cuno, abbot of Siegburg.[1] There Rupert expressed his annoyance, even anger, with Cuno not only for forcing him to interrupt work on a Matthew commentary (which Cuno himself had requested) at a key point (the exposition of the Sermon on the Mount), but also for doing so to ask him to write a work he was sure would stir up criticism. Wearied by the storms of controversy of his earlier life, Rupert demanded Cuno's indulgence as he meditated on those past conflicts and their causes, using as his theme-text, 'The poor man speaks, and they say, Who is this? And if he stumble they will overthrow him' (Ecclus. 13:29).[2]

He described how his detractors, who have 'gone far away and dwelled among famous teachers' at cathedral schools, reproach him like that poor man, since he has remained enclosed in a monastery since boyhood. 'But', Rupert said, 'I have seen the Wisdom of God; I have seen in some manner the Incarnate Word, Christ the Son of God. He was wholly golden, having as it were a body wholly formed from the finest gold and from it living waters poured forth into me with force through many pipes projecting from that body of his on every side'.[3] Others might find this a ludicrous claim, but Cuno would not, Rupert wrote, because he had been instrumental in providing Rupert with the material resources needed to write and 'by writing, to pour back for anyone that wanted the living waters pouring into me from that golden stamp and seal'.[4] Now Rupert prays that Christ may also kiss him 'with his whole mouth, his golden mouth ... so that the understanding of his secrets which is due his friends alone may not fail me and that I may learn more and more from that experience that the living outflow of Christ's fountain, continually running, is better than the tanks and cisterns of men'.[5]

Grounded in his awareness of this outpouring of Christ's Spirit, Rupert flatly contradicted the teachings of the Laon masters, among the most eminent theologians of his day, men 'to whom I knew belonged both eloquence and wit, as well as a great dignity of office and magisterium',[6] on the question of evil and the divine will. And on Christ's authority, not his own, he wrote the works, offensive to some, on the Divine Office, the Gospel of John, and others.[7] In addition to discussing his conflict with the Laon theologians and outlining specifically and publicly for the first time his claim to divine inspiration, Rupert also described here three occasions on which his enemies had tried to overthow him by twisting his words, including the famous conflict over the presence or absence of Judas at the Last Supper, making Book 1 of *Rule* an important biographical source.

After finishing his work on the Benedictine Rule, Rupert returned to Matthew's Gospel and his commentary, titled *On the Glory and Honour of the Son of Man*.[8] In an excursus in Book 12 he also returned to the topic of authority, recalling a conversation with Cuno some three years earlier in which he had revealed to his friend and patron that his exegetical writing was inspired.[9] Cuno was curious both about the number and length of Rupert's writings and about his unique confidence as an exegete. How could Rupert cover the same ground as the Fathers had done before, yet without deferring to them? Why was he so unconventional as an exegete? 'You almost never saw in me', Rupert reminded Cuno, 'those preparations characteristic of the holy Fathers, by which they readied themselves to labour fruitfully in these studies "as servants of God", just as the blessed apostle says, "in wakefulness, and fasting", [2 Cor. 6:4-5] and other good things whereby a person's understanding may be made clear, so as to be worthy to approach the holy and awesome scriptures of truth with good judgement'.[10]

In explanation, Rupert had recounted his visions and Cuno had insisted that Rupert write them all down for him. But Rupert had been unwilling to comply and now found that this failure interfered so much with his commentary (at a point at which he was using Ezechiel's vision of the four living creatures as a theme-text) that he had to stop and finally deal with the topic of his own visions. Rupert may also have been uneasy about the very sketchy description which he had given earlier in his fit of pique with Cuno and others, for there are several aspects of the description in *Rule* which make very little sense before comparison with the fuller narrative of eight visions in *Glory*, the last three of which are apparently alluded to in the earlier account. The first six are all directly linked with his gift of scriptural interpretation, the last two with his decision to be ordained. The narrative makes clear that Rupert believed that a charismatic gift of interpretation had been given him as a consolation by a merciful God during a time of personal loss as well as of unhappiness and self-doubt about his vocation as priest and monk. The decision to seek ordination, which resolved some of this inner turmoil, was thus connected with the appropriation of both gift and consolation and the two visions related to that decision are likewise linked thematically with the six which preceded them. The seventh recapitulates the first. The eighth and final vision repeats themes and symbols from the sixth, the climax of the first series.

He recounted that he had been gripped by a morbid obsession with what seemed to him the good fortune of the dead, who were no longer subject to the spiritual dangers of this world. This obsession produced his mixed emotions at the deaths of his two brothers, apparently his only siblings – they were taken away and he alone was left behind. He described his mental state vividly, detailing how it interfered with his ability both to understand and to appropriate the consolation offered by the Holy Spirit. Rupert described to Cuno how, while brooding over his loss and his sorrow at being alone to face the dangers of life, 'my eyes were opened, I saw the Son of God: while I was awake I saw him, the Son of Man, alive upon the cross. I did not see him with bodily sight but, that I might see, the eyes of the body grew dim and better, that is, inner, eyes were opened'.[11] He remained all night in prayer behind the altar in an oratory dedicated to the Blessed Virgin, embracing and kissing the image of Christ on the crucifix. Then he returned the crucifix to its place but the sweetness of the embrace remained with him and he remembered the Psalm, 'O taste and see that the Lord is good' (Ps. 33:9).

But Rupert continued to be oppressed with fear and grief. Falling into a trance-like state on two successive mornings, he experienced a vision of the Trinity in human form. In this vision, he saw and spoke with two of the three Persons during the offertory of a mass celebrated by a venerable bishop. At the climax of the dream, all three Persons together lifted Rupert up on a huge open book and one of them said, pointing to the altar's relics, 'Fear not, you will be greater than these'.[12] According to Rupert, Cuno himself interpreted this vision:

> There is no need for me to explain to your loving-kindness the opening of the book or the reason why the Person said those words while pointing to the golden memorials or

phylacteries of the saints; many have often heard and agreed with your judgement of me, that God has truly opened his book, that is, the holy scriptures, to me and that I say some things better than many opinions of the holy fathers whose memory is worthily celebrated in the holy church and shines like gold.[13]

Although he now understood this to be the vision's meaning, Rupert explained that at the time he continued to be troubled and uncomprehending. This second vision was followed by three more: of the Father, of an unidentified consoler, and of the Holy Spirit under two forms. In the second of these three (the fourth vision overall), Rupert is told on the eve of St. Matthew's Day (20 September) by a man of venerable appearance that he will conquer in eight years.[14] But so obsessed was he by the dangers of sin to the living that the only way to conquer seemed to be to die and thereafter he believed that he would die in eight years. The climax of this first cycle of visions occurred, not surprisingly, eight years later. When Rupert did not die, he was finally open to the real meaning of his second dream, to his divine gift of scriptural interpretation. This moment of understanding and appropriation also took place within a vision, the sixth of the series, which took place on the night of Ash Wednesday. Something that he described as being like a talent (probably something disk-shaped like a talent coin) and full of light descended from heaven, rested on his chest, and began to rotate. It poured forth light, whose substance was like liquid gold, until he was filled.[15]

However, Rupert soon realized that he could not appropriate the gift of interpretation conferred symbolically in the second and sixth visions until he was a priest. The acceptance of this new office was also expressed in visionary experiences, which recapitulate the themes and images of the first, second, and sixth visions. In the seventh vision, Rupert once again saw the figure of Christ on a crucifix come to life, embraced, and kissed Christ. This caused him to be filled with love for the priestly office and to consent at last to ordination.[16] Soon after, he had his final and most unusual vision. In it, the figure of a man lying flat and stretched out came down on top of Rupert. It literally made an impression on him, as a seal stamps wax, but far more deeply than even very soft wax could be impressed. He quotes in explanation 1 Corinthians 6:17: 'But anyone who joins himself to the Lord is one with him spiritually'. From that time forward, Rupert began to write as if he could not stop. Now that he had comprehended and appropriated God's gift of consolation and consented to become his priest, Rupert felt empowered to say that he was at one with God.[17]

Hildegard of Bingen

Some fifty years later, in 1175, a correspondence began between Guibert, a monk of Gembloux, and the well-known and by then elderly Benedictine abbess and teacher, Hildegard of Bingen, whom apparently he had only recently and briefly met.[18] In her side of the exchange, at his request, she answered a number of questions about the source of her knowledge and her famous visions (first described in the account, written about twenty-five years earlier, in her *Scivias*).[19] There in her *protestificatio*, Hildegard had described the defining moment in a life of visionary experience that had begun in her early childhood:

> And behold, in the forty-third year of my passing course, while I was intent upon a heavenly vision with great fear and tremulous effort, I saw a great splendour, in which a voice came from heaven saying to me:
> 'O weak mortal, both ash of ash and rottenness of rottenness, say and write what you see and hear. But because you are fearful in speaking and simple in explaining and unlearned in writing these things, say and write them not according to human speech nor the understanding of human creativity nor according to the will of human composition, but according to this rule: that you reveal by interpreting the things you see and hear among heavenly matters from above, in the wonders of God, just as also a hearer receiving his teacher's words makes them known according to the tenor of *his* speech, as he wishes, shows, and teaches. So then you also, O mortal – speak the things you see and hear; and write them not according to yourself or any other person, but according to the will of the One Who knows, sees, and disposes all things in the hidden places of his mysteries'.
> And again I heard a voice from heaven saying to me: 'Therefore speak these wonderful things and write and say them in the manner they were taught'.
> This happened in AD 1141 when I was forty-two years and seven months old: A fiery light, of the greatest flashing brightness, coming out of a cloudless sky, flooded my entire mind and so inflamed my whole heart and my whole breast like a flame – yet it was not blazing but glowing hot, as the sun makes anything on which its rays fall hot. And I suddenly experienced the understanding of the exposition of books, that is, of the Psalter, the Gospel, and of the other orthodox volumes of both the Old and the New Testaments, but nevertheless I did not thereby enjoy the interpretation of the words of their text, nor the division of syllables, nor a knowledge of cases and tenses.[20]

This defining vision has become so well known that we need not discuss it here in detail,[21] save to focus on the particular themes of mission and commission that show so clearly in Hildegard's own words. It is significant that she, like the prophets of old, was told not to impose herself or her own personality on her accounts of what she has seen, but instead solemnly commanded four times to speak and write what she sees and hears. In addition to this commissioning to speak and write, in this vision she received a new comprehension of the foundations of her religious faith and life. The knowledge of syllabification, cases, and tenses, which she was careful to disclaim came from her vision, was the stuff of primary education in Latin. She would likely have acquired them in a rudimentary form in her early years in the religious life, as part of her training in the *opus Dei*, the liturgy and the Benedictine offices. No one who has read her powerful but eccentric Latin can doubt her sincerity either in claiming an infusion of understanding of exposition, that is, of the interpretation of meaning, or in denying any infusion of syntax or literary style.

Much of the account in *Scivias* is actually directed toward explaining what this commissioning to speak was not. It was not like the other visions she had experienced since childhood, for they were kept in silence in her heart (and in fact she never said very much about their contents). Nor was it the result of dreams or ecstatic trances like the sibyls and oracles of pagan antiquity experienced (a point she had to make again about her visions in general in her correspondence with Guibert). This vision included a new understanding of the biblical text (and more than that, for in her desire to clarify matters for Guibert she elaborated on the gifts of the Light she saw, observing that 'just as the sun, moon, and stars appeared reflected in water, so the Scriptures, sermons, virtues, and some works formed by men shine in it for me'[22]), but this was not academic knowledge.

She emphasized in both *Scivias* and in her correspondence the overriding importance of communicating what she saw from that point on, an importance underlined and intensified by the repetition of the divine commission to speak and write what was revealed to her. Although she was silent in her childhood and youth, now that she had reached the robust strength of middle age what she saw and heard was no longer to be kept to herself, because it was no longer given her for herself alone. Writing to Guibert some thirty-five years after this commissioning vision, she remarked, 'My soul never lacks at any time that light named above which is called the semblance of the living Light ... and in it I see what I often say and what I reply to those asking about the splendour of the living Light'.[23] Failure to meet the responsibility of the divine commission resulted in illness initially: 'Although I did see and hear this, nevertheless ... I refused to write for a long time – not out of obstinacy but as an office of humility – until I lay on a bed of sickness, struck down by God's lash so that finally, compelled by many infirmities ... I set my hand to write'.[24] But in old age, when she suffered almost constant ill health, the heavenly visions brought their own reward, as she wrote to Guibert: 'because of the constant infirmity that I suffer, sometimes I weary of revealing the words and visions that are shown to me then. But still when my soul is seeing them by tasting, I am so transformed ... that ... I completely forget every sorrow and trouble'.[25]

The extraordinary likeness between the experiences of these two twelfth-century Benedictines has not generally been recognized by modern students of the theology and exegesis of the period. For a variety of reasons, both in our time and in theirs, Rupert's claim of an authority grounded in divine revelation has attracted less attention and acceptance than Hildegard's. For example, Barbara Newman recognized apparent similarities between the self-presentations of Rupert and Hildegard.[26] Ultimately she dismisses the similarities as superficial, characterizing Rupert's visions described in his *Rule* as involving 'no extraordinary charism' and of 'a purely subjective' content. She concludes that

> Rupert as a male religious writing in a highly traditional genre (exegesis), did not have to face opposition nearly as severe as Hildegard did, whether from his peers or from his own psyche.... His visions adorn and authenticate his writings, but they do not determine the whole.[27]

This judgement does not seem to do justice to Rupert's own words in *Rule* and *Glory*. Rupert may have been, as Newman observes, a male cleric engaged in a traditionally male clerical activity; but he was, or felt himself to be, under siege if not assault by a new breed of academic theologian trained in the cathedral schools. And in defence of his teaching and his right to be heard he asserted no less absolutely than Hildegard the authority of God. He offered his detractors not evidence of the depth and value of a monastic education but the claim that Christ had poured the living water of inspiration into him like liquid gold.

More recently Robert E. Lerner has located Rupert in a very different section of the visionary spectrum.[28] He links Rupert with two later theologians, Joachim of Fiore (c. 1132–1202) and Arnold of Villanova (c. 1235/40–1312/3), as a forerunner of what he calls their 'ecstasy defence', the claim that a new or even an apparently heterodox interpretation of the Bible is in fact the result of an inspired insight. There is an impropriety in using 'ecstasy' to describe the sort of inspired state described by Rupert, Joachim, Arnold, and even Hildegard, for Christian writers traditionally have seen *ecstasis*, the state of being outside oneself, as characteristic of pagan soothsayers or false prophets and rarely if ever the preserve of those truly inspired by God.[29] More importantly, there seems to be a basic difference between Rupert's situation and that of Joachim and Arnold as described by Lerner. Each of them offered an account of divine inspiration or guidance in a particular situation. Joachim sought guidance from the Holy Spirit in a new, and potentially anti-Augustinian, reading of Revelation historically; while Arnold was defending himself against a charge of heresy.[30] But if Rupert is using an ecstasy defence, it is for his whole life as a Christian teacher and not for any one teaching. In this he seems to have more in common with Hildegard for, as we have seen in his own words, Rupert was at a crisis of vocation, indeed (given his acknowledged desire for death) a crisis of life, when his visionary experiences opened up an entire realm of theological and exegetical understanding and commissioned him to write and teach what he had learned. Hildegard, too, was only commissioned to speak what she had learned in a vision about 'the orthodox volumes of both the Old and the New Testaments' after many years of troubling and largely untold visions, which may equally have brought her to a point of crisis.

Rupert and Hildegard, then, appear to have more in common than has generally been assumed.[31] This common ground lies in the realm where Hildegard is often viewed as standing not just pre-eminent, but alone: the realm of visionary inspiration. Is it possible, however, given their emphasis on visionary experiences, to go a step further and to use the category of 'prophet' or 'prophecy' in some meaningful way to describe them? Certainly this has been done by many in describing Hildegard in her own lifetime, and in more recent times as well.

What is a prophet, or perhaps better, what might Christians of the twelfth century like Rupert and Hildegard have thought that a prophet was? There are three sources that fed the tradition that they inherited: the Old Testament, the New Testament and apostolic tradition, and the work of exegetes in the patristic and early medieval period.[32] In the Old Testament, the prophet may be a charismatic leader like Samuel, who led the people as prophet and judge before the anointing of Saul.[33] But pre-eminently, the prophet was seen as one who receives the Word of the Lord to be spoken to a particular person or for a particular situation. Such prophets were not called out of the world but sent into it, with a particular message, usually one to be reported in the Lord's words, occasionally one to be acted out. The prophet's words, because they were not his or her own but the Lord's, were to be not simply heard but, once tested, to be obeyed. The test of true prophecy is given in the Mosaic Law: true prophets speak in God's name and not in the name of other gods; speak exactly and only the words the Lord puts in their mouths; and speak what will be proven true by the people's experience or will come about in the future (Deut. 18:15-22). Although there were elements of prediction in a prophet's actions (since the consequences of either obedience or disobedience often formed part of the message), the principal role of the prophet was not to foretell the future but to act as a messenger and an intermediary between Yahweh and the community of Israel.

In the early Christian community, as reflected in the New Testament and the works of the Apostolic Fathers, the role of a prophet changed: not only had the coming of the Messiah changed the relationship between God and the New Israel, but the Church living in the Roman Empire had radically different needs and choices than those of the more or less independent states of pre-exilic Israel and Judah. Those changed circumstances and the importance of the prophetic books of the Old Testament as a source for 'proof texts' that were fulfilled in the life, death, or resurrection of Jesus affected the early Christian attitude toward Old Testament prophecy. In retrospect, the Church saw prophecy in the Old Testament as chiefly directed toward predicting the events of the New Testament. But there continued to be individuals within the gathered community who were seen as exercising a prophetic ministry. In the New Testament, especially in the works of Paul, these prophets' function was seen very much in terms of the community to which they were sent and of which they were part. Paul particularly emphasized that a prophet should give an intelligible message and one that serves to build up the community (1 Cor. 12:4-31). These are different criteria for judging true prophecy than those of Deuteronomy, but they are in many ways easier to apply and the early Church no less than Israel believed that God would hold accountable those who did not heed a prophet's words.

This tendency to emphasize a didactic and communal role for the prophet was strengthened in later patristic writers by the orthodox reaction to Montanism. This second-century movement, with its emphasis on charismatic leadership and prophetic authority, was ultimately rejected as false by the Church, although it included no less an authority than Tertullian among its members, and it engendered wariness toward persons and groups that claimed a prophetic role. Following these earlier tendencies and drawing on the New Testament, the Latin tradition, exemplified by such writers as 'Ambrosiaster' and Cassiodorus, concluded that there were two kinds of prophecy.[34] One sort involved foretelling the future, and it was in this category that Old Testament prophecy tended to be included. The other sort, in a natural development of Pauline tradition, was a charisma of interpreting the Bible. Since prophets were to be sent to the new Israel to build up the community of the Church with their intelligible messages, what better form for these messages to take than that of interpreting the divine oracles? The work of these Latin writers was then codified and passed on to the twelfth century by the exegetes of the eighth and ninth century schools such as that of Auxerre.

Whichever of these three threads of the tradition we use, Rupert and Hildegard clearly conform, according to their own accounts of their experiences, to the prophetic mould. In Old Testament terms, each explicitly claimed to have received the Word of the Lord and to have been commissioned to speak and to write what he or she had been taught. The description of the prophet 'like Moses' (Deut. 18:15-22), the touchstone of true prophecy in Israel, shows the importance, from the prophetic point of view, of Hildegard's reiteration in her account of her vision in 1141 of the command to speak in exactly the words that she heard and no others. Both match the Pauline criteria of speaking an intelligible message that builds up a community. Hildegard was sent, as she and many others believed, to build up and reform a corrupt church in a corrupted age.[35] Rupert clearly thought that such works as his commentary on John were as necessary for combating heresy in his own day as the Fourth Gospel itself was in the evangelist's day.[36] And clearly both exercised the ministry of scriptural interpretation and claimed divine authority for doing so.

In an essay appearing in an anthology honouring the contribution of Walter Principe to medieval studies, however, it is not enough to stop with this insight into Rupert and Hildegard's sense of mission. Principe was convinced that, to avoid the dangers of antiquarianism, the study of medieval theology and exegesis had to produce not just a better understanding of medieval people or ideas but also importantly to develop understandings and insights which would illuminate modern thought and exegesis. So in this instance, we must also ask: what can an exegete or theologian, or indeed the Church itself, since that was the audience to which Hildegard and Rupert themselves looked, learn today from the study of these particular examples of medieval prophetic discourse?

The lessons are both positive and negative. On the one hand, Hildegard's role in the church in the Rhineland in the twelfth century, and the way in which her role and her gifts were recognized and validated in her own day, present a valuable model. However unpalatable to some (perhaps many) her activities and teachings may have been, coming as they did from a cloistered woman, nevertheless the medieval church came to validate and to value them. Other insights are now also coming to light from the study of such earlier exegetes as Rabanus Maurus, who (as Mayeski has demonstrated)[37] recognized prophetic ministries among his female contemporaries. Seen in this context, Hildegard's life and work can point to ways that the insights and vision of those on the margin can be incorporated into the core experience of the present-day church, without losing sight of its central truths or betraying its truest traditions. Rupert, too, reminds us that spiritual insight does not always come in the expected packaging: not only did he not have the proper education but even his friend Cuno said he looked like another Epicurus, 'a paltry fellow with a fat belly',[38] yet his reading of John's Gospel, imperfect though it may be, has much to offer a modern audience. Hildegard and Rupert thus show us ways in which to make all things new, surely the prophet's role in any age.

On the negative side, Rupert's experience too is instructive. He must bear some if not most of the responsibility for the failure of his conviction of inspired insight to be validated in his own day. Rupert was not without guilt in debasing spiritual insights by abusing them as debater's points in his controversies with those teachers, like the nascent schoolmen of Laon, with whom he bitterly disagreed. No one is very likely to recognize an inspired insight when it is used as a club to belabour one's enemies and no matter how convinced Rupert was of his own rightness, he might well have remembered his Master's advice to be wise as serpents (Matt. 10:16) as well as the more contemporary proverb about honey and vinegar. In the end, even the appreciation by later times of his contribution to exegesis was derailed by the use later made of his work in the equally bitter controversies of the Reformation and Counter-Reformation. If theology and exegesis in our day are to profit from visionaries like Hildegard and Rupert, we (and they) must be wary of the trap of controversy so bitter that it leaves no room for the Spirit of prophecy.

Notes

1 Rupert of Deutz, *In quaedam capitula Regulae S. Benedicti*, bk 1 (PL 170.477-538), henceforth cited as *Regula*. There is no modern edition of this work.

2 The only full-length treatment of Rupert's life and work in English remains the excellent study by John van Enghen, *Rupert of Deutz* (Berkeley: University of California Press, 1983).

3 *Regula*, col. 480C. This translation, and subsequent Latin translations in the text, are the work of the author; fuller translations of several of the texts discussed here (Rupert's apologetic preface to his commentary on John; his *Regula*, bk 1; Hildegard of Bingen's *Protestificatio* to *Scivias*; Guibert of Gembloux's first two letters to Hildegard and her initial reply) can be found at http://www.chass.utoronto.ca/~young/trnintro.html.

4 Ibid., col. 481A.

5 Ibid., col. 481A-B.

6 Ibid., col. 482D.

7 Ibid., col. 489D.

8 Rupert of Deutz, *De gloria et honore filii hominis super Mattheum*, ed. Rh. Haacke, (CCCM 29 [Turnhout: Brepols, 1979]); henceforth cited as *Gloria*.

9 This narrative has been discussed at length in section one of Abigail Ann Young, 'The Fourth Gospel In The Twelfth Century: Rupert Of Deutz On The Gospel Of John' (http://www.chass.utoronto.ca/~young/rdintro.html), a revision of 'The Commentaria in Iohannis Euangelium of Rupert of Deutz: A Methodological Analysis in the Field of Twelfth Century Exegesis', unpublished Ph.D. diss. (University of Toronto, 1984).

10 *Gloria*, ed. Haake, p. 366, ll. 132-8.

11 Ibid., p. 369, ll. 242-5.

12 Ibid., pp. 370-2; the words quoted are on p. 372, ll. 364, 366-7. It is an interesting and little-mentioned fact that Rupert is, so far as is now known, the first person in the Latin West to record such a vision of the Trinity in human form. See François Bœspflug, 'La Vision-en-Rêve de la Trinité de Rupert de Deutz', *Revue des sciences religieuses* 71/2 (1997) 205-29.

13 *Gloria*, ed. Haake, pp. 372-3, ll. 378-84.

14 Ibid., pp. 374-5.
15 Ibid., pp. 378-9.
16 Ibid., pp. 382-3.
17 Ibid., pp. 383-4.
18 Guibert's letters to Hildegard are printed as nos. 16-22 and 24 in *Guiberti Gemblacensis epistolae quae in codice B. R. Brux. 5527-5534 inueniuntur*, ed. Albert Derolez, 2 vols., (CCCM 66-67 [Turnhout: Brepols, 1988], 1.216-50, 254-7. Hildegard's replies are printed as nos. 103R, 106R, and 109R in *Hildegardis Bingensis Epistolarium*, ed. L. van Acker, CCCM 91-91A (Turnhout: Brepols, 1993), 1.258-68.
19 Hildegard of Bingen, *Scivias*, ed. A. Führkötter and A. Carlevaris, 2 vols. (CCCM 43-43A [Turnhout: Brepols, 1978]), 1.3-6.
20 *Scivias*, ed Führkötter and Carlevaris, pp. 3-4.
21 See Sabina Flanagan, *Hildegard of Bingen, 1098-1179: A Visionary Life* (New York: Routledge, 1989) and Barbara Newman, *Sister of Wisdom: St. Hildegard's Theology of the Feminine* (Berkeley: University of California Press, 1987) for full discussions and bibliography.
22 *Hildegardis Bingensis Epistolarium*, ed. van Acker, n. 103R (2.261).
23 Ibid., p. 262.
24 *Scivias*, ed Führkötter and Carlevaris, p. 5.
25 *Hildegardis Bingensis Epistolarium*, ed. van Acker, n. 103R (2.262)
26 Barbara Newman, 'Hildegard of Bingen: Visions and Validation', *Church History* 54 (1985) 163-75.
27 Ibid., 173.
28 Robert E. Lerner, 'Ecstatic Dissent', *Speculum* 67 (1992) 33-57; Lerner discusses Rupert (whom he refers to throughout as 'Robert of Liege') principally on pp. 34-8.
29 See M.A. Mayeski, '"Let Women not Despair": Rabanus Maurus on Women as Prophets', *Theological Studies* 58 (1997) 237-53, especially 240-1, for a brief discussion of the roots of this distinction, based both upon scriptural texts and the earlier church's repudiation of Montanism.
30 Lerner, 'Ecstatic Dissent', pp. 38-42 (Joachim), 42-6 (Arnold).
31 This attitude seems to be changing, however. Walter Berschin, 'Visione e vocazione allo scivere. L'autobiografia di Ruperto di Deutz', *Schede Medievali* 19 (1990) 297-303, has described Rupert's visions, translated part of the account from Book 12 of *Gloria* into Italian, and concluded that Rupert was 'un visionario di tipo profetico come più tardi Ildegarda di Bingen' (p. 302).
32 In the following discussion, I have relied on the discussions of Old Testament prophecy in F.I. Andersen and D.N. Freedman, *Hosea: A New Translation with Introduction and Commentary*, Anchor Bible, vol. 24 (Garden City, NY: Doubleday, 1980), pp. 40-52 and 143-51, and of prophecy in the Apostolic Age and in early Christian commentaries in Mayeski, 'Let Women not Despair', pp. 239-45.
33 Cf. 1 Sam. 3:30, 7:15-17.
34 See especially Ambrosiaster's discussion in PL 17.263A-C and the prefaces to Cassiodorus' *Expositio Psalmorum*, PL 70.13D, both quoted in Mayeski, pp. 241-2.
35 The best discussion of Hildegard as preacher and reformer and her attitudes toward the Church in her day is found in Newman, *Sister of Wisdom*.
36 The preface to his commentary on John suggests that one of Rupert's motives was correcting heresy, for he emphasized that aspect of the tradition about the gospel's composition. In fact he there placed those traditions in a pastoral context, showing John not only correcting false teaching but thereby increasing and bolstering the faith of ordinary

believers. For Rupert, the great danger of heretical teaching about the divinity of Jesus is the threat it presents to a believer's assurance of salvation, because if Jesus was not truly the Son of God, he was not a true heir to the kingdom, and if not a true heir, he could not associate others with him in his inheritance. John, by meeting that threat head-on in his gospel, helped not only his own contemporaries, whose salvation was threatened by persuasive teachers who reduced the status of Jesus Christ from that of full divinity and sonship, but also believers of Rupert's day. See *Commentaria in euangelium sancti Iohannis*, ed. R. Haacke (CCCM 9 [Turnhout: Brepols, 1969]), pp. 5-7, especially pp. 5-6, and section three of Young, 'The Fourth Gospel' (see n. 9).

37 Mayeski, 'Let Women not Despair', especially pp. 245-9.

38 *Regula*, col. 479C.

Chapter 3

There is a Text in this Classroom: The Bible and Theology in the Medieval University[1]

James R. Ginther

Modern Approaches to Medieval Scholastic Theology

Over the last century, students of medieval scholastic theology have embraced two different approaches in their research. The first concerns the theoretical conception of theology as a domain of abstract thought. Scholars of this approach entertain such issues as how medieval theologians defined their discipline, what the methods of investigation were, and how these masters related their discipline to others in the university. The principal question for scholastic theology has been: is theology a science?[2] – that is, a discipline that employs a structured method to investigate its principal subject. There has been some rewarding labour here, although there has been a tendency in the literature to gravitate to the opening question of the *Summa theologiae* of Thomas Aquinas.[3] However, the recent editorial work of Leonardo Sileo has provided another important textual gateway into this scholastic debate, although few scholars have fully embraced these sources.[4] Nonetheless, it is clear that most university theologians of the Middle Ages considered it important, if not necessary, to envision what their discipline was and how it was to function theoretically.[5]

The second approach has focused on the institutional features of theological education. Scholars of this field approach the textual remains of university teaching within the context of university regulations and charters, noting that the tripartite job description of a master of theology – namely to lecture, dispute and preach – was not only an ideal, but also an actual practice. The primary sources have been carefully assimilated into a portrait of how the faculties of theology functioned within the wider university context, both in terms of course regulation and the development of the university as a guild of masters.[6] Because of the careful work completed by modern scholarship, we have a reasonable picture of how theology was taught, and even how the various components of that teaching functioned together.[7]

It is troubling that these two approaches are rarely combined to produce a more holistic image of medieval theology.[8] Instead, we have two distinct visions of scholastic theology as a medieval discipline, one that thrives as a theoretical model, and another that embraces the day-to-day realities of teaching. One can understand why this segregated description persists: what scholars say and what they actually do, do not always necessarily cohere. This still remains a common assessment of the modern university. We all can develop grand theories for teaching and research, but at times we must still bend to the mandates of a dean, college president, or vice-chancellor who may conceive of the university in terms entirely different from the teachers and researchers.

The modern experience has indeed had a profound impact on the perception of the theology of the medieval schools. In the late nineteenth century, Roman Catholic seminarians and theologians were encouraged to adopt a 'medieval' approach in their teaching of philosophy and theology. The aim of this mandate, promulgated at first through the papal encyclical *Aeterni Patris* (1879), was to protect Catholic theology from the onslaught of modernism. By returning teachers to the medieval roots of theology, it was hoped by many, not least the papal curia, that nineteenth-century Catholic thinkers would have an alternative to contemporary theories that was substantive, intellectually challenging, and above all, orthodox. Herein lies a fine example of using historical sources as a fortress to protect contemporary theological ideals.[9] By appealing to the past, the papacy sought to ensure the growth of contemporary theology.

It is somewhat ironic, then, that documents like *Aeterni Patris* have had the reverse effect, namely that the portrayal of medieval theology has reflected more of the contemporary ideals of modern theology – such as systematics and philosophical theology – than modern theology did of its medieval counterpart.[10] While many scholars of medieval philosophy have moved beyond the neo-scholastic model,[11] the 'modern' depiction of medieval theology has remained almost intact. This traditional account still permeates much of the research in this area of medieval studies, and has indeed permitted some dialogue between the past and the present. That dialogue, however, has proceeded on modern terms, which can easily reduce dialogue to monologue. It may take some time, therefore, to wrest control of medieval theology from the traditional account, and transform what was originally a fortress into a launching pad for future research.

The Traditional Account of Scholastic Theology

The traditional account of medieval scholastic theology states that a new form of theological discourse emerged in the late eleventh century.[12] It was not entirely novel as much of scholastic theology drew from patristic sources, particularly Augustine and Boethius. What was new was the well-defined distinction between faith and reason, and soon the movement's motto became *fides quaerens intellectum* – 'faith seeking understanding'. The writings of St Anselm (1033–1109) are often considered as the watershed of this new movement, but we have to include as well the formative work of Anselm of Laon (d. 1117), Gilbert of Poitiers (c. 1080–1154) and perhaps even Peter Abelard (1079–1142).[13] All this theological musing focused on providing a rational explanation of items which had been heretofore placed in the category of *credibilia* – 'things to be believed'.

In many respects, the scholastic method was about liberation. Its participants obtained a new sense of freedom to engage critically the content of the Christian faith. They could raise questions and take various positions on theological points, much to the chagrin of more conservative thinkers.[14] Moreover, they could utilize patristic and canonical sources in a fresh manner. No longer was it simply a question of providing a relevant authority to support a theological position. It became necessary to create a network of consistency among the various authorities. Scholastics developed a new reading strategy for their sources, in which the intent was to produce a *ratio* which allowed for a concordance of apparent discordant sources.

Scholasticism also embraced a liberation from the biblical text.[15] Scholastic theology allowed for discourse to take place outside of biblical commentary, and this produced a more speculative form of theologizing. As the thirteenth century progressed, the traditional account continues, biblical commentary was eclipsed by commentary on the *Sentences* of Peter Lombard, a source which allowed for a greater flexibility in the theological agenda.[16] This programme was furthered by the opportunity of public debates, whose points of departure were not always specific biblical loci, but rather the abstract controversies of the academic and ecclesiastical communities.[17] Scholastic theologians, in effect, achieved a separation between theology and exegesis.[18]

This account has served historians well, as it has engendered an admirable collection of monographs and articles, all of which have gone a long way in elaborating the modern understanding of medieval thought. However, if one is willing to utilize the findings of those who have carefully explicated the practical realities of teaching in the medieval university, it becomes clear that the traditional account is in need of some correction. In the first place, the history of medieval education reminds modern historians and theologians alike that teaching in the medieval university was text-based – and the sacred science was no exception. Theology began and ended in an authoritative text, and that text was not any magisterial *summa*, nor even the *Sentences* of Peter Lombard; but rather, the Bible.[19] Secondly, this text-centred teaching strategy is echoed in the writings of those who grappled with the theoretical outlines of their sacred discipline. Regardless of how a theologian constructed the nature of theological discourse, however he enscribed the rules of analysis for, and engagement with, the discipline's subject matter, he acknowledged the discipline's commitment to the Bible as the epi-centre. Hence, introductory articles of scholastic *summae* as well as disputed questions concerning the nature of theology, included sections on the nature of biblical exegesis.[20] A good theologian embraced a rational approach to theology, and that approach had a significant place for the reading of sacred Scripture.

To challenge the traditional account is one thing, and perhaps few at the beginning of this new century would object.[21] Coming to terms, however, with the implications of returning the Bible to the heart of medieval theology is another matter altogether.

There may have indeed been a text in the classroom of medieval scholastic theology, but it was of a configuration that differed greatly from the modern notion of a classroom text. Reconstructing a more holistic picture of medieval theology cannot simply be a question of identifying the central text, and describing what it contains. For the Bible, this can be somewhat misleading. We can begin by saying that the biblical text is defined by the established canon of Old and New Testament books, and that it was read mainly in Latin.[22] However, students and masters did not always encounter the Bible as a whole book. Rather, they were exposed to the various constituent parts of the sacred text, and often in small fragments. Most probably students of theology, when young boys, had learned to read by using a Psalter.[23] They heard biblical reading in the liturgies of feast days and Sundays. They heard minute portions of text in sermons. If they were ordained in the major orders, they used lectionaries, gospel books, and graduals for their public and private Bible reading. As students read through the Fathers, they also encountered scriptural *lemmata*. Even when a student followed a strategy for reading the entire canon, that very strategy often emphasized the difference between the various books, grouping them together in terms of genre and level of difficulty.[24]

This fragmented reading points to a significant feature of the medieval Bible, and it has major implications for medieval theology. When we speak of medieval exegesis, it is necessary to conceive of Bible reading not only within a certain conceptual framework, but also in terms of the reader's physical encounter with the text. This means that we pay attention both to the forces that shape the mental pre-conditions for reading, and to the text's physiognomies. This requires us to exercise our historical imagination in a different manner. It is not uncommon, for example, to note that one medieval scholar must have had the writings of another open and on his desk while he wrote his commentary. As common as this imagery is, and indeed helpful when we think about sources, it can sometimes misrepresent the actual historical events. It pre-supposes three physically independent elements in the picture: the reader, the text under study, and the source(s) employed in the reading. Such a portrayal can obscure the fact that the reader also encountered the sacred text at hand in many different ways, as already noted. The alternative, then, is to envision a reader, the text under study, and that same text embedded in the sources which he is exploiting. Sometimes that embedding was a physical reality for the *whole* text, particularly if the reader was using a glossed Bible. As equally important, however, is the fact that the reader would also embrace the portions of the sacred text within other texts, sometimes during his reading, or often as a recollection of past encounters with that text. In other words, the medieval exegete experienced the Bible as a dispersed text.

Describing the Bible as a dispersed text is not simply a reconfiguration of medieval exegesis in terms of intertextuality.[25] My aim here is not to examine the intertextuality of the Bible, since medieval exegesis did not concern itself *a priori* with the construction of the biblical text. One may consider, however, commentary as an *a posteriori* reconstruction of the Bible, and therein we must pay careful attention to the intertextual functions of commentary. In this instance, we may provisionally consider the Bible as the intertext *par excellence*, because it acted as the textual anchor to any and all exegetical activity in medieval scholastic theology. Hence, I would argue that the Bible as a dispersed text is a form of *delimited intertextuality* – an oxymoron to some degree, but a term that embraces the expansiveness of the exegetical act, as well as its textual and interpretive boundaries.[26] It is delimited because the medieval exegesis began with a stable text of the Bible, defined by the canon. However, that stability did not mean that readers embraced it as a complete text at all times. Instead, the Bible was read as part of other texts, or it was reorganized according to an external principle. Even when confronted with a complete Bible, the medieval reader did not necessarily treat it as a unit. Indeed, this may be one further reason why scholastics began to develop concordances and distinctions, which allowed them to navigate around the whole text in various ways, and with differing exegetical intentions.[27]

If we consider the Bible as a dispersed text, then how does this affect our understanding of the work of theology in the medieval schools? I will explore this question by examining some sources of theological discourse from the first half of the thirteenth century, with principal reference to the writings of Robert Grosseteste (c. 1170–1253), Alexander of Hales (c. 1186–1245), Hugh of St-Cher (d. 1268), Richard Fishacre (d. 1248), and Thomas Aquinas (c. 1225–1274). To appreciate the medieval Bible as a dispersed text first requires a change in the analytical model used to investigate exegetical sources. Instead of relying solely upon a theoretical analysis of exegesis (that is, the fourfold sense of Scripture), we must treat medieval scholastic exegesis as an historical act. As historians of theology, we need to identify how a scholastic exegete fulfilled his task, and what textual and cultural tools he exploited in the process since it is in these very tools that he also encountered sacred Scripture. By doing so, we will be able to examine how this dispersed text functioned in medieval scholastic theology. Moreover, to embrace fully the implications of the Bible as a dispersed text, we must not limit our enquiries to the literary remains of biblical commentary. The act of disputation has a relevant role to play here, and in two specific ways. First, disputation acted as another medium for the sacred text to be dispersed, and indeed one can find the imprint of Scripture and its exegesis in the disputed questions of the scholastic era. Second, I will argue that disputation also took the place of meditation as a means to develop the powerhouse of memory. If sacred Scripture could travel in a variety of media, and in various configurations of citation and allusion, then the theologian needed to be able to identify those elements of the Bible in other texts. As most theologians committed the Bible to memory, engaging in disputation provided an ideal pedagogical venue for the memory to be enhanced, for the disputation was an event in which the student and master equally engaged and exploited the biblical *lemma* and its multi-valent *sententia*. In establishing the internal configurations of these theological activities, we shall see that there was no complete separation of theology and exegesis; rather they proceeded in tandem.

Exegesis as an Historical Act

In order to consider scholastic exegesis as an historical act, we must first recognize that it functioned as an integral part of a curriculum, and that it was primarily within the brief of teaching masters. Each regent master, within each faculty, was responsible for overseeing a small group of students, a *schola*. If we are to appreciate the dynamics of university education in the Middle Ages, we must understand that the pedagogical locus was not the discipline's faculty, but rather the various *scholae* that were the constituent parts.[28] The *schola*, in fact, predates the origins of the university: a master attracted a group of students who formed his teaching unit, the school. They paid him directly for his services, and he maintained the curriculum and enforced the requisite discipline. With the establishment of universities, the schools became part of a faculty, but the master retained full control of his individual school. He could no longer expect a regular income from his students,[29] but the other side of the transaction remained fully intact. The *auditor* or *scholaris* sat at the feet of his master, until he was ready to be examined for graduation. He heard his master lecture, although he might be allowed to attend the lectures of other masters and bachelors.[30] The master's school would also hold private disputations, in which two students debated with one another. The resolution to the debate would be provided by the master, which is the main reason why these disputations should be considered as belonging to the master and not the students.[31] Students would also attend public or faculty disputations, in which a master could employ students from outside his own school as participants. This happened only at certain times in the year, and so for the most part a student gleaned his education from a single master.

From the magisterial perspective in any faculty of theology, there were three duties to perform: to lecture, to dispute, and to preach. To lecture meant to expound sacred Scripture, that is to provide a comprehensive reading. Only masters were permitted to engage in spiritual exegesis. Hence, the term ordinary lecture (*lectio ordinaria*) referred to a magisterial reading of the Bible.[32] To dispute, as we have just noted, meant to lead the school in a debate on a certain passage of scripture, or on a doctrinal point. According to the Franciscan chronicler, Thomas of Eccleston, leading a disputation was indeed a magisterial responsibility. Among the many Franciscan convents established in England in the first half of the thirteenth century, some only had a bachelor of theology as the lector, who could then only comment on sacred Scripture; others had fully-fledged masters who could lead disputations.[33] The reason for this lay in the determination, which was an authoritative statement, and therefore required a fully trained person to pronounce it. Finally, a master was to preach. This could take one of three forms: he could preach to a convent's chapter if the master were the lector for a mendicant order; or as a regent master before the whole university congregation; or thirdly, before a lay audience.[34] Preaching was not separate from the other two academic responsibilities. In the words of Peter the Chanter, preaching was the final adornment of the house of God that theologians were called to build, as lecturing was the foundation, disputation the walls, and preaching the roof.[35]

Let us focus for a moment on the foundation for this house. In order to investigate exegesis in medieval scholastic theology, we must begin with a catalogue of authentic works – an obvious point of departure, but one that is not always easy to locate. If we take Alexander of Hales as a prime example, it is instructive to note that there has been little critical discussion of his biblical exegesis.[36] The main reason for this is that we lack editions of any sort for any of his commentaries, save for a very good edition of his prologue to his commentary on John,[37] and hence we cannot expect any serious discussion of his exegesis until this editorial challenge has been taken up.[38] Moreover, where we do have editions of texts, as is the case with Thomas Aquinas, it is of some regret that they have been virtually ignored in the modern configuration of that thinker's theological vision. Thomas himself spilled far more ink for his commentaries on the Bible than he did on Aristotle, and yet it is the Philosopher who looms large in Thomistic studies. A corrected modern vision of medieval scholastic theology must begin with a clear understanding that sacred Scripture was both the beginning and end of the scholastic theological enterprise.

Once we have placed exegesis in its rightful place, it remains to establish a general methodology for examining these texts. We need to have a better idea of the nature and the mechanics of medieval exegesis. In his biography of Cassiodorus, James O'Donnell noted that we are still in the infancy stage of our understanding of medieval exegesis. For all the magisterial advancements by scholars such as Beryl Smalley and Henri de Lubac, we have yet to establish a comprehensive methodology for reading these medieval texts. Their construction is of such a foreign fabric, so alien are they to our modern way of reading and interpreting texts, that we often proceed down their corridors of reasoning and explanation in a partially blind state.[39] It is sometimes unclear why we encounter so many disparate ideas in one book, and thus we are unsure how to bring together these ideas to form a coherent and unified pattern of exposition. Although we can examine the issues and assertions within the commentary under study, connecting them with general trends in scholastic theology, and can even make some observations about the exegete's sources, it remains to answer the question: how exactly did he do it?

I would like to make a modest suggestion, one that at the very least takes into account the Bible as a dispersed text. To interpret the Bible *in scholis* was to engage in two distinct, but clearly related, actions. First, there was reading the text. It was carefully examined but never in isolation, for there were four basic inter-related filters or lenses, which aided the expositor: patristic or authoritative commentaries, including canon law; the *Glossa ordinaria* that encircled the text; the liturgical function of the text at hand; and the theory of the Four Senses of Scripture. By pointing to these textual influences, we must do much more than just simple source criticism, for it is here that the idea of the dispersed text is a force with which we must reckon. We need to dispense with the image of medieval exegesis as a two step process: read the text, and then read the sources. Instead, these two steps could happen simultaneously. We ought to envision in what context the expositor has experienced the text now before his exegetical eye. Is it, for example, a central text to a specific liturgical feast or function?[40] Does the master encounter the text either in part or in whole in the patristic sources he has consulted? In what context does the *Glossa ordinaria* place the *lemma* at hand? Is the exegete quoting from a canon law collection, and in what way does that section of canon law focus his exegesis? And finally, in what ways do the guidelines for spiritual exegesis shape his interpretation?

Sometimes it will be impossible to answer some or any of these questions, since we cannot trace with any confidence the specific material sources that the expositor has used. However, even if we can answer these questions in part, we may at least be able to see how and why the teaching master has employed other passages of the sacred text as a means of expounding the *lemma* under scrutiny. We need to have a careful look at how the interpreting portion of Scripture arrives in the mind of the exegete, for as a dispersed text a biblical citation was normally embraced as part of another text or context. Understanding the way in which a biblical *lemma* is received is a fundamental factor for describing medieval exegesis as an historical event.

The second related action of scholastic exegesis is the presentation of the findings to the students of the school. This involved: exploitation of classical and scholastic rhetorical forms, within the context of the *studium*; occasional influence of, or reference to, contemporaneous events and controversies; and critical engagement with other masters. While the immediate context of the exegesis was the school, the form of teaching reflected the general characteristics of the *studium* or university. Many masters of the sacred page were graduates of the faculty of arts, and therefore had that faculty's methods of investigation and communication firmly imprinted on their intellectual outlook.[41]   Robert Grosseteste illustrates this point well. Before he was a master of theology, he had been well-educated in the liberal arts, and especially in the quadrivium.[42]   He wrote a number of treatises on the natural world, as well as on metaphysics and mathematics.[43]   It is not surprising therefore that a scientific perspective can be found in his exegesis of the sacred page. The other two factors are sometimes more difficult to establish, especially for Grosseteste. For example, I have yet to find a single instance in his commentary on the Psalms in which he mentions a contemporary event. When he notes the opinions of others (*quidam dicunt*), the ones traced to date indicate an engagement with patristic sources, and not contemporary thinkers.

We must be careful not to separate the assessment of rhetorical and institutional context from the actual act of exegesis. As Martin Irvine has recently pointed out, commentary remains embedded in textuality. It is an attempt to replicate the text as object, but with additional guidelines or parameters that can be used for any subsequent reading.[44]   In exegesis, this means that there is a physical replication of the biblical text in the form of *lemmata* from the text as object, as well as additional pericopes which are used as explicative keys. More importantly, these are arranged, connected, or juxtaposed for the sake of a rhetorical strategy, such as addressing a contemporary doctrinal problem, or explaining past expositions of this or similar texts. Commentary is yet another way for the biblical text to be dispersed.

As a dispersed text, the Bible could not be contained within a classroom lecture. Just as Scripture spilled out of the sources of exegesis, so it also seeped into all work of the medieval scholastic theologian. As much as the traditional account would like the work of medieval theology to be neatly compartmentalized into exegesis and theology, the nature of the medieval Bible prevented any simple division of labour. Instead, any account of medieval theology must confront how the exposition of the discipline's central text worked its way into the other facets of theology in the medieval university. A full account of scholastic engagement with the Bible cannot end with the classroom lecture: we must begin there, and then continue to trace the path of the dispersed text into the other major function of the master of the sacred page. It is to the disputation that we now turn.

Disputation as Medium for Dispersion

The disputed question is often reputed to have been the repository of the infamous scholastic method. However, William Courtenay has recently pointed out that we must be careful not to attach too much metaphysical significance to what was basically a pedagogical practice. Disputation did not necessarily herald the birth of a new theological method, but rather provided a means for students to develop certain critical skills. Courtenay, in order to reintroduce a more balanced look at disputation, has suggested that historians consider these events as equivalent to jousting tournaments. They were opportunities for intellectual play that had a practical purpose, namely to hone the student's ability to gather disparate details and organize and assess them in order to support a supposition.[45] The disputant as a *homo ludens* does capture the general intent of these debates, particularly for the quodlibetal questions where the aim was to test the limits of a master's knowledge, as well as his ability to address *ex tempore* any and all questions.

The pedagogical nature of disputation returns the historian once again to the textbook of theology. Since the beginning of the scholastic period, masters had raised *quaestiones* that concerned both the problems that specific biblical loci had spawned, as well as general theological questions. As the teaching of theology became more formalized, it was not uncommon for lectures on the Bible to end with a series of questions, raised either by the master himself or drawn from his audience. This practice continued right up to the fourteenth century, and in some instances posing and answering questions became a teaching method in its own right.[46] While there was a link between the *quaestio* found in a lecture and the *quaestio disputata*, they are not the same thing. Instead, the latter emerged as a separate pedagogical event in the early thirteenth century. The process of having two students take opposing points of view, with the Master later providing a final resolution to the problem (*determinatio*), remained unchanged for the whole of the scholastic period.

The link between the *quaestio* and the *disputatio* was the exegesis of the Bible, a point that is often neglected in the modern literature. Robert Grosseteste provides once again an instructive example. Among the questions disputed during his regency at Oxford, one is entitled *De veritate*, and modern scholars have employed this text as a means of examining Grosseteste's epistemology.[47] Such an approach can be supported by the content of the question, since Grosseteste provides a careful assessment of Anselm's definition of truth. However, the point of departure for the question is of equal importance. The question opens by asking: If Christ claims to be the truth in the singular, as he does in the Gospel of John, what does this have to say about the nature of truth? Must one speak only of one truth, or is it licit to consider many truths?[48] In other words, the question is an attempt to come to terms with the theological implications of a reading of Scripture.

Moving from *lectio* to *disputatio* appears to have been a common occurrence. In his commentary on Galatians 2, Grosseteste rehearses the patristic controversy over the role of the Mosaic Law in early Christianity. He presents a short argument as to why it would seem better to follow Augustine rather than Jerome in this debate, and he concludes the section by noting that such topics will be best left to a disputation.[49] The use of the future tense implies that a disputed question was part of Grosseteste's teaching programme, and indeed it is not surprising to discover that his major work on the relationship between Law and Gospel, *De cessatione legalium*, opens with what appears to be the remnants of a disputed question.[50] Grosseteste was not the only one to outline this relationship between lecture and disputation. A more celebrated case is found in the writings of Hugh of St-Cher's commentary on Isaiah 38. There he addresses the problem that Isaiah prophesied the death of the King, Hezekiah, who then did not die. Did Isaiah prophesy falsely, Hugh asks, and, even more seriously, if Isaiah's statement was based on God's foreknowledge did this mean that God's foreknowledge was mutable? Hugh does attempt to answer the question, but his explanation brings him into the general realm of a definition of prophecy and away from the meaning of the biblical text.[51] Hugh's aim was to explicate carefully the text, using the original intent of the author as the guide to establishing the spiritual exposition.[52]

These two examples demonstrate a clear link between the lecture and the disputation, which points to disputation as another medium by which the Bible was dispersed. However, as many students of medieval scholastic theology will note, there are a number of instances when little mention is made of the Bible in a disputed question, and indeed it would seem that philosophical enquiry becomes the preoccupation of the disputant. Perhaps this is most relevant to study of the commentaries on the *Sentences.* Did not this text become the real centre of theological education in the thirteenth century, since it further bolstered the disputed question? After all, for those who embraced the new theology of this period, the *Sentences* were a textual locus to invoke the *modus inveniendi* of scientific theology. The development of doctrine can be traced quite clearly in these texts, and modern scholarship would be well-served by the production of more critical editions of these important sources.[53]

To understand the place of the *Sentences* in scholastic theology, and its relationship with Scripture, we need to remind ourselves who commented on the work. We are told in the traditional narrative that a new age began when Alexander of Hales led his school in an exposition of the *Sentences* sometime between 1225 and 1229.[54] After that, more and more theologians lectured on the Lombard's work, and by mid-century, it was a common practice in the curriculum. However, there are two points that we must include to update this narrative. First, Alexander was hardly the first commentator on the *Sentences*, and indeed his *Gloss* reflects the way the previous generation had examined this important source.[55] Connected to this point is that only one commentator followed in his footsteps at Paris, Hugh of St-Cher.[56] It would be another fifteen years before more theologians would embrace this text.[57]

Second, the majority of those who did lecture on the *Sentences* were bachelors, and not masters. By the 1240s, it would appear that only after four years of hearing magisterial and cursory expositions of the Bible, were these bachelors permitted to hold public lectures on the *Sentences*. By the end of the century, commenting on the *Sentences* became the major textual production necessary for completing the theology course. In other words, these commentaries were the 'doctoral dissertations' of the faculty of theology. To present *Sentence* commentaries as the major source for scholastic theology is thus equivalent to tracing the intellectual history of a department or university by examining only the work of its graduate students. Such a strategy does indeed tell you very important things about the institution, but it by no means tells the whole story. The rest of the story, as equally important, lies in the work of the regent masters, and we find that recorded in their determinations to disputed questions, and above all, in their magisterial comments on Scripture. We cannot forget the *Sentences* and its billowing clouds of witnesses that surrounded it, but this text cannot stand as the sole representative for scholastic theology.

There is a further reason why this cannot be so. Around 1242, the Dominican Richard Fishacre began to lecture on the *Sentences* at Oxford. He caused quite a stir, not because he was the first to do so, but rather because he insisted on lecturing *ordinarily* on this text. A certain bishop of Lincoln attempted to stop him, and was only dissuaded by a papal letter directing that bishop to allow Fishacre to dispense with the standard rules of university lecturing. For the pope, such lectures on the *Sentences* would further the apologetic task of the Dominicans, namely to combat heresy.[58]

Fishacre seems to have been aware of the fact that he was breaking with tradition, and so addresses the status of the text before himself and his students. Allow me to quote him at some length.

> There is a division of this science because there are two things in human nature (*in natura media*), the motive virtue and the apprehensive virtue, and these are also called the affect and the aspect. Now, the supreme nature is the highest good and the highest truth. Thus this science, which is about one [subject] from two, has two parts: one concerns the unity of the affect with the highest good; the other concerns the unity of the aspect with the highest truth.... Therefore that part of this science which concerns the union of the affect with the highest good in this life, pursues moral teaching (*moribus instruendis*), but the other part which concerns the union of the aspect and the highest truth in this life pursues difficult questions which ought to be disputed concerning the articles of faith.

Both these parts, I admit, are contained in the canon of Sacred Scripture, though indistinctly. Nonetheless modern masters teach moral doctrine when they lecture on the sacred books; the other, more difficult part is reserved for disputation. This more difficult part found in that book called the *Sentences* has been excerpted from the canon of Sacred Scripture.[59]

Fishacre admits that ultimately the content of the *Sentences* originates with sacred Scripture. Lombard's text is yet another example of the Bible as a dispersed text. Even when confronting a source that encouraged a speculative method, it was not divorced from the sacred text, but rather another opportunity to rediscover the Bible.[60] *Lectio* and *disputatio* shared the same ultimate source, and were both centred on sacred Scripture.

One final point needs to be made about the functionality of disputation, and again the Bible as a dispersed text illuminates. A dispersed text requires a good memory: as the text could travel in smaller units, the ability to memorize the text allowed a reader to be able to identify which elements of a text were biblical, and how they could be used to build an argument. There were a number of techniques both monastic and scholastic thinkers employed to memorize the Bible, including lemmatic lists, distinctions, images, and other mnemonic devices.[61] What drew it all together, at least for the monastic audience, was meditation. Here is where the fruit of memory was discovered, and plucked from the trees of the forest of ideas and images – if one can take liberty with a similitude of Hugh of St-Victor's.[62] Meditation allowed one to take the data read and memorized, and chew it over, ruminate, and regurgitate. In this way, the reader could apprehend not only the basic meaning of the text, but with his meditation, the student could make new connections and draw out other meanings from the text.

The way Mary Carruthers has described monastic meditation, in both of her recent monographs, reminded me of how Peter the Chanter described disputation: it was where one chewed over the doctrine of Christian faith.[63] Moreover, listen to how Hugh of St-Victor described the act of meditation:

> [Meditation] is bound by none of study's rules or precepts. For it delights to range along open ground, where it fixes its free gaze upon the contemplation of truth, drawing together now these, now those ideas, or now penetrating into profundities, leaving nothing doubtful, nothing obscure. The start of learning, thus, lies in *lectio*, but its consummation lies in meditation.[64]

This description could easily be applied to scholastic disputation. In the heat of debate, the two students marshalled evidence from Scripture, authorities, and other arguments to make their case. They roamed the countryside of theological thought, in search of landmarks and points of interest that would advance the central argument. Every point suggested was examined, challenged, and verified. Nothing was left obscured in imprecise or unclear terms. In the disputed question, the students, under the direction of the master, reconstructed theological truths of the *lectio* in new forms in order to come to grips with the profundities of doctrine.

A good scholastic exegete could not shun the disputed question: it was an essential feature of the reading of scripture. Questions had arisen from the lecture, and their separation in the early thirteenth century protected not only the biblical lecture, but also the disputation as well.[65] For scholastic theologians, each task was important, and relevant to the other. There was no separation of theology from exegesis, only distinctions made between the forms of inquiry. One could not proceed to disputation without first succeeding at exegesis. The best example of this comes from a text that few have considered a gateway to medieval exegesis, namely the *Summa theologiae* of Thomas Aquinas. It is not surprising that Thomas invokes Scripture on occasion; however, what is fascinating is the fact that in constructing his case, the turning point of the argument, the *sed contra*, is often a citation from Scripture.[66] In other words, what directs the argument is not simply the rational argument, but one that stems from an intimate and abiding knowledge of the sacred text. This should not be surprising, for in his inception sermon when he became a master of the sacred page, Thomas argued that the *lectio* is where one grapples with theological truth.[67] The disputation, the scholastic article, is where the implications of that truth are distinguished and examined. There were also pastoral dimensions to the task of disputation. In his commentary on the Psalms, Grosseteste makes the case that the health of the church depended upon the pastoral mastication of scriptural teaching. Without it, the church as a whole could not digest the truth of salvation. Grosseteste also speaks of the entire church learning to chew over the truth of Scripture, but it first must begin with the mouth of the church, that is, the leadership.[68]

One can see that disputation furthered the intimate experience with Scripture. To make an argument allowed theologians and their students to strengthen their abilities to store, collate, and recall portions of the sacred text. Like meditation, disputation furthered the art of memory. The schools may have abandoned the *otium* of the monastic life, as they were caught up in the joust of debate, but the intention of meditation remained an important principle for the faculties of theology: to acquire knowledge of Scripture and its meaning, and to commit it to memory so that it could be recalled, examined, and, above all, lived out.

Conclusion

This historical approach to medieval scholastic theology is not necessarily revolutionary, nor even original. It has been latent in more recent scholarly works, and in particular in the work of those who have been pursuing medieval exegesis itself. It has been my attempt here to *articulate* the methodological considerations of a more comprehensive analysis of the period and its sources. While I have drawn from some contemporary literary theory, I remain convinced that it is the study of the sources in conjunction with theoretical approaches, as opposed to those theoretical constructs on their own, that will yield a far more rigorous and accurate account of medieval scholastic theology. Indeed, while there has been a recognition of the similarity in textuality between premodern and postmodern thought, we must address this as an equivocal and not univocal similitude. At the very least, the pedagogical context of medieval theology should remind us that the theology of the medieval university is ultimately an alien world to the modern scholar.

Hence, both future historical study of, and any contemporary dialogue with, medieval theology must embrace this alterity. At the very least, modern scholars must accept that medieval theologians had a deep and abiding knowledge of Scripture. The memorization of Scripture was not simply an act of piety, nor were its contents of interest only to textual critics and those interested in biblical history; rather, the biblical text was the foundation for all theological reflection.[69] Moreover, that abiding knowledge of the text allowed medieval theologians to embrace a variety of sources. If we are willing to acknowledge the discursive force of patristic sources and even the *Glossa ordinaria*, there is no reason why we cannot apply the same degree of influence to the liturgy. It is a modern fiction that only Byzantine theology was charged by its liturgical context, for theology in the West was shaped by the act of communal worship. It is more than clear that the liturgical calendar, both in terms of daily and annual activities, shaped the context of medieval education, and it would further our understanding of theological discourse if modern scholars would pay attention to the liturgical sources. Some excellent work in sermon studies has recently been completed in this regard, and it yields a positive model for proceeding.[70]

Sources such as the fathers and the liturgy, along with the memorization of Scripture were some of the ways in which exegesis and disputation remained bound together. We must dispense with a model that emphasizes separation between these two acts, and instead take these historical figures as they were: masters of the sacred page.[71] Not only will this recognition pave the way towards a more accurate and comprehensive view of medieval scholastic theology, it may in the end also provide some guidance on how the various branches of modern theology may establish fruitful interchanges, and even gratifying dialogue.

Notes

1   This essay has a two-fold origin: first from chapter two of my doctoral thesis: James R. Ginther, 'The *Super Psalterium* of Robert Grosseteste (c. 1170-1253): A Scholastic Psalms Commentary as a Source for Medieval Ecclesiology', unpubl. PhD diss. (University of Toronto, 1995). I am grateful for comments on the chapter which Walter Principe conveyed in a letter written in the Autumn of 1995. Many of them have been incorporated here. The second origin is a paper presented at the Fifth International Medieval Congress, University of Leeds, 12-15 July 1999, which was completed as part of my preparation for a monograph on Grosseteste as a theologian. I am grateful to Dr. Mary Swan of the Centre for Medieval Studies, University of Leeds, for her comments on a draft of this paper.

2   The seminal work remains M.-D. Chenu, *La théologie comme une science au XIIIe siècle*, third edition (Paris: Vrin, 1957); but see also A. Köpf, *Die Änfange der*

theologischen Wissenschaftstheorie im 13. Jahrhundert (Tubingen: Mohr, 1974); and Brian Gaybba, *Aspects of the Medieval History of Theology, 12th to 14th Centuries,* Studia Originalia, 7 (Pretoria: University of South Africa, 1988).

3 *ST* 1.1.9-10.

4 Leonard Sileo, *Teoria della scienza teologica,* 2 vols., Studia Antoniana cura pontificii Athenaei Antoniani Edita, 27 (Rome: Antonianum, 1984).

5 In addition to the texts edited by Sileo, see also the contribution by Robert Grosseteste, *Hexaëmeron,* ed. R.C. Dales and S. Gieben, Auctores Britannici Medie Aevi, 6 (London: British Academy, 1982), 1.1.1-2.2 (pp. 49-51); Richard Fishacre's prologue to his *Sentence Commentary* in R. James Long, 'The Science of Theology according to Richard Fishacre', *Mediaeval Studies* 34 (1972) 71-98; the arguments of St Bonaventure and his school in G.H. Tavard, 'St. Bonaventure's Disputed Question *De theologia',* *Recherche de théologie ancienne et médiévale* 17 (1950) 187-236; Robert Kilwardby, *De natura theologiae,* ed. F. Stegmüller, Opuscula et Textus: Series Scholastica, 17 (Münster: Aschendorff, 1935); and Henry of Ghent, *Summa questionum ordinarium* (Paris: Bade, 1520; rprt. St Bonaventure, NY: Franciscan Institute, 1953), aa. 6-20, (fols. 35r-122v), as just a few additional examples.

6 On the guild structure and its relation to history of the medieval university, see Betsey Price, 'A Master by any other Means', *Renaissance and Reform* n.s. 13 (1989) 115-34.

7 See H. Rashdall *The Universities in Medieval Europe,* ed. F.M. Powicke and A.B. Emden, 3 vols. (Oxford: Clarendon Press, 1936), esp. 1.471-496, 3.158-159; G. Leff, *Paris and Oxford Universities in the Thirteenth and Fourteenth Centuries* (New York: Wiley, 1968); A.B Cobban, *The Medieval Universities: their Development and Organization* (London: Metheun, 1975); William J. Courtenay, *Teaching Careers at the University of Paris in the Thirteenth and Fourteenth Centuries,* Texts and Studies in the History of Mediaeval Education, 18 (Notre Dame IN: University of Notre Dame Press, 1988); the collected essays in *Manuels, programmes de cours et techniques d'enseignement dans les universités médiévales,* ed. J. Hamesse (Louvain-la-Neuve: Institut d'Etudes Médiévales de l'Université Catholique de Louvain, 1994), and the resources produced by Olga Weijers, *Terminologie des universités au XIIIe siècle* (Rome: Ateneo, 1987).

8 One fine example in which the two approaches are gracefully combined is William Courtenay, *Schools and Scholars in Fourteenth-Century England* (Princeton, NJ: Princeton University Press, 1988).

9 Walter H. Principe, 'The History of Theology: Fortress or Launching Pad?' in *The Sources of Theology,* ed. J.P. Boyle, Current Issues in Theology, 3 (Chicago: Catholic Theological Society of America, 1988), pp. 19-40.

10 On the impact of *Aeterni patris,* see Gerald McCool, *From Unity to Pluralism: the Internal Evolution of Thomism* (New York: Fordham University Press, 1989); and E.A. Synan, 'Latin Philosophies of the Middle Ages', in *Medieval Studies: An Introduction,* ed. J.M. Powell, Second Edition (Syracuse: Syracuse University Press, 1992), pp. 314-32, at 322-4.

11 In some respects, this shift in the scholarship began with the seminal work of Etienne Gilson. While the neo-scholastic project informed Gilson's attempt to identify a 'Christian Philosophy' drawn from medieval thought, he nonetheless pointed out to scholars the necessity of rigorous historical and textual research, facets not always found in the writings of neo-scholastics. For a recent example of this historical method in action, see John Marenbon, *Later Medieval Philosophy* (London: Routledge, 1987).

12 I have drawn this account from the following sources: G. Fritz and A. Michel, 'Scolastique', *Dictionaire de théologie catholique*, 14,2.1691-1728, esp. 1695-1715; M.A. Hotze, 'Scholastic Theology', *New Catholic Encyclopedia*, 12.1153; I.C. Brady, J.E. Gurr, and J.A. Weisheipl, 'Scholasticism', *Ibid*, 12.1153-1170; *A Scholastic Miscellany: From Anselm to Ockham*, ed. E.R. Fairweather, Library of Christian Classics (Philadelphia: Westminster Press, 1956), pp. 17-32; D. Knowles, *The Evolution of Medieval Thought* (New York: Vintage Books, 1962), pp. 79-106; A.M. Landgraf, *Introduction à l'histoire de la littérature théologique de la scolastique naissante*, trans. A.-M. Landry and L.-B. Geiger, Publications de l'Institut d'Etudes Médiévales, 22 (Montreal: Institut d'Etudes Médiévales, 1973), pp. 21-41; J. Pelikan, *The Christian Tradition: a History of the Development of Doctrine, Volume 3: The Growth of Medieval Theology (600-1300)* (Chicago: University of Chicago Press, 1978); J.J.E. Gracia, 'Scholasticsm and Scholastic Method', *Dictionary of the Middle Ages*, 11.55-58; B. Price, *Medieval Thought: An Introduction* (Oxford: Blackwell, 1992), pp. 119-44; and Ulrich G. Leinsle, *Einführung in die scholastische Theologie* (Paderborn: Ferdinand Schöningh, 1995), esp. pp. 111-69.

13 For Anselm of Laon, the authoritative work remains O. Lottin, *Psychologie et morale aux XIIe et XIIIe siècles, Tom. 5: Problemes d'histoire litteraire : l'ecole d'Anselme de Laon et de Guillaume de Champeaux* (Gembloux: Duculot, 1959). For the theology of Gilbert, see L.O. Nelson, *Theology and Philosophy in the Twelfth Century: A Study of Gilbert Porreta's Thinking and the Theological Expositions on the Doctrine of the Incarnation during the Period, 1130-1180* (Leiden: Brill, 1982); but a recent work has expanded the modern portrait of Gilbert: Theresa Gross-Diaz, *The Psalms Commentary of Gilbert of Poitiers: From* Lectio divina *to the Lecture Room*, Brill's Studies in Intellectual History, 68 (Leiden: Brill, 1996). The most recent biography of Abelard is M.T. Clanchy, *Abelard: a Medieval Life* (Oxford: Blackwells, 1997); but the findings of David Luscombe, *The School of Peter Abelard: the Influence of Abelard's Thought in the Early Scholastic Period* (Cambridge: Cambridge University Press, 1969), are still relevant. Abelard's impact on the development of medieval theology may not have been as great as it was first suggested: see Marcia L. Colish, 'Systematic Theology and Theological Renewal in the Twelfth Century', *Journal of Medieval and Renaissance Studies* 18 (1988) 135-56.

14 It is in this narrative framework that the conflict betwen Peter Abelard and Bernard of Clairvaux is cast. But see C. Stephen Jaegar, *The Envy of Angels: Cathedral Schools and Social Ideals in Medieval Europe, 950–1200* (Philadelphia: University of Pennsylvania Press, 1994), pp. 229-36, who suggests that this controversy concerned the much larger issues of authority and the virtuous life in teaching.

15 Pelikan, *The Growth of Medieval Theology*, pp. 223-9, 255-67.

16 Jacques Verger, 'L'exégèse, parente pauvre de la théologie scolastique?' in *Manuels, programmes de cours et techniques d'enseignement dans les universités médiévales*, Actes du Colloque international de Louvain-la-Neuve (9-11 Septembre 1993), ed. J. Hamesse, Publications de l'Institut d'Etudes Médiévales, 16 (Louvain-la-Neuve: Université Catholique de Louvain, 1994), pp. 31-56.

17 Benardo C. Bazàn, et al., *Les questions disputées et les questions quodlibétiques dans les facultés de théologie, de droit et de médecine*, Typologies des Sources du Moyen Age Occidental, 44-45 (Turnhout: Brepols, 1985). See Edward Synan, et al., 'A disputed question: Whether whatever is known is known in the divine ideas', 15 June 1983, in *From Cloister to Classroom: Monastic and Scholastic Approaches to Truth. The Spirituality of Western Christendom III*, ed. E. Rozanne Elder, Cistercian Studies, 90

(Kalamazoo, MI: Cistercian Publications, 1986), pp. 154-77, for a modern reenactment of a disputed question.

18 Chenu, *La théologie comme science*, pp. 15-52; Beryl Smalley, *The Study of the Bible in the Middle Ages*, second edition (Notre Dame: University of Notre Dame Press, 1964), pp. 293-94; G.R. Evans, *Old Arts and New Theology: The Beginnings of Theology as an Academic Discipline* (Oxford: Clarendon Press, 1980), pp. 91-100.

19 H. Denifle, 'Quel livre servait sur la base à l'enseignement des maîtres en théologie dans l'université de Paris?' *Revue Thomiste* 2 (1894) 149-61.

20 See *ST* 1.1.9-10; the edited texts in Sileo (above note 4); Grosseteste, *Hexaëmeron*, ed. Dales and Gieben, 1.2.1-2 (pp. 50-51); and the summary of the Franciscan school in Paris: *Summa fratris Alexandri*, ed. PP. Collegii S. Bonaventurae, 4 vols. (Quaracchi: College of St Bonaventure, 1944-1958), 1.3-7 (1.5-14).

21 See Bert Roest, 'Scientia and Sapientia in Gilbert of Tournai's *(E)rudimentum doctrinae*', in *Les vocabulaires des écoles des mendiants au moyen âge*, ed. M.C. Pacheco, Actes du Colloque Porto (Portugal), 11-12 Octobre 1996, Études sur le Vocabulaire Intellectuel du Moyen Age, 9 (Turnhout: Brepols, 1999), pp. 164-79, at 164-165; Leslie Smith, 'The Use of Scripture in Teaching at the Medieval University', in *Learning Institutionalized: Teaching in the Medieval University*, ed. J. van Engen (Notre Dame, University of Notre Dame Press, 2000), pp. 229-43.

22 The standard work for the history of the medieval vulgate is Samuel Berger, *Histoire de la vulgate pendant les premiers siècles du moyen âge* (Paris: Hachette, 1893), but it is in need of significant revision. In the meantime, there are more focused studies such as: M.T. Gibson, *The Bible in the Latin West*, The Medieval Book, 1 (Notre Dame IN: University of Notre Dame Press, 1993); Laura Light, 'Versions et révisions du texte biblique', in *Le Moyen Age et la Bible*, ed. P. Riché and G. Lobrichon, Bible de tous les temps, 4 (Paris: Beauchesne, 1984), pp. 55-93; and the collected articles in *The Early Medieval Bible: Its Production, Decoration and Use*, ed. R. Gameson (Cambridge: Cambridge University Press, 1994).

23 M.B. Parkes, 'The Literacy of the Laity', in *Literature and Western Civilization: The Medieval World*, ed. D. Daiches and A.K. Thorlby (London: Aldus Books, 1973), pp. 555-76.

24 Smalley, *The Study of the Bible in the Middle Ages*, pp. 88-9.

25 See *Intertextuality: Theories and Practices*, ed. M. Worton and J. Still (Manchester: Manchester University Press, 1990), esp. the introduction (pp. 1-44). For the role of intertextuality in modern biblical hermeneutics, see Anthony C. Thiselton, *New Horizons in Hermeneutics* (London: HarperCollins, 1992), pp. 499-508.

26 See Umberto Eco, *The Limits of Interpretation* (Bloomington: Indiana University Press, 1990).

27 The advent of single-volume Bibles is not indicative of a shift in any reading strategy, but rather a question of making the text *available* to scholars in transit, namely itinerant preachers. See Christopher de Hamel, *A History of Illuminated Manuscripts* (Oxford: Phaidon), pp. 113-20, for a physical description of the single-volume bible manuscripts. For their relationship to preaching, see Richard and Mary Rouse, '*Statim invenire*: Schools, Preachers, and New Attitudes to the Page', in *Renaissance and Renewal in the Twelfth Century*, ed. R.L. Benson and G. Constable (Cambridge, MA: Harvard University Press, 1982), pp. 201-25, at 221-2, where they state: 'At this juncture we have come to the type of the book [i.e. a single volume text] that can only be searched, for it cannot be read'.

28 Rainer Christoph Schwinges, 'Admission', in *A History of the University in Europe, Volume I: Universities in the Middle Ages*, ed. H. de Ridder-Symoens (Cambridge: Cambridge University Press, 1992), pp. 171-94, at 173-4, 179.

29 Since the Third Lateran Council of 1179, theological education was supposed to be free – at least in theory: Olaf Pedersen, *The First Universities: studium generale and the Origins of University Education in Europe* (Cambridge: Cambridge University Press, 1997), pp. 148-9. This was due to the fact that teaching masters secured their income through ecclesiastical benefices, and so no longer relied upon student fees. However, medieval universities continued to charge matriculation fees, and masters fought bitterly for a share of this revenue: J. Verger, 'Teachers', in *A History of the University in Europe, Volume I: Universities in the Middle Ages*, ed. H. de Ridder-Symoens (Cambridge: Cambridge University Press, 1992), pp. 144-68, at 151-4; Schwinges, 'Admission', pp. 185-7.

30 It is unclear when bachelors obtained their teaching responsibilities. The earliest record points to the 1240s, a period in which a number of curriculum innovations were introduced in the faculty of theology at Paris: Weijers, *Terminologie des universités au XIIIe siècle*, pp. 378-81; M.B. Hackett, *The Original Statutes of Cambridge University* (Cambridge: Cambridge University Press, 1970), pp. 73, 120-21.

31 Bernardo C. Bazàn, 'Les questions disputées, principalement dans la faculté de théologie', in *Les questions disputées et les questions quodlibétiques dans les facultés de théologie, de droit, et de médecine*, Typologie des Sources du Moyen Age Occidental, 44-5 (Turnhout: Brepols, 1985), pp. 58-70, 129-36.

32 Weijers, *Terminologie des universités au XIIIe siècle*, pp. 306-15, 324-35.

33 Thomas of Eccleston, *De adventu fratrum minorum in Angliam*, ed. A.G. Little (Paris: Fischbacher, 1909), p. 50. This same procedure appears to have continued well into the fourteenth century: see A.G. Little, 'Theological Schools in Medieval England', *English Historical Review* 55 (1940) 624-30.

34 On university preaching, see Jean Longère, *La prédication médiévale* (Paris: Etudes Augustiniennes, 1983), pp. 75-77, 147; and M.M. Davy, *Les sermons universitaires parisiens de 1230-1231*, Etudes de philosophie médiévale, 15 (Paris: Vrin, 1931).

35 Peter the Chanter, *Verbum abbreviatum*, PL 205.25. See *Roberti Grosseteste quondam episcopi Lincolniensis Epistolae*, ed. H. Luard, Rolls Series, 25 (London: Longman, 1861), no. 123, pp. 346-7.

36 The closest we come to a general analysis is Beryl Smalley, *The Gospels in the Schools* (1985), pp. 141-71; but see also the general comments of Ignatius Brady, 'Sacred Scripture in the Early Franciscan School', in *La Sacra Scrittura ei Francescani* (Rome: Ediciones Antonium, 1973), pp. 65-82, at 69-74.

37 Abigail A. Young, 'Accessus ad Alexandrium: the *Prefatio* to the *Postilla in Iohannis Euangelium* of Alexander of Hales (1186?-1245)', *Mediaeval Studies* 52 (1990) 1-23.

38 There is also the question as to whether Alexander commented on the Psalms: see Brady, 'Sacred Scripture in the Early Franciscan School', p. 73; and F. Stegmüller, *Repertorium biblicum medii aevi*, 11 vols. (Barcelona: Matriti, 1950-1980), pp. 1149-50 (2.68).

39 James O'Donnell, *Cassiodorus* (Berkeley: University of California Press, 1979), pp. 136-37; Karlfried Froehlich has noted that we still await the writing of a comprehensive history of medieval exegesis: 'St. Peter, Papal Primacy, and the Exegetical Tradition, 1150-1300', in *The Religious Roles of the Papacy*, ed. C. Ryan, Papers in Medieval Studies, 8 (Toronto: PIMS, 1989) , pp. 3-44, at 7n.

40 The impact of liturgy on the reading and exegesis of sacred Scripture is examined in Daniel Sheerin, '*Sonus* and *Verba*: Varieties of Meaning in the Liturgical Proclamation

of the Gospel in the Middle Ages', in Ad Literam: *Authoritative Texts and their Medieval Readers*, ed. M.D. Jordan and K. Emery Jr. (Notre Dame: University of Notre Dame Press, 1992), pp. 29-69.

41 Monika Asztalos, 'The Faculty of Theology', in *A History of the University in Europe. Volume I: Universities in the Middle Ages*, ed. H. De Ridder-Symoens (Cambridge: Cambridge University Press, 1992), pp. 409-41, at. 416-17.

42 James McEvoy, *The Philosophy of Robert Grosseteste* (Oxford: Clarendon Press, 1982); A. Crombie, *Robert Grosseteste and the Origins of Experimental Science* (Oxford: Clarendon Press, 1958).

43 James McEvoy, 'The Chronology of Robert Grosseteste's Writings on Nature and Natural Philosophy', *Speculum* 58 (1982) 614-55.

44 Martin Irvine, *The Making of Textual Culture:* Grammatica *and Literary Theory, 350-1100*, Cambridge Studies in Medieval Literature, 19 (Cambridge: Cambridge University Press, 1994), pp. 244-7.

45 Courtney, *Schools and Scholars*, pp. 29-30.

46 Two extant examples point to this trend. First, the only comments on the Psalms by Stephen Langton survive as a set of *quaestiones*, which may have acted as his lectures: see Riccardo Quinto, '*Doctor Nominatissimus*'*: Stefano Langton (?1228) e la Tradizione delle sue Opere*, Beiträge zur Geschichte der Philosophie und Theologie des Mittelalters, Neue Folg, 39 (Münster: Aschendorff, 1994), pp. 58-71. Secondly, in the fourteenth century, John Buridan lectured on the *Physics* of Aristotle by only posing questions: see Pedersen, *The First Universities*, pp. 255-8.

47 See Stephen P. Marrone, *William of Auvergne and Robert Grosseteste: New Ideas of Truth in the Early Thirteenth Century* (Princeton NJ: Princeton University Press, 1983), pp. 144-56, where the date of the text is incorrectly given as c. 1220–1225: the text in fact belongs to his magisterial period, c. 1229/30–1235. The text as it stands now, reads like a determination, and not a *reportatio* of the disputation, that is, it is not an account of everything stated by the participants in the disputation; but rather, summarizes the arguments by the Master as he proceeds to his final conclusion. However, there are a number of textual markers to indicate that the text originated as a disputed question.

48 *De veritate*, in L. Baur, *Die Philosophischen Werke des Robert Grosseteste, Bischofs von Lincoln*, Beiträge zur Geschichte der Philosophie des Mittelalters, Texte und Untersuchungen, 9 (Münster: Aschendorffsche Verlag, 1912), p. 130: '"Ego sum via veritas et vita". Hic ipsa Veritas dicit se esse veritatem. Unde dubitari non immerito potest, an sit aliqua alia veritas, an nulla sit alia ab ipsa summa veritate? Si enim nulla est alia veritas, tunc veritas est unica et singularis nec recipit distributionem aut pluralitatem, ut dicatur "omnis veritas", aut "multae veritates". – Sed e contra in Evangelio legitur: "Ipse docebit vos omnem veritatem"'.

49 Robert Grosseteste, *Expositio in epistolam sancti Pauli ad Galatas*, ed. J. McEvoy, CCM 130 (Turnhout: Brepols, 1995), 2.19 (p. 62): 'Sed hae quaestiones melius tractabuntur disputando quam legendo et exponendo'.

50 Robert Grosseteste, *De cessatione legalium*, ed. R.C. Dales and E.B. King, Auctores Britannici Medii Aevi, 7. The relationship between this treatise and his Galatians commentary was forcefully presented by James McEvoy, 'Robert Grosseteste on the Ten Commandments', *Recherche de théologie ancienne et médiévale* 58 (1991) 167-205.

51 Hugh of St-Cher, *Postilla in Isaiam*, in *Cardinalis Hugonis de St-Caro opera omnia*, 8 vols. (Venice: Pezzana, 1732), 4.83v, where he ends his assessment by noting: 'Quid autem sit Prophetia videre in speculo aeternitatis, disputationi relinquimus'. For the relevant disputed question, see the edition of Hugh's *Quaestio de prophetia* in Jean-

Pierre Torrell, *Théorie de la prophétié et philosophie de la connaissance aux environs de 1230: la contribution d'Hugues de Saint-Cher*, Spicilegium Sacrum Lovaniense, 40 (Leuven: Spicilegium Sacrum Lovaniense Etudes et Documents, 1977), pp. 20-31.

52 Hugh notes that Isaiah had a two-fold intention in mind: 'Intentio auctoris similiter duplex: literalis et spiritualis. Literalis intentio est Judaeos ab idolatria et aliis vitiis revocare. Spiritualis intentio est omnes malos a vitiis deterrere et ad desiderium aeternorum provocare. Attenduntur autem quatuor circa intentionem, scilicet benificiorum Dei commemoratio, delictorum exprobatio, suppliciorum comminatio, praemiorum promissio'. *Postilla In Isaiam*, 4.2r.

53 Nancy Spatz, 'Approaches and Attitudes to a New Theology Textbook: the *Sentences* of Peter Lombard', *Studies in Medieval Culture* 39 (1997), 57-52. Our knowledge about the development of *Sentence* commentaries is severely hampered by the fact that some of the earlier commentaries remain unedited. Hence, the forthcoming critical edition of Richard Fishacre's *Sentence* commentary will be definitely a boon to the study of medieval theology. However, we still lack any complete edition of the commentaries of Hugh of St-Cher, Roland of Cremona, and Richard Rufus, to mention but three of the early commentaries. These commentaries would provide essential clues to the eventual acceptance of Lombard's work as a teaching text, filling in the gap between Alexander of Hales and Thomas Aquinas. A full listing of all medieval commentators on the *Sentences* may be found in F. Stegmüller, *Repertorium commentariorum in Sententias Petri Lombardi*, 2 vols. (Würzburg: Schöning, 1947). See also the corrections offered by Victorin Doucet, 'Commentaires sur les *Sentences*: supplement au repértoire de M. Frederic Stegmüller', *Archivum Franciscanum Historicum* 47 (1954) 88-170.

54 Alexander of Hales, *Glossa in quattuor libros Sententiarum Petri Lombardi*, ed. PP Collegii S. Bonaventurae, 4 vols. (Quaracchi: College of St Bonaventure, 1951–1957).

55 James R. Ginther, 'Theological Education at the Oxford Studium in the Thirteenth Century: A Reassessment of Robert Grosseteste's Letter to the Oxford Theologians', *Franciscan Studies* 55 (1998) 83-104.

56 For Hugh's *Scriptum* see John Fisher, 'Hugh of St. Cher and the Development of Mediaeval Theology', *Speculum* 31 (1956) 57-69; and Walter Principe, *Hugh of Saint-Cher's Theology of the Hypostatic Union*, Studies and Texts 19 (Toronto: PIMS, 1970), pp. 13-25, 163-243, where there is a partial edition of book 3.

57 *Glossa*, ed. PP. Collegii S. Bonavenaturae, 1.66*. Cf. M.-D. Chenu, 'Maitres et bacheliers de l'université de Paris, v. 1240', *Etudes d'histoire littéraire et doctrinale du XIIIe siècle* 1 (1932) 11-39.

58 Long, 'The Science of Theology', pp. 72-3. Cf. Ginther, 'Theological Education', pp. 103-104.

59 Long, 'The Science of Theology', pp. 96-7.

60 See Spatz, 'Approaches and Attitudes', pp. 35-9, for similar considerations by earlier *Sentence* commentators.

61 Mary Carruthers, *The Book of Memory: A Study of Memory in Medieval Culture* (Cambridge: Cambridge University Press, 1990), esp. pp. 122-55.

62 Hugh of St-Victor, *Didascalicon*, ed. C.H. Buttimer (Washington: Catholic University Press, 1939), 5.5 (p. 103): cited in Carruthers, *Book of Memory*, p. 165.

63 Carruthers, *Book of Memory*, pp. 156-88; idem, *The Craft of Thought: Meditation, Rhetoric, and the Making of Images, 400–1200* (Cambridge: Cambridge University Press, 1998).

64 Cited in Carruthers, *Book of Memory*, p. 162.

65 It is not entirely precise to speak of a separation between *lectio* and *questio*. It would be better to argue that the *quaestiones* from the lecture spawned a separate pedagogical function, namely the *quaestio disputata*. See above, n. 46.

66 Dr. Philip Lyndon Reynolds made this observation in a recent conversation. For example, a quick examination of the first eleven questions of the *Summa*, which contains 54 distinct articles, reveals 21 instances in which Thomas uses scripture to turn the question. There are 20 other articles in which a citation from a church father forms the *sed contra*. For the remaining 13 articles, Thomas either presents a logical argument or a citation from Aristotle as the article's turning point.

67 The sermons are printed in Thomas Aquinas's *Opuscula theologica*, ed. R.A. Verardo et al., 2 vols. (Turin: Marietta, 1954), 1. 441-3. They are translated in Simon Tugwell, *Albert and Thomas: Selected Writings*, Classics of Western Spirituality (New York: Paulist Press, 1988), pp. 355-60.

68 In Ps. 70.15 (Bologna, Biblioteca dell'Archiginnasio MS A.983, fol. 38vb). See James R. Ginther, 'A Scholastic Idea of the Church: Robert Grosseteste's Exposition of Psalm 86', *Archives d'histoire doctrinale et littéraire du moyen âge* 66 (1999) 49-72, at 65-6.

69 This statement can also be applied to the fourteenth century: W.J. Courtenay, 'The Bible in the Fourteenth Century: Some Observations', *Church History* 54 (1985) 176-7; idem, 'Programmes of Study and Genres of Scholastic Theological Production in the Fourteenth Century', in *Manuels, programmes de cours et techniques d'engseignement dans les universités médiévales*, ed. J. Hamesse (Louvain-la-Neuve: Institut d'Etudes Médiévales de l'Université Catholique de Louvain, 1994), pp. 325-80, at 338-40. In a more recent study, Courtenay states that the Bible in the fourteenth century was not 'the central text as far as the *preparation* of an academic theologian....' (his italics). However, he qualifies this observation by noting that it is an overstatement to suggest that the lecturing on the *Sentences* 'supplanted the Bible as the central text for university theological training at Paris, Oxford, Cambridge, and in theological faculties and *studia* elsewhere from the thirteenth to sixteenth centuries' (p. 245). Instead, historians can argue that the *Sentences* did have a 'shaping effect' on the theological education, but not to the exclusion of biblical commentary.

70 Maura O'Carroll, *A Thirteenth-Century Preacher's Handbook: Studies in MS Laud Misc. 511*, Texts and Studies, 128 (Toronto: PIMS, 1997). O'Carroll's mastery of Dominican liturgy is a sobering reminder that one needs to have a sophisticated grasp of the liturgical context, in order to assess the influence of the liturgy in medieval theology. See also William T. Flynn, *Medieval Music as Medieval Exegesis*, Studies in Liturgical Musicology, 8 (Lanham MD: Scarecrow Press, 2000).

71 Joseph de Gellink, '*Pagina* et *Sacra Pagina*. Histoire d'un mot et transformation de l'objet primitivement désigné', in *Mélanges Auguste Pelzer. Etudes d'histoire, littéraire et doctrinale de la scholastique médiévale offertes à Monseigneur Auguste Pelzer*, Recueil de Travaux d'Histoire et de Philosophie, 3me Série, fasc. 26 (Louvain: Bibliothèque de l'Université, 1947), pp. 23-59, esp. 41-52.

Chapter 4

Christology in the *Quodlibets* of Guerric of Saint-Quentin: A Precursor of Thomas Aquinas?

Jean-Pierre Torrell, OP
translated by Charles Principe, CSB

Walter Principe devoted a large part of his research in the medieval field to preparing a critical edition of the *Quodlibets* of Guerric of Saint-Quentin. That edition was just reaching completion when he entered into eternal life. However, an introduction was still needed that would place these texts in the historical context of the evolution of ideas and also clarify their theology. At the request of the Pontifical Institute of Mediaeval Studies, I assumed this task in fraternal homage to our departed friend. The following pages give a small sample of that much larger project, which has recently been published and includes the text of the *Quodlibets*. After a brief presentation of this little-known theologian, we shall touch on some aspects of his Christology.

Guerric and his Works

His biography is easily summed up in a few lines. A native of Saint-Quentin, located at that time in Flanders (which explains the name *Flandrensis* sometimes given him), Guerric joined the Friars Preachers (c. 1225) while he was a Doctor (?) of Medicine and Master of Arts of the University of Paris, where he had likely already taught. At first, he was a reader at Bologna, then Master of Theology in Paris, where from 1233 he occupied the second chair at Saint-Jacques. Whereas the first chair, that of Hugh of St-Cher (since 1230), had been acquired by the Dominicans in 1229 by Roland of Cremona, already a master when he entered the Order of Preachers, the second chair had been acquired in 1230 by the entry of the secular master John of Saint Giles, who moved shortly afterwards to Toulouse. Guerric was therefore the fourth Dominican regent master in theology. He would remain so until 1242.[1]

Nine years was an exceptionally long period. It may be surmised that Guerric was thus able to exercise a marked influence on the succeeding young generations during his regency. However, we have hardly any details about this period, outside of the fact that he was one of the participants in the disputation of 1238, convened by William of

Auvergne, to examine the plurality of benefices. In all likelihood, Guerric was among those theologians targeted by the condemnation of 13 January 1241. By this condemnation, Bishop William and the masters of the faculty denounced the error, widely held since the beginning of the century, which affirmed that it was impossible for angels as well as men to see God in His essence. There exist, in fact, two versions of Guerric's treatment of the subject of the beatific vision. In a first question, prior to the condemnation of 1241, he maintained the aforesaid impossibility; while in the second, subsequent to the condemnation, Guerric's teaching falls into line with the new official position.[2] His death occurred perhaps before that of John of La Rochelle (3 February 1245), and certainly before that of Alexander of Hales (21 August 1245).

The outlines of the literary heritage of Guerric have gradually become clearer owing to the patient work of scholars throughout the twentieth century.[3] If, in spite of much research, no one has yet succeeded in finding a possible Commentary on the *Sentences* by Guerric, a very large number of Questions have been successfully identified, and his glosses on Scripture have also been discovered. Although the notes taken during these presentations are often very poor, those on the Book of Isaiah and the Wisdom literature do allow us to form an idea of the general features of Guerric's exegesis and through it to observe the first Dominican school in action.[4] Guerric seems to have been the first to introduce in the study of Scripture a method of explanation based on the four causes. Until then that method had been reserved to the Faculty of Arts. By using it, he was able to highlight the content of the text with great vigour. In this he foreshadowed his successors, Albert the Great and Thomas Aquinas. The same is true of his conception of the literal sense of Scripture, which is rather close to that of Thomas, for whom the allegorical sense is included in the literal sense. Beryl Smalley admitted that if historians were allowed to show their preferences, she would have eagerly shown a special admiration for Guerric.[5]

The *Quodlibets*

In order to appreciate fully the importance of Walter Principe's edition, we must realize that Guerric was one of the two originators of that typical activity of the medieval university, the quodlibetal disputations. If we cannot be absolutely sure that he was the first to carry on debates in this new style (since it appears at the same time in his contemporary, Alexander of Hales), still we are here at its very beginning.[6] It is all the more invaluable to have at one's disposal this impressive corpus of nine *Quodlibets*, since, except for a few fragments, it is the only published text of Guerric, and it has no equivalent in the edited literature of that period.

Like all Questions *de quolibet*, those of Guerric group together several different topics, often quite varied and even unrelated, sometimes following one another without any logical connection. Hence, they reflect the free style of the original oral discussion. In these texts we have counted more than one hundred different questions, and some *Quodlibets* contain between fifteen and eighteen. It will be quickly noticed, however, that the condition in which these texts have reached us is a little disappointing. They are *reportationes* in the rough notes taken during the disputation by those present without their being checked by the master. The result is great brevity in the treatment of certain questions. Moreover, given the abbreviated style of the *reportatio*, the texts are sometimes difficult to understand, though in general they are intelligible and we have every reason to believe they are accurate. This can be verified when we have two parallel versions which, despite their clear verbal differences, convey the same doctrine. Some of these notes are certainly the work of experienced reporters, but even then they have not been rewritten by the master and therefore do not have the same finished appearance as the *Quodlibets* of a later period. Their fragmentary character also poses a serious problem for anyone wishing to form an idea of Guerric's theology. Much could be said of their content and of what it reveals about the author's theological method, but it will be more useful to offer an example of it in the field of Christology.

The Motive of the Incarnation

Several articles in these *Quodlibets* concern Christ. Unequal in substance, they certainly do not allow us to give a complete account of Guerric's Christological doctrine. However, his most important exposition on the subject commands our immediate attention: 'Would the Son of God have become incarnate if man had not sinned?' (*Quodlibet* 7.1.1).[7] This question was certainly not unknown to authors before him, but Walter Principe rightfully emphasized that no one had as yet posed it so clearly or discussed it so fully.[8] There is no need here to repeat his study, but for our part we would insist more strongly on Guerric's originality.

Indeed, previous authors, from Rupert of Deutz through Robert Grosseteste to Alexander of Hales, had been unanimous in emphasizing at least the possibility of the Incarnation even if man had not sinned, but Guerric is the first author known to have taken the contrary position. Without claiming to be a thorough demonstration, his option is nonetheless extremely firm. This independent spirit is all the more remarkable since it leads Guerric to adopt a carefully considered position, taken only after examining the arguments given by previous authors, especially the one that the Incarnation put the final touch to the beauty of the universe (7.1.11-2).

Even without much research, it is easy to find in later literature a few authors who remembered his line of reasoning. Immediately after Guerric, Eudes Rigaud (1242) also thought that God would not have become incarnate if sin had not taken place; and, like Guerric, he emphasized how grateful those who have been the object of so much love should be.[9] The same position is prominent in St Bonaventure's *Commentary on the Sentences*. Like Guerric he held for a redemptive Incarnation. If Bonaventure granted more clearly that God alone could give an answer to the hypothetical question of the Incarnation without sin (*novit ille qui pro nobis incarnari dignatus est*), he too stressed that meditating upon this great divine event nurtures piety.[10] The position adopted by these two Franciscan authors (to whom one must add Roger Marston and Raymond

Rigaud) is the more remarkable because their confreres will later rally overwhelmingly to the theme of an Incarnation for the sole completion and beauty of the universe. This theme is found originally in Robert Grosseteste[11] and later more briefly in Alexander of Hales.[12] Guerric will not convince Albert the Great, his immediate Dominican successor, but only Thomas Aquinas. Although Thomas's position is more fully developed, including more explicitly the reservation that God could have acted otherwise, he too will be modest enough to say that this position only seems preferable to him. That is well known, but it is not emphasized enough that he also repeats that nothing awakens so much the love of man for God as the remembrance of what God has done for him. If it is impossible to assert that Thomas had Guerric in mind, one cannot deny the affinity of their positions.[13]

Without giving it the same real importance, Guerric also raises the question of the necessity of Christ's passion for man's redemption. This theme is introduced by a famous saying of Augustine repeated endlessly by the scholastics: God could have saved us in another way, but none was more suitable (5.1b.8)[14] Guerric takes this up again in his *determinatio*, in which he explains, however, that this statement does not claim in any way to decide what is possible or impossible for God. It is based on a fact of common experience: there is no better way to reconcile an enemy than showing him benevolence. Therefore, the supreme goodness of God owed it to itself to show forth supreme benevolence, and that is accomplished by the passion, since 'no one has greater love than this, to lay down one's life for one's friends' (John 15:13) (5.1b.14). Under this negative form we can recognize the positive argument advanced for the motive of the Incarnation (7.1.12). Guerric remains faithful to himself. And if it is true, he adds, that the humility of the Incarnation was greater than Adam's pride, and that we could have been liberated by any one of Christ's works if he had so willed, that was not the actual case, for there was another means more suitable (*convenientior*) for us, namely the passion (5.1b.15).[15]

Problems Concerning the Hypostatic Union[16]

After these fundamental questions, the scholastic taste for argumentation leads Guerric to take up a more abstract problem: When we speak of the Incarnation of God, can we say that the divine essence became incarnate? Since the divine essence is just as simple as the divine person, what can be said of the one can therefore be said also of the other, and thus we should be able to say that the divine essence became incarnate (4.2b.38). Guerric concedes equal simplicity in the divine essence and divine person, but he still stresses some differences. By definition the essence is communicable, while the person by definition is incommunicable. This diversity calls for a difference in formulation: the essence did become incarnate but it was the essence as found in the Son. In itself, the essence is common to the three persons, and what is said of all is also said properly of each (4.2b.39).

That brief response is completed by another that examines the various aspects of the problem posed by the 'unitability' of the divine nature (*de unibilitate naturae divinae*).

Three questions are raised: Was the Son 'unitable' (*unibilis*)? Were the Father and the Spirit also 'unitable'? What then is special about this union with relation to the other unions (9.1.2)? The problem is approached beginning with the notion of the incommunicability of the person as recalled in the previous passage: if the person were truly incommunicable, the Son of God would not have been able to unite himself to human nature (9.1a.3).

Guerric's *solutio* develops extensively the necessary distinctions and thus furnishes a fine example of a *determinatio magistralis*. We must distinguish, he asserts, a twofold way of being communicable (*communicabile*). In one sense, 'communicable' means what can be possessed in common by several; in a second sense, it denotes what can be united to another.

1. Communicability in the first sense can be understood in three ways. First, this quality is possessed by several so that each possesses its *secundum virtutem et potentiam*. This is how the divine essence is communicable to the three persons of the Trinity. Second, communicability is possessed by several things with respect to being, but not with respect to power (*secundum esse, non secundum posse*). This is how the different species of a genus participate in the whole being of the genus, but not in all its power (for the differences are in the power of the genus, but not in that of the species; only the specific difference is found in acts in each of the species). Third, communicability is possessed by several things, for instance, in the case of an effect that is common to them. Thus the creative essence is found in all things and can be shared in by all, for it communicates to all of them the effect of its uncreated substance (9.1a.8).

The divine person is not communicable in any of these modes. It is not communicable *per effectum*, for the effect is not attributable to the person but to the essence. The Trinity acts in fact according to what is common to the three persons, and that is why we say: *indistincta sunt opera Trinitatis*. Nor is the divine person communicable *per virtutem*, for power is not proper to the person but common to the three, so that the person cannot communicate itself through its power as if that were proper to it. For the same reason, it is evident that the divine person is not communicable *secundum esse*, since its being is not proper to it (9.1a.9).

2. As said above, in its second sense 'communicable' denotes what can be united to others. Once more this is confirmed in two ways: first, in a unity of nature, in the way that the soul communicates with the body (it is clear that the person is not communicable in this way); second, in a unity of person, and here again it is evident that the person is not communicable, for communicability implies equality. So, if you want to reason as follows: 'the person of the Son is unitable, therefore it is communicable', or inversely, 'it is not communicable, therefore it is not unitable', I say (*dico*), responds Guerric, that the argument is not conclusive, for unitability does not imply equality, whereas communicability does. Both arguments involve a sophism as to the 'accident' (*sophisma accidentis*).[17] It is obvious that communicability implies equality or parity, for to say '*communicabile*' is to say '*communiter habile*' (9.1a.10). Guerric feels no need to be more specific, but it is clear to him that in raising the hypothesis based on the

incommunicability of the person of the Son, he has reserved for that person the possibility of uniting itself.

It still remains for him to examine an objection, namely that union would entail dependence. He replies that it all depends on whether one is thinking of a passive union or of an active union. In the case of a passive union it is true that the unitable reality is dependent upon the other, but this is not how the Son of God was united. On the other hand, in the case of a purely active union (that is to say, a union in which the initiative is taken by the unitable reality), the unitable experiences no dependence or lack with regard to the other. This is the way the person of the Son was unitable, not just verbally but by nature. For by his own nature the Son had the power to unite himself to humanity, a power he held from the Father, and so it was natural for him (9.1a.11).

We had to follow quite closely the argumentation in this article in order to give a sample of Guerric's style as a debater. We cannot treat as fully all the questions raised. The next question can therefore be handled more briefly.

A priori nothing seems to stand in the way of the Father and the Holy Spirit being able to unite themselves to humanity by the same title as the Son, since it has just been established that the Son could do so by nature, and his nature is the same as that of the other persons (9.1b.12).[18] But since it is easier to understand that a person already born of the Father from all eternity could be born of a woman in time, this argument is enough to show that the Incarnation of the Father or the Spirit would have been less suitable. This amounts to an impossibility, the objection concludes, since, according to Anselm, 'however slightly unsuitable something might be in God, it is in fact impossible' (9.1b.13).

In Guerric's eyes, this line of reasoning is too absolute. He intends to show that what would be impossible if one considered only God in himself can very well be possible in relation to his works (9.1b.14). Or better still, one can try to adopt the viewpoint of God's goodness, since, according to Damascene, it is that superabundant goodness which is the cause of all things.

We can consider this goodness in itself, as having no desire or norm other than pouring itself out. Or we can consider it insofar as it is a law according to which God binds himself so as to act *secundum virtutem et potentiam*, that is, he compels himself to act in the most fitting manner (*summe convenienter*) (9.1b.15).

One need only skim though the Wisdom of Solomon to understand that God's goodness is at work in two ways; in the first way, precisely as goodness, he brought about each of the good things with which we are familiar. Second, taking goodness as law and order (*bonitas ut est lex et ordo*), he acted in the most well-ordered way: *sicut summe bonus est, ita summe bene et convenienter operatur*. Since the union of God with man is the most perfect expression of this well-ordered universe with which we are familiar, this union originates in goodness as law, not in goodness as goodness. Consequently, we can say with regard to this union that 'the least inappropriateness would have been impossible', not only on the part of God himself but also on the part of his works. And in this sense it was impossible for the Father or the Holy Spirit to be united to humanity.

Nevertheless, this would have been possible, and remains so, if we consider the goodness of God as such (9.1b.16).

Again, Guerric considers whether it is fitting to express things differently, by using for instance the Dionysian axiom '*bonum diffusivum sui*'. But for Guerric, that authoritative statement is not convincing (9.1b.17). So he has recourse to arguments from suitability (*congruitates*) to explain why the Son became incarnate rather than the Father or the Holy Spirit.

The first of these arguments is based on the fact that the Son was the actual occasion of the devil's fall, as well as that of man, for the devil claimed a certain equality with God, something appropriated to the Son. On his part, man wanted to be equal in knowledge, but knowledge too is appropriated to the Son. That is why the restoration of fallen nature belonged to the Son (9.1b.18). It also belonged to the Son to restore all things since it is through him that all things were created. Moreover, since he is the very image of God, it was up to him to restore that image. And since he is the heir, he should confirm the promise of the inheritance. Again, because he is Son by nature, it is through him that adoptive sonship ought to be confirmed (9.1b.19-22). To this series of arguments, doubtless considerably abridged by the reporter, is added the authority of Anselm: 'Only the offended person can punish or pardon'. Now it is certainly the Son who was offended, since, as we have said, the devil claimed to be equal with him, while man laid claim to the Son's knowledge. So, it belonged to the Son to punish or pardon. He preferred to pardon, 'himself bearing our faults in his body on the Cross' (9.1b.23).

The quotation above is from the First Epistle of Peter (2:24) and has the advantage of emphasizing the relevance of Guerric's accumulation of the arguments from fittingness. The apparent exactness of the previous arguments is unable to hide the fact that theologians cannot answer *a priori* this sort of question. That may be what Guerric wishes to point out by taking up again the main themes from Scripture on the subject. Only *a posteriori* may the theologian hope to discover the internal consistency of the Incarnation. In light of that, it is rather striking to note that Thomas Aquinas – who treated the same question but far more fully and subtly[19] – also returns finally to arguments from fittingness to account for the Incarnation of the Son rather than of another person of the Trinity. Thomas advances almost the same arguments as Guerric: the Son's restoration of creation as its exemplar and author, the themes of eternal inheritance and adoptive sonship, as well as the appropriateness of repairing through the Son – who is the true wisdom of God – the disorderly appetite for knowledge that had led man to his ruin.[20] We need not necessarily conclude from this that Guerric influenced Thomas, but if we have here a common legacy of Christian tradition, each of them treated it in quite similar terms.

As for the third consideration (is the hypostatic union the closest of all unions?), Guerric's response leaves no room for hesitation. Leaving aside the supremely blessed union of the three persons in a single essence, the union of two natures in Christ is the greatest one (*maxima*) possible. Guerric gives a whole series of reasons for this and concludes as follows: Since from the beginning the three persons were united in a single nature, it was therefore fitting to complete the perfection (*consummatio*) of everything by uniting the three natures (soul, body, and divinity) in a single person (9.1c.28-9).

Various Questions concerning Christ

Besides the major themes in Guerric with which we have just dealt, there remain a few questions scattered here and there that are treated at various lengths. Some of them are disposed of so quickly that one suspects faulty work by the reporter. For example, when Guerric is asked if Christ alone possessed all the virtues, he answers tersely that Christ alone possesses all the virtues 'fully,' or again, *excellenter* (6.9.68-9).

We set aside certain questions regarding the conception and formation of the body of Christ: was its formation, like ours, extended in time (*successiva*) or instantaneous (*subita*)? Without hesitating, Guerric asserts that from the first instant the body of Christ was informed, his soul was infused in it, and that this soul possessed perfect knowledge and virtue (5.1c.18-32). In this matter, he shows himself to be as strict an Aristotelian as Thomas Aquinas when it comes to the distinction between the body's conception and animation. This question, over which physiology and theology used to get along so well together, is now completely out of date.

The preceeding passage raises a more directly metaphysical and even dogmatic question, stemming from an authoritative statement of John Damascene. Damascene declared that the union of the divinity to flesh was effected '*mediante intellectu*'.[21] According to Guerric, the scholastics were divided as to how this was to be understood. For some[22] – and rightfully so (*bene*)[23] – this mediation is not to be taken as an ordered succession in time. One must rather think of a mediation of fittingness and dignity, since the soul is more worthy and simpler than the body (nearer then, one may conclude, to the divinity). For others, this mediation is not only one of suitability but also of causality. By reason of his plenitude of grace, the soul of Christ would be clothed with a certain quality which it would have imprinted on his body, making it more apt for this union. This quality remains present in the body even in its separated state, and this would explain how the divinity could remain united to the body of Christ during the three days in the tomb (5.1c.31). If the objection is made that God could have arranged things otherwise (that is, without using the mediation of the soul), Guerric responds: 'Of course he could have done so, but that would not have been appropriate, for it is not fitting for the greatest things to perform small operations. So that, although the Divinity could have done this, it preferred to entrust to the form (that is, the soul) the task of disposing the matter, for that was the fitting thing to do' (5.1c.32).

Those last reflections give a hint of the seriousness of the problem. It is a known fact that theologians were concerned with it since Origen had placed the soul of Christ at the forefront of Christological discussion and stressed its intermediary role. To cite only two authors, in the East and the West, Gregory of Nazianzen as well as Augustine had also insisted on the mediating role of the soul in the Incarnation. Augustine even went so far as to say that the union of two spirits, the soul and the Word, was easier to understand than the union of a spirit and a body in ordinary human generation.[24] While it is unlikely that Guerric was acquainted with Origen and Gregory, he could have had access to Augustine. In any case, his text indicates clearly that he knew about this theological tradition, which was already well established. Shortly after, Thomas Aquinas's solution to the problem would be the same as Guerric's. Aquinas ruled out, of course, any notion of temporal succession, but if the soul is an intermediary in the assumption of the body, it is because it is its form. Flesh had to be informed by the soul to make a truly human body capable of being assumed by the Word.[25] As for the permanence of the union between the flesh and the divinity during the three days of Christ's death, this also is explained by the permanence of the aptitude thus created.[26]

Another question linked to Christ's physical nature comes as a surprise. Supposing that Christ did not have to suffer the passion, would he have died of old age? The discussion opens with two arguments claiming that this was impossible. On the one hand, God, who preserved the body of Christ from corruption when he was in the tomb, could likewise have preserved it from the deterioration of old age (5.1a.3). On the other hand, it is established that Christ took nothing from our humanity except in view of what was useful for us, and it is hard to see the use of his death if it were caused by decrepitude (5.1a.4). Guerric's answer witnesses to a firmly established doctrine: Christ did not merely acquire our human condition, he assumed it willingly. From that moment on, it was necessary for him to die, and if he had not arranged to die in the manner we know, he would have died in another way (5.1a.5). No argument can be based on the preservation of Christ's body in the tomb in order to infer his preservation from death itself. It was not for the purpose of preserving his body that he had assumed it but to redeem the human race (5.1a.6). And when it is claimed that death from old age would have been of no use to us, this must be said to be untrue. On the contrary, such a death would have been of great value to us as an example to turn us away from evil and draw us to love. But one must admit that we would have been less drawn to love in that way than by his death through his passion, and that is why the latter was more fitting for our good (5.1a.7).

This response, which reconciles both the necessity of dying connected with the corporal nature of man and the voluntary character of Christ's death, seems a perfectly reasonable conclusion. Augustine, in passing, had stated this as an obvious fact.[27] Nevertheless, retrieving it did not come easy in the history of theology, and only since Peter Lombard does it appear to have become a commonly held position.[28] While many authors see the necessity of Christ's dying only as a consequence of sin,[29] it is all the more interesting to note that Guerric first replies to the question not from their viewpoint but by appealing to an intrinsic necessity connected to the very nature of the human composite. We must await Thomas Aquinas for a more precise development of this question, but we are certainly on the path that leads to him.[30]

A few remarks must be added concerning the coexistence in Christ of the suffering of the passion and the joy of the beatific vision. Like all the scholastics, Guerric holds that Christ's soul was at the same time totally united to God and totally united to his body. It was therefore necessary for his soul to possess completely within itself all the properties attached to each of these two unions as well as the ensuing conditions, namely fruition and passion. Thus Christ was at once *viator* and *comprehensor*, but in such a way that neither one of these two states undermined the other (5.1e.35-40; 9.4.75-6). We do not wish to read into these rather rudimentary texts more than they contain, but we can still point out that, here once more, Guerric sets out on a path that Thomas Aquinas will not be slow to follow.[31] According to Guerric, the joy of the vision and the pain of the passion in the soul of Christ did not spill over on one another so as to cancel each other out. The joy was just as total as the pain. However, he does not explain how this could be. This is precisely the point where Thomas will introduce his distinction between the essence of the soul and its various powers. Since the higher powers have God as their object, they can only rejoice. On the contrary, the lower powers can suffer from what wounds them. While the soul, which is the unique subject of all these powers, is said to suffer or rejoice according to its essence, the various powers do not interfere with one another in their natural function, for in Christ, Providence arranged that they have no interconnection.[32] However, there is still a long road to cover before arriving at a formulation of these matters with that kind of clarity, and indeed the only one to do so will be Thomas Aquinas.

Obviously, these few pages cannot do justice to Guerric or to his Christology, which was assuredly much more developed. The other questions in his *Quodlibets* – on God and his works, on the Trinity, the human soul, eschatology, etc. – also reveal a well-informed theologian who is competent and even bold. We had approached him in the hope of confirming his possible influence on Thomas Aquinas. Even though much remains to be done to demonstrate this more convincingly, it seems to us that what we have found in Guerric's teaching concerning Christ allows us to consider this working hypothesis as not completely without foundation.

Notes

1   All the specialized dictionaries give a more or less complete entry on Guerric. The oldest ones need to be updated. Our preferred references are B.-G. Guyot, 'Guerric de Saint-Quentin', *Dictionnaire de Spiritualité* 6 (1967) 1121-2, and the complementary bibliography in the anonymous entry: 'Guerric de Saint-Quentin', *Dictionnaire d'histoire et de géographie ecclésiastique*, t. 22 (1988) col. 726.

2   Cf. H.-F. Dondaine and B.-G. Guyot, 'Guerric de Saint-Quentin et la condamnation de 1241', *Revue des sciences philosophiques et théologiques* 44 (1960) 225-42.

3   As a simple reminder: F.-M. Henquinet, 'Les écrits du Frère Guerric de Saint-Quentin OP' *Recherches de théologie ancienne et médiévale* 6 (1934) 184-214, 284-312, 394-409; 'Notes additionnelles sur les écrits de Guerric de Saint-Quentin', *Recherches de théologie ancienne et médiévale* 8 (1936) 369-88, and B.-G. Guyot, 'Quaestiones Guerrici, Alexandri et aliorum magistrorum Parisiensium' (Praha, Univ. IV.D.13), in *Archivum fratrum praedicatorum* 32 (1963) 5-125.

4   B. Smalley, 'A Commentary on Isaias by Guerric of Saint-Quentin, OP' in *Miscellanea Giovanni Mercati*, vol. II: Letteratura medioevale, 'Studi e Testi 122', Città del Vaticano,

1946, pp. 383-97; idem, 'Some thirteenth-century Commentaries on the Sapiential Books', *Dominican Studies* 2 (1949) 318-55 (for Guerric, consult especially pp. 348-55); 3 (1950) 41-77, 236-74.

5   B. Smalley, *The Study of the Bible in the Middle Ages*, pp. 297-8.

6   J.F. Wippel, 'Quodlibetal Questions Chiefly in Theology Faculties', in B.C. Bazan, G. Fransen, J.F. Wippel, D. Jacquart, *Les Questions disputées et les questions quodlibétiques dans les facultés de théologie, de droit et de médecine* (Turnhout, 1985), pp. 151-222 (at p. 157) is really quite evasive. Glorieux enables us to be more precise: since with Guerric and Alexander of Hales we are at the very beginning of this literary genre, its appearance at Paris can be placed between 1230 and 1235, among the mendicant orders; cf. P. Glorieux, 'Aux origines du Quodlibet', *Divus Thomas* (Piac.), 38 (1935) 502-22; for Guerric see especially pp. 515-17.

7   From here on, we shall adopt a simplified reference system, using the numbers of the newly-published edition: Guerric of Saint-Quentin, *Quaestiones de quolibet*, ed. W.H. Principe and Jonathan Black, Studies and Texts, 143 (Toronto: PIMS, 2002). Thus 7.1.1 sends the reader to Quodlibet 7, article 1, paragraph 1. Sometimes there is added a subdivision indicated by a letter (1c).

8   Cf. W. Principe, 'Guerric of Saint-Quentin, OP, on the Question: *Utrum Filius Dei esset incarnatus si homo non peccasset?*', in *Ordo sapientiae et amoris ... Hommage au Professeur Jean-Pierre Torrell ...*, ed. C.-J. Pinto De Oliveira, Studia friburgensia 78, (Fribourg, [Suisse], 1993), pp. 509-37 (cf. p. 510); consult also J.-Fr. Bonnefoy, 'La Question hypothétique *Utrum si Adam non peccasset... au XIIIe siècle*', *Revista española de teología* 14 (1954) 326-68; G.M. Grech, *De ratione incarnationis in primitiva schola dominicana ac franciscana* (Melitae, 1939), who proposed already a first edition of this Quodlibet of Guerric, as well as various other texts of Richard Fishacre, Robert Kilwardby and Ulrich of Strasbourg.

9   '*Debemus et infinitas gratiarum actiones cum fecerit pro peccatoribus quod non fecisset si essemus iusti*', partial edition of *Sent.* III, d.21 resp., in J.M. Bissen, 'De motivo incarnationis. Disquisitio historico-dogmatica', *Antonianum* 7 (1932) 314-36; cf. p. 335.

10 Bonaventure, *Sententiae* III, d.1 a.2 q.2, *Opera omnia*, t. III, ed. Quaracchi, pp. 23-5; cf. p. 25 a: 'Plus enim excitat devotionem animae fidelis, quod Deus sit incarnatus ad delenda scelera sua quam propter consummanda opera inchoata'.

11 Cf. D.J. Unger, 'Robert Grosseteste, Bishop of Lincoln (1235-1253), On the Reasons for the Incarnation', *Franciscan Studies* 16 (1956) 1-36.

12 Alexander, *Quaestiones antequam esset frater*, q. 15, membrum 4, nos. 46-9, ed. Quaracchi, 1960, t. 1, pp. 208-9.

13 Thomas Aquinas, *Sententiae* III, d.1 q.1 a.3; *ST* 3.1.3. According to Principe, Guerric's influence would be more clearly discernible on Bonaventure and Eudes Rigaud than on Thomas. It will be difficult to ratify that judgement if one recalls certain texts: *SCG* 4.54 (ed. P. Marc) n. 3926: 'Nothing prompts us so much to love someone as experiencing the love he bears us (*Nihil autem sic ad amorem alicuius nos inducit sicut experimentum illius ad nos*)'. Cf. also *ST* 3.46.3: '(through the passion of Christ) man has learned how much God loves him and has thus been prompted to love him in return (*per hoc homo cognoscit quantum Deus hominem diligat, et per hoc provocatur ad eum diligendum*)'. Apart from a few different terms, Guerric really has the same idea: 'If God had had to become incarnate even if man had not sinned, it would not then have been for man (*propter hominem*) that God would have become incarnate; so that man would hardly have reason to be grateful to God because of the Incarnation. Why should I give thanks to someone for something he had to do for me out of necessity? Christ's Incarnation would not then have the powerful attraction (*vim attractivam*)

it now has. For nothing exerts such an attraction on us as the thought that our Creator took our flesh and in it suffered for us. That is what attracts man to the utmost (*Sed nihil ita attrahit sicut cum cogitamus Creatorem carnem assumpsisse et in ea passum fuisse pro peccatis nostris: hoc enim est quod maxime attrahit hominem)'* (7.1.12).

14 This is the very theme of one of the texts edited by W. Principe, '*Quaestiones* Concerning Christ from the First Half of the Thirteenth Century: I. *Quaestiones* from the Bibliothèque Nationale, Paris', *Mediaeval Studies* 39 (1977) 1-59 (cf. pp. 36-9). See also A.M. Landgraf, 'Das Axiom *Non alium modum possibilem Deo defuisse, cuius potestati cuncta aequaliter subiacent, sed sanandae nostrae miseriae convenientiorem modum alium non fuisse nec esse oportuisse'*, in idem, *Dogmengeschichte der Frühscholastik* II-2 (Regensburg, 1954), pp. 254-87.

15 When Guerric says here: 'quolibet operum suorum poteramus liberari si ad hoc ea retulisse', he is emphasizing two things found more clearly and forcefully in Thomas Aquinas. For Thomas, the first is even a real leitmotif: all the actions and passions of Christ bring salvation (cf. *ST* 3.48.6). The second is less frequently repeated but firmly attested all the same: each and every one of Christ's actions takes its definitive meaning solely from the divine intention that directs them and causes them to find their fulfilment solely through the passion (cf. for example: *Compendium theol.* I 231; *Quodlibet* II q.1 a.2 [2] and ad 3-4). Regarding this second point in particular, consult our book: *Le Christ en ses mystères. La vie et l'oeuvre de Jésus selon Thomas d'Aquin*, t. II (Paris, 1999), Chap. IX: 'Le plus grand amour'.

16 We speak of hypostatic union for the sake of brevity; but unless it has escaped our attention, this expression is not found in Guerric's *Quodlibets*. In what follows, the reader should take into account that we set aside deliberately any reference to the major books of W. Principe on the hypostatic union in the works of William of Auxerre, Alexander of Hales, Hugh of Saint-Victor, and Philip the Chancellor. Needless to say, they would provide the indispensable background for assessing accurately Guerric's doctrine. But it is just as evident that the brief reporters' notes we shall now examine do not deserve treatment of that sort. One can compare only what is comparable.

17 As we know, the *sophisma* (or *fallacia*) *accidentis* is the first of the errors *extra dictionem* in reasoning (accident being taken here in the broad sense of predicate). That form of sophism occurs when one reasons as if the predicate was suitable to the subject when such is not the case, and vice versa. This is exactly the type of sophism Guerric is here criticizing. More information on this subject can be found in the apocryphal opuscule long attributed to Thomas Aquinas: *De fallaciis*, cap. XI, ed. leon., t. 43, pp. 411-13.

18 This question is not exceptional; it is even classic in the schools of the time; cf. for example W. Principe, *Quaestiones...* I, pp. 27-31, 41-2.

19 *ST* 3.3: *De modo unionis ex parte personae assumentis*; 3.3: *De modo unionis ex parte naturae humanae assumptae*. Note in passing that the theme of the incommunicability of the person, which occupied Guerric so much, occupies only a very secondary place in Thomas: cf. *ST* 3.3.1 ad 2.

20 Cf. *ST* 3. 3.8.

21 Among other theologians, Peter Lombard passed on this authoritative statement of Damascene, *Sententiae* III, d. 2, c. 2, t. II, ed. Quaracchi, p. 29. But the problem was known well before him: cf. A.M. Landgraf, 'Das Axiom "Verbum assumpsit carnem mediante anima" in der Frühscholastik,' in *Dogmengeschichte der Frühscholastik* II/I (Regensburg, 1953), 150-71.

22 One can think of Alexander of Hales, *Quaestiones antequam esset Frater*, q. 15, membrum 3, n. 42, p. 206, who speaks of a *medium secundum ordinis congruentiam*, but dismisses any idea of a *medium conjungens* (exercising real causality; the second hypothesis in Guerric's text).

23 It is hard to determine if Guerric adopts this position. According to one of the two reporters, whose text we have followed, these first authors are right (dicunt quidam *et bene*), while according to the other reporter, the opinion of the second ones would be preferable (alii dicunt *et probabilius*). Given the development that follows, it does appear that Guerric sides with this second point of view.

24 Cf. Augustine, *Letter* 137 II 8-III 11: PL 33.519-20.

25 Cf. *ST* 3.6.1, especially.

26 Cf. *ST* 3.6.1 ad 3.

27 Cf. Augustine, *De peccatorum meritis et remissione* II xxix 48: PL 44, 180.

28 P. Lombard, *Sententiae III* d.16 c. 1, pp. 103-4. Cf. A.M. Landgraf, 'Die Sterblichkeit Christi', in *Dogmengeschichte der Frühscholastik* III/I, pp. 199-272; this study, which furnishes considerable documentation, stops unfortunately before the period we are concerned with.

29 It really seems that this is the case of Alexander of Hales, who speaks only of final causality; cf. *Glossa in quatuor libri Sententiarum*, t. III, d. 16, ed. Quaracchi, 1954, pp. 170-2.

30 Cf. Thomas Aquinas, *Sent.* III, d. 16 a. 2; *ST* 3.14.2.

31 This fact deserves all the more to be pointed out since, unless we are mistaken, this problem had not often been brought up until then. In the collection of texts edited by W. Principe, only one touches on the theme of the greatness of Christ's suffering; cf. *Quaestiones...* II, pp. 36-7.

32 Cf. *ST* 3.46.8c. and ad 1; but see also q. 14 a.1 ad 2; q. 15 a.5 ad 3. One may also consult J.-P. Torrell, 'Saint Thomas d'Aquin et la science du Christ: une relecture des Questions 9-12 de la *Tertia Pars* de la "Somme Théologique"', in S.-Th. Bonino, ed., *Saint Thomas au XXe siècle*. Actes du Colloque du Centenaire de la 'Revue Thomiste', 25-28 Mars 1993, Toulouse (Paris, 1994), pp. 394-409 [p. 399].

Chapter 5

Efficient Causality and Instrumentality in Thomas Aquinas's Theology of the Sacraments

Philip Lyndon Reynolds

A distinctive and original feature of Thomas on Christ's saving work is his application of concepts of efficient causality. Thomas maintains not only that God is the efficient cause of grace, salvation, and resurrection, but that God uses Christ's humanity and the sacraments as efficient instrumental causes. Thomas rejects the opinion that the sacraments are merely occasions for God's unmediated influence and argues instead that they are efficient instrumental causes of grace.[1] Likewise, he argues that Christ as a human being is an instrumental efficient cause of grace,[2] that the Passion of Christ is an instrumental efficient cause of our salvation,[3] and that Christ's resurrection is an instrumental efficient cause of the general resurrection.[4]

It is not easy to see how God uses creatures instrumentally, for whereas we understand our instruments through what they *enable* us to accomplish, nothing enables God to do anything, since God is already omnipotent. Nevertheless, by assuming that 'the work of grace is no less orderly than the work of nature', Thomas links natural philosophy to the theologian's inquiry into grace and salvation.[5] The explicit way in which he appropriates notions of causality from natural philosophy and applies them in theology is interesting today in part because religion always appropriates ideas from its secular context. Thomas establishes paradigms of causality by citing examples from everyday life or natural philosophy, and he shows how they fit the theological relationships that he wants to explicate. But the significance of ideas depends on their context, and it is not clear whether the notions that Thomas appropriates and translates into new contexts retain the same sense. It is not always clear even that they have any explanatory force at all. Nor is it clear how one should construe the development of such appropriations over the course of Thomas's career.

Scholars agree that Thomas attributes real efficient instrumental causality to Christ's human nature in the *tertia pars* of the *Summa theologiae* (1271–1273). But they agree too that in his *Scriptum super Sententias* (based on his teaching as a sententiary bachelor in Paris, 1252–1254), Christ's humanity is only a dispositive (*disponens*) and meritorious cause, and not truly an efficient cause. As Jean-Pierre Torrell has noted recently, scholars do not always agree about the intervening phases, but hardly anyone contests that such a development occurred.[6] Bernard Catão emphasizes this development in his elegant study of salvation and redemption in St Thomas.[7] While conceding that there is no single, overarching theory in Thomas's treatment of Christ's saving work, Catão argues that by the time Thomas composed the *Summa contra gentiles* (completed by 1265) and disputed the questions *De potentia* (1265–1266), he attributed 'true instrumental efficiency' and 'a real instrumental power' to the humanity of Christ. In Thomas's mature work, Catão argues, the meritorious and instrumental aspects of the atonement are 'properly distinct' and the objects of 'two complementary points of view'.[8]

Considered in the light of this consensus, what Thomas actually says about the instrumental causality of Christ's humanity in his later works may seem disappointingly meager, and his precise intentions unclear. Thomas certainly affirms that Christ in his human nature (*Christus homo*) is an efficient instrumental cause of our salvation, but it is not clear how this affirmation is related to the other explanations (that Christ saves us by example, by merit, by satisfaction, by sacrifice, and so on). Thomas does not explain *how* God uses Christ's humanity instrumentally.

Why have scholars regarded the development as self-evidently substantive and important? The answer lies in a distinguishing position of the Thomist school. As long as theologians argued about the causality of the sacraments, most Thomists maintained that the sacraments were 'physical' causes of grace. According to the traditional versions of the theory, the physical causality of the sacraments is essentially independent of their signification: a pen may signify writing, but its significance has no role in its instrumental causality. The idea that the sacraments cause grace 'physically' is probably due to Cardinal Cajetan.[9] It reflects controversies that arose after Thomas, especially the Thomists' opposition to the competing theory of 'moral causality', whose original proponent may have been Melchior Cano. The moral theory attributes a certain value to the sacraments that derives from Christ's acts and merits and induces God to bestow grace. Both the moral and the physical theories were products of the counter-reformed Catholic tradition, with its tendency to so objectify the work of the sacraments (which confer grace *ex opere operato*) that it seemed independent of human experience.

By noting that the physical theory postdates Thomas and was shaped by later controversies, I do not mean to imply that it is *ipso facto* inconsistent with Thomas's intentions. That remains to be shown (if it can be shown, for Thomas could not have foreseen what his account of sacramental causality would look like in the context of later controversies). The physical theory follows what Thomas says to the letter, and Thomists maintained it and vigorously defended it largely because of Thomas's authority.

Scholars perceived an analogous notion of physical causality in Thomas's account of Christ's saving work.[10] Torrell concedes that the term 'physical' is not Thomas's and has misleadingly mechanical connotations. He prefers instead to characterize the efficiency of Christ's humanity as 'réelle et intrinsèque'.[11] Nevertheless, the concepts of physical and real efficiency are essentially the same. Scholars have modified the physical interpretation in the light of an historical reading of Thomas's works. His analysis of how Christ's Passion and resurrection are causes in the early sententiary commentary seems inconsistent with physical causality. Because there is no such analysis in the later works, scholars reason that Thomas eventually came around to the view that Christ's Passion and resurrection were physical causes. But one could interpret the change differently: as indicating that Thomas became more reticent about explaining how Christ saves us.

It is worth pursuing a minimalist interpretation because the theory that the sacraments and Christ's human acts are physical causes of grace, salvation, and resurrection is unintelligible.[12] Proponents of the sacramental theory have been unable to give a satisfactory account of what the sacraments *per se*, through their own innate causality, contribute to the primary causality. Nor have they identified the instrumental 'motion' by which a sacrament transmits spiritual and, indeed, supernatural influence to the soul.[13] It will not suffice to affirm that God uses the sacraments in a mysterious way that we cannot understand, for the physical theory presupposes that the agent uses a *natural* causal power in the instrument. Thomas's genius may astound me, but I can understand how his pen, as he moves and directs it, gets his words onto the page. What natural power in water, when directed by a higher cause, washes sin from the soul?

Robert Masterson notes that broadly understood, the notion of an instrumental cause 'can be applied to any combination of diverse causes, insofar as one is subordinated to the others ministerially'. But he distinguishes this broad sense from the proper one, and following John of St Thomas, he goes on to divide proper instrumental causes into moral, logical, and physical causes and to argue that the sacraments are physical instrumental causes.[14] But Thomas does not make distinctions of this sort. He certainly maintains that God is the principal efficient cause of grace,[15] which is therefore a quality in the soul, the result of a real and intrinsic renewal, and not only an extraneous divine favour.[16] He also maintains that God uses creatures as instruments of grace. But in his discussion of sacramental causality, Thomas offers only two alternatives: either the sacrament is an occasional cause (which is to say that it is not really a cause at all), or it is an instrumental cause.

In answer to whether God alone is the cause of faith, Thomas argues that external causes, such as miracles and persuasive words, are not sufficient in themselves to cause faith because they work only if God first makes the soul receptive to them. This is why the same words or signs engender faith in some persons but not in others. God himself, the chief or proper agent, directly causes the assent of the believer to the external message.[17] One might call instruments of this sort 'post-dispositive causes', since their mediating influence presupposes the disposing of the subject by the primary agent. But it would not be wrong to regard the preacher as an instrumental cause of faith, although he would not be one by the standards of John of St Thomas or Masterson.

As a first step toward reassessing Thomas's application of causal models to Christ's saving work, I shall focus in this article on his treatment of sacramental causality. I have three aims: first, to clarify the problem that Thomas wanted to resolve by arguing that the sacraments were instrumental causes; second, to argue that his solution is itself extremely problematic, especially if one construes it in the traditional way; and third, to suggest that a minimal interpretation may resolve such problems. I shall argue that when Thomas characterizes a creature as an instrumental cause in relation to the supernatural primary agent, he means only that God uses the creature *in some way* to achieve an effect.

Thomas's Intentions

To appreciate why Thomas regards the sacraments as instrumental causes, one needs to put his treatment in its historical context, first in a general way, and second by considering Bonaventure's treatment. According to both Thomas and Bonaventure, the chief objection to the thesis that sacraments are efficient causes is that corporeal things cannot be efficient causes of spiritual effects because agents are nobler than their patients. Bonaventure concludes that the sacraments cannot strictly be efficient causes, whereas Thomas introduces the notion of instrumental efficient causality to obviate the same objection. Bonaventure's more elaborate treatment represents the *status quaestionis* that Thomas presupposes, and it reveals by contrast the economy of Thomas's treatment.

Parisian masters of theology around the middle of the thirteenth century were still dealing with the problems and implications of advances made about a century earlier. Hugh of St-Victor, the *Summa sententiarum*, and Peter Lombard had established that the sacraments proper – the sacraments of the New Law in contradistinction to those of the Old Law – caused the grace that they signified.[18] As Hugh explains, Christ instituted Baptism to signify the cleansing of sin because water naturally 'represents' the Holy Spirit as what spiritually cleanses us. In addition to representation and institution, sacramental efficacy requires the blessing (*sanctificatio*) of a minister. Once it has been sanctified, the sacrament 'contains' the grace that it signifies.[19] This 'not-only-but-also' account presupposes that the sacrament's causality is somehow dependent on its signification. Thus Hugh teaches too that the sacraments have an instructive, pedagogical purpose that befits our fallen condition. They induce humility in us; they teach us about interior, spiritual things through exterior, visible things; and they provide salutary external works that induce interior virtues.[20] Theologians had always affirmed that the sacraments were 'sacred signs'. What was new was the clear distinction between a *mere* sign and a causal sign. But the new emphases in sacramentology were also products of an ethos of humanism and naturalism, in which theologians were keenly aware both of the natural properties of created things and of their symbolic value.

Parisian masters of the two or three generations before Thomas and Bonaventure, by borrowing concepts current in natural philosophy, tried to state more precisely how the sacraments caused grace. They needed to mitigate as well as to save the insights of their twelfth-century predecessors, according to whom the sacraments (Christ's *sacra medicamenta*) were not so much performances as corporeal substances – water, wine, bread and oil – that 'contained' the power of grace as a physician's bottle or box contained a healing medicine.[21] Such materialism seemed to imply that through some acquired quality, a material substance was magically empowered to bring about spiritual results. Nevertheless, thirteenth-century theologians were less concerned with explaining sacramental causality than with using the idea to differentiate the sacraments of the New Law (such as Baptism) from the sacraments of the Old Law (such as circumcision), and with inquiring whether the paradigm fitted sacraments other than Baptism and Eucharist. (The case of Marriage was especially problematic.) The vocabulary of efficient causality remained fluid and confused. Terms such as 'dispositive', 'occasional', and *sine qua non*, when used to characterize causes, were equivocal. Thomas seems to have found in the term 'instrumental' the clarity he was looking for, yet he did not clear up confusion about the other terms.

It is very likely that in the background of treatments of sacramental causality were larger questions about intermediate causes and the immediacy of God's natural and supernatural presence to creatures. Theologians sometimes regarded creation and 're-creation' as analogous and reasoned that God created grace directly and *ex nihilo*, a thesis that might rule out the possibility of God's using the sacraments as intermediate causes.[22] But neither Thomas nor Bonaventure shows any sustained concern to link the question of how the sacraments cause grace to these larger issues. The chief spiritual effect or *res* of a sacrament is grace, but the problem, as Thomas construes it, is not that a natural agent cannot cause a supernatural effect, but that a corporeal agent cannot cause a spiritual effect. It is therefore not clear that the development in Thomas's position was metaphysically motivated, although he naturally appropriated whatever causal models were current and seemed metaphysically probable.[23]

Bonaventure's Position

In his commentary on the *Sentences* (edited 1254–1256), Bonaventure goes some way toward clarifying the questions that had emerged. Bonaventure first asks whether the sacraments 'contain' grace (as twelfth-century theologians had said). Sacraments certainly do not contain grace essentially, as a vessel contains water. Grace is essentially present only in the soul. Yet because they confer grace on those who present no obstacle, they may be *said* to contain grace.[24] Bonaventure next asks whether the sacraments are efficient causes of grace.[25] His answer is a qualified *no:* spiritual things are nobler than corporeal things, and no effect is nobler than its cause.[26] Against this one might argue that even a corporeal sign instituted by human beings can cause some spiritual effect in us, such as knowledge or emotion. For example, a circle marked on the door of a house causes one to know that one can obtain wine within, and the sight of a gibbet or the tokens of war can frighten someone. How much more, therefore, can a divinely instituted sign have spiritual effects. But this argument fails because signs do not cause efficiently but rather 'dispositively or occasionally'. The soul is the efficient cause of one's cognitive and affective responses to signs, for it actively derives knowledge from the sign, and the acquired knowledge in turn causes the emotional response. This is why the sight of a gibbet scares some persons but not others.[27]

In his response, Bonaventure rehearses two explanations, both of which he finds probable. According to the first, the sacrament is a *sine qua non* cause of the sanctifying grace (*gratia gratum faciens*) conferred with the sacrament, although it is the efficient cause of the character or some other spiritual mark (*ornatus*), which is not sanctifying but preternatural grace (*gratia gratis data*).[28] The sacrament is also a disposing cause of the healing and strengthening of mental faculties. It is not clear how this first solution solves the objection that bodies cannot be efficient causes of spiritual effects (for *gratia gratis data* is a spiritual effect too). Bonaventure explains what he means by a *sine qua non* cause with the help of an example.[29] The fires of purgatory have a salutary effect on the soul. Fire has its own natural power, but the subject is spiritually receptive to this power because of a prior grace in the soul. Likewise, two concurrent causal influences heal and strengthen one's mental faculties when one receives the sacraments: an interior grace working directly on the soul, and the exterior work of the sacrament. The exterior work renders the interior grace more effective (*efficacior*).[30] On this view, a sacrament is what I have called a 'post-dispositive' cause: God makes the soul spiritually receptive to the natural causality of the sacrament. But Bonaventure does not say what the exterior work is. Nor does he explain the causal role of the *sacramentum et res* (the character or *ornatus*) in relation to the twofold influence. His model seems to presuppose that there is some subjective, rational response on the part of the patient, a presupposition that does not obviously fit infant Baptism.

According to the second probable theory, a sacrament is only an occasional cause. It is efficacious by virtue of a divine ordination, which is a relational rather than absolute power.[31] When Elisha told Namaan the leper to bathe in the Jordan and Namaan was healed (2 Kings 5:10–14), there was no causal power either in the words of Elisha or in the water of the Jordan. God's power alone was the efficient cause of the cure, although Namaan's devotion and obedience were disposing causes. If God had decreed that henceforth, any leper who bathed in the Jordan would be healed, we should say that the water of the Jordan healed leprosy, but it would do so only by an extraneous ordination. Likewise, God's saving power is not present in the sacraments but rather accompanies them. God has ordained that appropriately disposed persons will receive certain graces when they receive the sacraments, just as an intrinsically valueless token, by the order of a king, may be redeemed for a hundred pounds.[32] On this view, a sacrament is a sign so instituted by God that worthy recipients receive, directly from God, the healing power signified by the sacrament. Its effectiveness is due entirely to an extraneous 'ordination', a kind of compact (*pactio*).

In the *Breviloquium* (1256–1257), an introductory compendium of theology for Franciscan students, Bonaventure eliminates the dialectic of *quaestiones* and arguments for and against a thesis. In treating each topic, he first states dogmatically what one must believe and then presents some reasons (*rationes*) to help the reader understand it. Here Bonaventure simply explains that although grace is neither substantially contained in nor efficiently caused by the sacraments (since grace is substantially present only in the soul and God alone infuses it), the recipient somehow, by a divine decree, obtains grace 'in them and through them'.[33] Although Bonaventure linked the notion of a divine decree to the occasional theory in his sententiary commentary, the notion that one obtains grace in and through the sacraments may suggest that the occasional theory is at best incomplete. (Bonaventure speaks of a divine decree here, following Peter Lombard, to emphasize that God's power is not restricted to the sacraments: God may confer saving grace in other ways.) But he does not suggest *how* the sacraments confer grace. His lapse into a primitive, unexplicated account shows that he found current explanations both unnecessary and unconvincing.

Thomas's Position

Thomas reduces the question of sacramental causality to its bare outlines: either (a) the sacrament is an instrumental cause or (b) it is merely an occasional cause (which Thomas, unlike Bonaventure, calls a *sine qua non* cause). To illustrate the latter theory, Thomas, like Bonaventure, gives the example of a token of nominal intrinsic value that can be redeemed for gold by virtue of a king's order. Thomas objects that if the sacrament were effective only thanks to an extraneous *ordinatio* or *pactio,* the sacrament's role would be merely that of a sign; but their being more than signs is precisely what distinguishes the sacraments of the New Law (the sacraments proper) from those of the Old Law.[34] Considered against the alternatives that Thomas offers, his conclusion that the sacraments are instrumental causes means only that they contribute something of their own natural efficacy in some way to the operation. He does not explain *what* they contribute. His position is therefore similar to Bonaventure's in the *Breviloquium* and consistent with Bonaventure's first theory (involving the *sine qua non*, 'post-dispositive' cause) in the sententiary commentary.

In Thomas's view, the crucial objection to affirming that sacraments cause grace is that corporeal agents cannot cause spiritual effects, since an agent is always nobler than its patient and effects are never nobler than their causes.[35] Both the human soul (the patient) and the effect (grace) are spiritual and are therefore nobler than any corporeal stuff. Thomas points out in reply that even a human artisan can use a corporeal instrument to produce something that is commensurate with human art and nobler than the instrument. An agent can use an instrument to produce an effect that is fully proportionate to itself and transcends the limited powers of the instrument because causal power belongs to an instrument only transiently and secondarily. The instrument, as such, is a *movens motum*: it moves another only inasmuch as it is itself moved by the principal agent, in which the instrumental power properly and permanently inheres. Thomas outlines an analysis of instrumental causality in general when he deals with the problem of sacraments as causes, and also when he discusses the two 'operations' of Christ (divine and human).[36]

Thomas's account of the causality of the sacraments develops in the course of his career only by becoming simpler. In his early *Scriptum* on the *Sentences,* Thomas argues that the sacraments are instrumental efficient causes in the strict sense only of the character or some equivalent adornment of the soul (*ornatus*). The character or *ornatus* in turn disposes the subject to receive grace from God (infallibly, if there are no obstacles). Hence the sacrament itself is strictly not an instrumental cause of grace but a disposing cause.[37] In later works, Thomas argues simply that the sacrament is an instrumental cause of grace, without explaining how the *sacramentum et res* (such as the baptismal character) mediates causally between the *sacramentum tantum* (the sensible sign) and the *res tantum* (grace).

When Thomas discusses sacramental causality in the *Scriptum,* he makes two distinctions, which he regards as different from each other and independent: (i) that between a disposing and a perfecting cause, and (ii) that between a principal agent and its instrument. The first two are related as (a) what causes the disposition for an ultimate form and (b) what induces the form itself. The second two are related as (a) the first mover (*primum movens*) and (b) that which moves inasmuch as it is moved (*movens motum*).[38] This 'dispositive' model is clearly important to Thomas at this stage of his career, for he applies it in other contexts. He makes a similar twofold distinction later in the *Scriptum,* when he discusses the powers that Christ bestows upon his ministers. Here the crucial question is whether created agents can cause supernatural effects. Thomas argues that among the various ways in which something can co-operate with an agent, only two can apply to creatures in relation to God: (i) they can act as mediators through which the principal agent induces its effect; or (ii) they can dispose something to receive the effect of the principal agent. All natural causes are in some sense instruments of God's action in the first sense, but God reserves certain actions to himself alone, namely, creation and re-creation (the reformation of the soul through grace). In these cases, the secondary cause only disposes and never mediates. When one human being generates another, nature disposes matter to receive the soul, but God himself directly creates and infuses the soul into the matter. Likewise, ministers collaborate with God in the work of grace only by disposing subjects to receive grace from God. When the efficacy of a minister's disposing work depends on the efficacy of something in him, such as his teaching or his merits, it is *ex opere operante*; when it does not, as when he dispenses the sacraments, it is *ex opere operato.*[39]

Thomas abandons the strictly dispositive model in later works and no longer distinguishes between instrumental and disposing causes. Hence Cajetan and most Thomists thereafter maintain that the sacraments are 'perfective' rather than dispositive instrumental efficient causes of grace. To account for the change, Cajetan argued that after commenting on the *Sentences,* Thomas realized that because grace is a quality and not a substance, its production is not creation *ex nihilo* but the modification of an existing substance, and therefore that it is not metaphysically impossible for a created agent to be an instrumental cause of grace. But there is no indication of this reasoning in Thomas's own words.[40] I suspect that in Thomas's mature view, the manner in which God uses any intermediate cause is uncertain and mysterious. Proclus's theory that the First Cause is more closely related to its effects than the intermediate causes (a theory that provided him with a rationale for theurgy) tends to undermine the very notion of causal mediation. Thomas knew of Proclus's idea in part through the first proposition of the *Liber de causis*, according to which a first cause exerts more causal influence over its effects (*plus est influens super causatum suum*) than a secondary cause, a principle that he applies in his treatment of transubstantiation.[41] When God is the agent, the distinction between intermediate and disposing causes collapses, since creatures collaborate in God's work yet God is immediately present in the effects.

Scholars who see a positive development from merely dispositive to real or physical instrumental causality in Thomas's treatment of the sacraments and of Christ's saving work are on shaky ground, for Thomas himself abandons the distinction. Even in the *Sentences*, Thomas uses the term 'disposing' and its cognates more broadly, to include modes of causality different from the merely preparatory one defined above. In a discussion of Christ's 'grace of union', Thomas counts as another sort of disposing cause the medium that intervenes between a cause and the achievement of some perfection, such as a transparent medium in relation to light. Here the conducting medium acts 'as if it were an instrument' of the perfection.[42] When Thomas says in the *De potentia* that the sacraments justify 'instrumentally and dispositively', it is unlikely that he still retains the distinction he made in the *Sentences*, for there is no other indication of it, but one must presume that he has some distinction in mind.[43] When Thomas calls the sacraments 'disposing instruments' of grace in the disputed questions *De veritate* (1256–1259),[44] it is not clear whether the term 'disposing' qualifies or explicates the term 'instrument'. In the *Summa theologiae*, when Thomas considers why God cannot confer on a creature the power to create, he argues that an instrumental cause can convey the action of the superior cause only insofar as it works *dispositively* in relation to the effect.[45] But here Thomas uses the term 'dispositively' merely to indicate that the instrument's contribution to the effect, while real, is subordinate *in some way* to the principal agent. If Thomas had decisively rejected the dispositive theory, he would surely have tidied up his vocabulary. What changed was Thomas's sense of how much he could explain.

Throughout his career, Thomas maintains that God uses sacraments as instrumental causes of some spiritual effect, whether of a disposing condition (the character or *ornatus*) or simply of grace itself. To the objection that corporeal agents cannot cause spiritual effects, Thomas replies that because an instrument moves only inasmuch as it is itself moved by the primary agent, the instrument (as moved) may produce an effect that transcends what the instrument can achieve itself.[46] A craftsman may use an inanimate object, such as a saw or an adz, to produce a work of human skill and art, such as a bench or a bed. Hence there is no reason why a material instrument cannot produce a spiritual effect. An instrument's power, in relation to the principal effect, is existentially incomplete, while the corresponding power of the principal agent is permanent and existentially complete. The instrument's power is transient in the sense that it passes *through* the instrument and does not belong to it.[47] Thomas describes the transience as a *motus*, and he reminds us that according to Aristotle, a motion is indefinite, being no longer *that* but not yet *this*.[48]

Since Thomas regards forms as the sources of causal powers, he sometimes explains the transience of the sacrament's power by saying that the power cannot be attributed to a form that is complete in the instrument:

> Something can produce an effect in two ways. In one way, as something that acts *per se.* Something is said to act *per se* when it acts through some form inherent in itself as a completed nature, whether it has this form from itself or from another, and whether naturally or violently. It is in this manner that the sun and the moon are said to illumine, and that fire, red-hot iron and hot water are said to heat. In another way, when something produces some effect instrumentally: it does not produce the effect through a form inherent in itself, but only inasmuch as it is moved by something that acts *per se.*[49]

If the complete effect is a consequence of *any* complete form in an agent, then, regardless of whether the form is innate in the agent itself or educed from the agent by another cause,[50] and regardless of whether the form is present naturally or violently, the agent is a *per se* cause and not an instrument. By this demanding standard, one should not say that God uses the sun as an instrumental cause of warmth and generation. But Thomas does not try to meet this standard when he discusses the grace of Christ and the instrumentality of Christ as head of the Church, where he likens Christ in his human nature to the sun and to fire as the first, essential causes of light, generation, and heat.[51] Likewise, when he argues that God raises Christ first and others through Christ's resurrection, Thomas appeals to the 'natural order' by which a first cause influences distant objects through proximate objects, and he cites as an example the way in which air conducts the heat of a fire.[52] Thomas uses artificial causes as examples when he discusses the causality of the sacraments, but natural causes when he discusses Christ's saving work. Interpreters have overlooked these apparent inconsistencies, but they are significant. They indicate not that Thomas is muddled, but that he applies his borrowed causal paradigms flexibly and adapts them freely to the matter in hand.

Problems with the 'Physical' Interpretation of Thomas's Theory

One might say that a principal agent uses a physical instrumental cause just as a carpenter uses an adz to fashion a bench; and in that case, Thomas maintains that the sacraments are physical causes of grace. But the problem with such comparisons is that they presuppose unstated judgements as to which features of the simile are essential or salient and as to how close one expects the equivalence to be. Like Aristotle, the schoolmen often translate a concept by analogy from one context to another.[53] Even when a scholar induces a universal *ratio* by analysing such examples, the standard examples remain to remind us that a concept has been analogically extended.[54] For example, Christ is the source of grace as the sun is the source of light or generation;[55] God sends forth his Son as a branch 'emits' a flower.[56] Since the aim of such analogies is to explain something, the concept is always easier to understand in its original setting. But analogies are open to a range of interpretations. Which details of the example are important? One should not assume that when Thomas characterizes a sacrament as an instrumental cause and compares it to an adz, he is placing adzes and sacraments in the same genus of cause. But if he is not saying this, what is the point of the comparison?

Perhaps one might say that an instrumental cause is physical or real to the extent that the means, inasmuch as it is moved by the principal cause, can itself be regarded as the efficient cause of the effect in question: the adz is what cuts the wood, and insofar as it is moved by the carpenter, it fashions the bench. The saw does not merely dispose the bench for the unmediated work of the carpenter; nor does it induce the carpenter to fashion the wood; nor does it induce the wood to fashion itself according to the carpenter's plan; nor does it tell the wood what to do. The effect is entirely due to a transient condition or 'motion' in the instrument (such as the accurately directed back-and-forth movement of a saw). The causal influence, insofar as the agent uses the medium instrumentally, *passes entirely through the instrument.* The instrument *comes between* the primary agent and the effect, yet it *embodies* the causal influence entirely, albeit only transiently. But a sacrament cannot be an instrumental cause of grace in this sense because there is no proportion or connection between the visible means and the invisible effect. The intentionally directed adz is an efficient cause of the wooden artifact in a manner that a sacrament, howsoever moved by God, cannot be an efficient cause of grace. Thomas does not really solve Bonaventure's objections.

The problem is the lack of 'proportion' between the instrument and the effect, for although it 'moves inasmuch as it is moved', an instrumental cause is not only a conduit of influence: it also contributes its 'proper operation' to the principal causality that it serves. It is because the subordinate causality participates the principal one that we use different instruments for different effects: a pen for writing, an adz to fashion wood, and so on. Because the sacraments cause what they signify, each has a visible, material effect that is proportionate to the principal effect for which it is an instrument. The immediate effect of baptismal water is washing (*ablutio*); the immediate effect of sacramental oil is anointing, whereby the skin glistens.[57] Each sacrament has two effects, external and internal, visible and invisible: Baptism washes the flesh without and cleanses the soul within.[58]

Such accounts of the twofold causality of the sacraments seem obvious and illuminating until one starts to think about them. Thomas's standard examples of instrumental causes do not fit. Thomas cites as examples of instrumental causality the craftsman using a tool, such as a saw or an adz, to make a piece of furniture, such as bench or a table,[59] and the way the nutritive soul uses heat, which naturally dissolves and consumes, to digest food and to convert it into flesh.[60] Yet such instruments do not have two separate effects, as the sacraments do. The result of using a saw to make a bench is not two effects but one: not cut wood *and* a bench but a bench fashioned from wood. Thus Thomas says that while the proper operation of a saw is *to cut*, the operation of the craftsman who uses the saw is *to cut accurately* and thereby educe the intended artificial form.[61] Fire *heats*; the smith uses fire *to heat iron*.[62] The result of applying a physical instrumental cause is not two effects but a single effect that may be considered under two *rationes* or formal aspects: as a simple physical effect, and as a work of human art. Corporeal cleansing and the remission of sins, on the contrary, are clearly separate and numerically different.

Again, the effectiveness of any physical instrumental action is dependent on the effectiveness of the instrument *per se*: a carpenter cannot make a satisfactory bench with a crooked saw or a blunt adz, and the nutritive soul cannot perform its work adequately if the body's heat is too intense or too weak. But the sacramental efficacy of Baptism does not depend at all upon the physical efficacy or washing-power of water: a sprinkle is enough. Perhaps the instrumental role of washing (*ablutio*) in Baptism is not physical but symbolic.

The obvious examples of corporeal instruments resulting in purely spiritual effects are not physical causes, like adzes, but signifiers, such as written or spoken words. If the instrumental *motus* of the sacrament is its consecration and reception in a faithful context, in accordance with its institution, its natural contribution is perhaps what Hugh called its representation: its natural fitness for a certain intentional symbolism. Thomas himself sometimes seems to assume that the sacraments cause by signifying, although unlike Bonaventure, he does not try to define in this context the mode of causality by which signs, such as words, communicate ideas. In the *De veritate*, replying to the objection that a corporeal agent cannot have an effect in the soul, Thomas points out that the sacrament has three natural effects: first, there is the outward, corporeal effect (such as to wash or to anoint); second, there is the effect *per accidens* on the soul through sensory perception; and third, there is the spiritual effect, whereby the sacrament touches the soul 'inasmuch as it is perceived by the soul in the intellect as a certain sign of spiritual cleansing'.[63] The 'spiritual' power to which Thomas refers here is not supernatural but natural: it is the result of interpreting a sign. When Thomas asks, in the *Summa theologiae*, whether there is a power to cause grace in the sacraments, he considers the objection that there cannot be a spiritual power in a material object. He replies that while a spiritual power cannot be in a material object as something permanent and existentially complete, it can be present as a transient, instrumental power. But the example he gives is again semantic: the sacrament has a spiritual power 'just as in the sensible spoken word itself, inasmuch as it proceeds from the conception of a mind, there is some spiritual power that arouses the understanding of someone'.[64] But semantic causes are not physical causes; they are not strictly efficient causes, as Bonaventure observes.

In his treatment of the sacraments, Thomas's standard examples of instrumental causes, such as the saw and the adz, do not match very closely what he needs to explain. There are hints in his work that the sacraments cause not so much by physically causing as by signifying, which seems to be a different matter entirely and to imply different paradigms, but Thomas neither develops this line of thought nor considers the objections that would arise. Unless Thomas was muddled and never thought the issue through, his intentions were strictly limited. In applying borrowed, analogically extended causal models to the sacraments and to Christ's saving work, Thomas proceeds *formaliter*, demonstrating the order between the causes without attempting to explain how they achieve their effect.

Toward a Minimal Interpretation

Thomas reduces the debate over sacramental causality to its bare essentials: unless the sacrament contributes no causal influence of its own at all (a position that is clearly unacceptable), it must be an instrumental cause of some sort. Therefore when Thomas affirms that the sacraments are instrumental efficient causes of grace, all he necessarily implies, as a sufficient condition for this characterization, is that the instrument contributes *in some way* to the efficient causing of grace by God. An instrument is an efficient cause inasmuch as the primary agent that uses it is an efficient cause.[65] Likewise Christ's humanity is an instrument of salvation inasmuch as God uses it as a means to cause salvation. Summarizing the various 'modes' in which Christ's Passion saves us – by merit, by satisfaction, and so on – Thomas explains that each mode corresponds to a way of considering the Passion vis-à-vis some aspect of Christ's twofold nature. The Passion of Christ is an efficient cause 'inasmuch as it is compared to his divinity'.[66] Thus defined, the efficient instrumental causality of Christ's Passion subsumes all the other means that Thomas posits (sacrifice, redemption, and so on), since each presupposes the hypostatic union. Nevertheless, Thomas does not commit himself to any complete account of what it subsumes but rather leaves the matter open. It is not what Thomas says that should strike us here but what he does not say.

The modesty in Thomas had a modest estimate of what he could contribute professionally to the understanding of faith, and a sharply defined sense of the limits of rational explanation. As a pious believer, Thomas was certain that God conferred grace through the sacraments, and that God somehow used the natural efficacy of the sacraments to this end. Such was the traditional view: the consensus was far too strong to be set aside. Moreover, this interpretation fitted Thomas's intuition that God redeemed, illumined, and perfected human beings through creatures, so that creatures collaborated with God in their own way: grace perfects nature. The occasional theory was a clever explanation, but too clever. In such matters, the more difficult position was safer and less likely to leave out something important. Such was the conservative response to Arius, to Berengar, and to Abelard.

The modesty in Thomas's method produces different results in different contexts. In his account of how Christ's Passion saves us, where he had two problematic examples of single-minded rationalism in mind (Anselm and Abelard), Thomas presents multiple explanations without making any attempt to reduce them to a single, overarching theory: the Passion saves us by merit, by satisfaction, by redemption, by sacrifice, and by efficient causality.[67] To show that the Incarnation was the most fitting means for God to save us, Thomas suggests ten ways in which it is conducive to salvation (at least eight of which are 'subjective', pertaining to how Christ's example moves and instructs us); and he adds that there are several other ways, which transcend human understanding.[68] Adolf Harnack perceptively described Thomas's account of the atonement as *multa, non multum*: many things but not much.[69] But Harnack failed to appreciate *why* Thomas did not say much.

In Thomas's treatment of the sacraments, instead of multiplicity, one finds simplicity. To defend the thesis that the sacraments cause grace, Thomas merely rebuts, formally, abstractly and in principle, the chief objection: that corporeal causes cannot have spiritual effects. The objection fails because the sacraments are instrumental causes. He goes to some lengths to explain in general how instrumental causes work, but he does not try to explain how the sacraments work. Thomas is remarkably reticent and indefinite as to precisely how God uses created instruments, and scholars have misconstrued his silence as a substantive doctrine. One might interpret or develop Thomas's simple model in a variety of ways, going beyond where he chose to stop, yet without doing violence to his thesis.

What lessons might a theologian who respects Thomas learn from his treatment of the sacraments? Thomas's theology remains interesting and challenging today in part because (like his *Summa theologiae*) it is unfinished. It invites further speculation. But at the same time, Thomas's modesty reminds his readers that the quest of 'faith seeking understanding' is always unfinished, and that religious belief is rooted in liturgical practice. Thomas is sometimes reticent and indefinite as to the precise means by which God sanctifies, and even obstinate in his refusal to pursue the inquiry far. But he is sure that in causing salvation, wisdom and grace, God uses created things, natural causes, and human responses.

Notes

1 *Scriptum super Sententias* 4.1.1.4, qua. 1; *Quaestiones disputatae de veritate* 27.4; *ST* 3.62.1–2. For Thomas's *Scriptum super Sententias*, I cite the Parma edition of the *Opera omnia* (1852–1873, repr. New York, 1948–1950), vols. 6 and 7. For the *ST*, I cite the Ottawa edition (published by the Institute of Medieval Studies, Ottawa, in 5 vols., 1941–1945). For the *De veritate*, I cite from the Leonine edition of the *Opera omnia* (vol. 22).

2 *ST* 3.8.1, ad 1 (2479a).

3 *ST* 3.48.6, resp. (2739).

4 *ST* 3.56.1, ad 2 (2787b).

5 *ST* 3.1.5, arg. 3 (2420a): 'Opus gratiae non est minus ordinatum quam opus naturae'.

6 J.-P. Torrell, 'La causalité salvifique de la résurrection du Christ selon saint Thomas', *Revue Thomiste* 96 (1996) 179–208. See especially p. 180: 'Entre le commentaire des *Sentences*, où il n'accorde à l'humanité du Christ qu'une causalité dispositive à l'égard de notre salut, et la *Somme de théologie*, où il lui reconnaît une véritable causalité efficiente instrumentale, sa pensée a connu diverses étapes.... Les auteurs ne sont pas toujours d'accord sur le moment où les situer ... mais le simple fait de cette maturation n'est guère contesté...'.

7 Bernard Catão, *Salut et rédemption chez s. Thomas d'Aquin. L'acte sauveur du Christ* (Paris: Aubier, 1964), a work that was a recommended text in Walter Principe's seminar on Christ's saving work in Thomas Aquinas and his contemporaries when I was a student at the Pontifical Institute in the 1980s.

8 Ibid., pp. 142–43.

9 See Bernard Leeming, *Principles of Sacramental Theology,* 2nd edition (London: Longmans, 1956; rpr. Westminster, MD: Newman Press, 1960), pp. 334–35.

10 E.g., M.-Benôit Lavaud, 'Saint Thomas et la causalité physique instrumentale de la sainte humanité et des sacrements', *Revue Thomiste* 32 (1927) 305 ff., 313, 315; N. Crotty, 'The redemptive role of Christ's resurrection', *Thomist* 25 (1962) 100–101; Torrell, 'La causalité salvifique de la résurrection', p. 188.

11 Torrell, 'La causalité salvifique', pp. 191–2.

12 Cf. Joseph Pohle, *The Sacraments: A Dogmatic Treatise,* trans. A. Preuss, vol. 1 (St Louis: Herder, 1915), p. 154. A proponent of the moral theory, Pohle argues that although the physical theory not only cannot be proved on grounds of authority but is also unintelligible, it is not *ipso facto* false, just improbable.

13 The scope of this article does not permit me to review attempts to explain the metaphysics of the physical theory. For examples, see C. Spicq, 'Les sacrements son cause instrumentale perfective de la grace', *Divus Thomas* (Piacenza) 32 (1929) 337–56; C.V. Héris, *The Mystery of Christ, Our Head, Priest and King,* trans. D. Fahey (Cork & Liverpool: Mercier Press, 1950), pp. 81–9, 140–42; Robert Reginald Masterson, 'Sacramental graces: modes of sanctifying grace', *Thomist* 18 (1955) 311–75. See also Masterson's article 'Instrumental causality' in *New Catholic Encyclopedia.* Héris argues that the *being* of the instrument (independently of its essence) is the means of grace, but as well as being unintelligible in itself, his theory is inconsistent with Thomas's assumption that causality depends on forms. Masterson treats the signification of the sacrament as an artificial form and argues that God uses this form as the means, but such causality is either non-physical or unintelligible.

14 R.R. Masterson, 'Sacramental graces: modes of sanctifying grace', *Thomist* 18 (1955) 343–4.

15 *ST* 1-2.112.1 (1373–4).

16 *ST* 1-2.110.1 (1363–4).

17 *ST* 2-2.6.1, resp. (1440).

18 Hugh, *De sacramentis christianae fidei* 1.9.2 (PL 176.317–19). *Summa sententiarum* 4.1 (PL 176.117B): 'Sacramentum vero non solum significat, sed etiam confert illud cujus est signum vel significatio'. Peter Lombard, *Sententiae in IV libris distinctae,* ed. PP. Collegii S. Bonaventurae, 2 vols. (Rome: Collegii S. Bonaventurae ad Claras Aquas, 1971–1981), 4.1.4 (2.233): 'Sacramentum enim proprie dicitur, quod ita signum est gratiae Dei et invisibilis gratiae forma, ut ipsius imaginem gerat et causa existat'.

19 *De sacramentis christianae fidei* 1.9.2 (PL 176.317D): 'sacramentum est corporale vel materiale elementum foris sensibiliter propositum ex similitudine repraesentans, et ex institutione significans, et ex sanctificatione continens aliquam invisibilem et spiritualem gratiam'.

20 Ibid., 1.9.3 (PL 176.319–22).

21 See Philip L. Reynolds, *Food and the Body* (Leiden: Brill, 1999), pp. 127–31.

22 Bonaventure, *Commentaria in quatuor libros Sententiarum* 4.1.1.un.4, *quaestio lateralis,* arg. 2 *pro parte negativa,* in *Doctoris seraphici S. Bonaventurae opera omnia,* ed. PP. Collegii S. Bonaventurae, 10 vols. (Quaracchi: College of St Bonaventure, 1894–1902), vol. 4. p. 20b: 'gratia ex nihilo et subito creatur'.

23 When Thomas argues in the *Scriptum* that the sacraments are disposing causes, the model of dispositive causality he has in mind is that in which an agent prepares matter for the reception of a form. Dondaine suggests that Thomas gets this causal model from Avicenna, according to whom the sublunary efficient causes of generation merely prepare matter to receive forms from the superior giver of forms (*dator formarum*). Theologians during the first half of the thirteenth century may have found in Avicenna's model a way to save both the reality of intermediate, created causes and the perfection and immediacy of God's action. Dondaine suggests that Thomas later abandoned Avicenna's model and found in the notion of instrumental causality (which he got from Aristotle and Averroës) a better way to achieve the same ends. See H.-D. Dondaine, 'A propos d'Avicenne et de saint Thomas: de la causalité dispositive à la causalité instrumentale', *Revue Thomiste* 51 (1951) 441–53.

24 Bonaventure, *Commentaria in quatuor libros Sententiarum* 4.1.1.un.3, resp. (vol. 4, p. 17).

25 Ibid., 1.1.un.4 (4.19 ff.).

26 Ibid., arg. contra 1 (4.19b) and 6 (20a). See also arg. 3 *pro parte negativa*, in the subsidiary question whether the sacraments are dispositive causes (20b).

27 Ibid., arg. 4 (19a) and ad 4m (4.22a).

28 In Bonaventure, *gratia gratis data* is any grace that is morally neutral and does not make the subject pleasing to God. Thomas usually restricts the scope of the term further, to graces given to the subject for the benefit of others, such as charisms and priestly powers.

29 Note that Thomas uses the term *sine qua non* not in this sense but to characterize an occasional cause (as in Bonaventure's *second* theory).

30 Ibid., resp. (4.21b).

31 Ibid., (4.23–4).

32 I.e., of gold or silver.

33 Bonaventure, *Breviloquium* 6.1, in *Opera omnia* (Quarrachi edition), 5.265b: 'sacramenta dicuntur gratiae vasa et causa, non quia gratia in eis substantialiter contineatur nec causaliter efficatur, cum in sola anima habeat collocari et a solo Deo habeat infundi; sed quia in illis et per illa gratiam curationis a summo medico ex divino decreto oporteat hauriri, licet Deus non alligaverit sum potentiam sacramentis'.

34 *ST* 3.62.1, resp. (2821b).

35 *ST* 3.62.1, arg. 2 (2821): 'Nullum corporale agere potest in rem spiritualem, eo quod agens honorabilius est patiente, ut Augustinus dicit'. *Scriptum super Sententias*, 4.1.1.4, qua 1, arg. 3 (460b–61a): 'nobilius est agens patiente, secundum Augustinum ... et secundum Philosophum ... et iterum causa dignior est effectu. Sed tam anima rationalis quam gratia praevalent sensibilibus elementis'. Cf. Aristotle, *De anima* 430a10–17; Augustine, *De Genesi ad litteram libri duodecim*, 12.16, ed. J. Zycha, *Corpus Scriptorum Ecclesiasticorum Latinorum*, 28.1 (Vienna: F. Tempsky, 1894), pp. 401–2. Cf. *Auctoritates Aristotelis* 6, De anima 3, n. 150 (ed. J. Hamesse [1974], p. 187): 'Agens est nobilius et honorabilius passo et forma materia'.

36 On the instrumentality of Christ's *operatio* as a human being, see *ST* 3.19.1, resp. (2551b–2a).

37 *Scriptum super Sententias* 4.1.1.4, qua 1, resp. (463a): 'Ad ultimum autem effectum, quod est gratia, non pertingunt etiam instrumentaliter, nisi dispositive...'. Cf. ibid., 18.1.3, qua 1, resp. (813b): 'baptismus non agit ut principale agens; sed ut instrumentum, non quidem pertingens ad ipsam gratiae susceptionem causandam etiam instrumentaliter, sed disponens ad gratiam, per quam fit remissio culpae'.

38 *Scriptum super Sententias* 4.1.1.4, qua 1, resp. (462b–3a).

39 *Scriptum super Sententias* 4.5.1.2, resp. (525).

40 For a critical review of the interpretation, see B. Leeming, *Principles of Sacramental Theology* (1960), pp. 324–9. For presentations of it, see M.-Benôit Lavaud, 'Saint Thomas et la causalité physique instrumentale de la sainte humanité et des sacrements', *Revue Thomiste* 32 (1927) 305 ff., 313, 315; N. Crotty, 'The redemptive role of Christ's resurrection', *Thomist* 25 (1962) 100–101; J.-P. Torrell, 'La causalité salvifique de la résurrection', *Revue Thomiste* 96 (1996) 188.

41 Cf. *ST* 3.75.5, ad 1 (2944a); *ST* 3.77.1, resp. (2959); *Quaestiones de quolibet* 3.1.1, ad 1 (Leonine edition, vol. 25.2, p. 242).

42 *Scriptum super Sententias* 3.13.3.1, resp. (143b).

43 *Quaestiones disputatae de potentia* 3.4, ad 8 (Marietti edition, *Quaestiones disputatae*, vol. 2 [1965], p. 48a): 'sacramenta iustificare dicantur instrumentaliter et dispositive'.

44 *Quaestiones disputatae de veritate* 27.4, ad 3 (Leonine edition, vol. 22, p. 806): 'et sic sacramenta dicuntur esse causa gratiae per modum instrumentorum disponentium'.

45 *ST* 1.45.5, resp. (288a).

46 Thomas seems to imply that a cause's being *movens motum* is a sufficient condition for instrumental causality: see *De veritate* 27.4, resp. (805a): 'Haec enim est ratio instrumenti in quantum est instrumentum, ut moveat motum'. But the condition applies equally to any intermediate cause in an essentially ordered sequence, such as an intermediate truck in a train.

47 *De veritate* 27.4, ad 4 (806).

48 *Scriptum super Sententias* 4.1.1.4, qua 2, resp. (463b).

49 *De veritate* 27.4, resp. (805a).

50 I.e., regardless of whether it is (i) essential or proper-accidental or (ii) contingent.

51 *ST* 3.7.12, resp. (2476a); 3.7.13, resp. and ad 2 (2477b and 2477b–8a); 3.8.5, resp. (2483a).

52 *ST* 3.56.1, resp. (2787a).

53 I refer to analogy in Aristotle's sense of a comparison between relations, and not in the peculiarly scholastic sense whereby analogy is akin to Aristotle's *pros hen* equivocation.

54 A *ratio* is a formal aspect of a thing, a way of conceptualizing it. While the same thing may be considered under several *rationes,* the schoolmen often regard the *ratio* as equivalent to the essence of the thing, especially when the thing itself by definition involves relations and functions (such as the property of being a head in relation to a body). Hence a definition is an account of a thing's *ratio,* and more precisely an analysis of the *ratio* in terms of genus and species (although in this strict sense, neither God nor created individuals are definable).

55 *ST* 3.7.13, resp. (2477b).

56 *ST* 1.43.2, resp. (271a). The point is that the relation of 'sending' (*missio*) between Father and Son is one of origin, and is neither like that by which a master sends a servant nor like that by which a counsellor sends a king to war.

57 *Scriptum super Sententias* 4.1.1.4, qua 1, resp. (463a): 'Hujusmodi autem materialibus instrumentis competit aliqua actio ex natura propria, sicut aquae abluere, et oleo facere nitidum corpus'. See also *De veritate* 27.4, ad 2m (806): the primary operation of the sacraments is to justify; secondary operations include washing and anointing (*abluere vel ungere*).

58 *Scriptum super Sententias,* 4.1.1.4, qua 1, resp. (463a): 'Et hoc est quod Augustinus dicit, quod aqua baptismi corpus tangit, et cor abluit; et ideo dicitur, quod sacramenta efficiunt quod figurant'.

59 Ibid., 1.1.4, qua 1, resp. (463a); *ST* 3.19.1, resp. (2551b–2a); *ST* 3.62.1, ad 2 (2822).

60 *Scriptum super Sententias* 4.1.1.4, qua 1, resp. (462b). *De potentia* 3.4, resp. (46b).

61 *De veritate* 27.4, resp. (805a): 'serra habeat aliquam actionem quae sibi competit secundum propriam formam, ut dividere, tamen aliquem effectum habet qui sibi non competit nisi in

quantum est mota ab artifice, scilicet facere rectam incisionem et convenientem formae artis'.

62 *ST* 3.19.1, resp. (2552a): 'calefacere est propria operatio ignis; non autem fabri, nisi quatenus utitur igne ad calefaciendum ferrum'.

63 *De veritate* 27.4, ad 2: 'spiritualiter vero attingit ipsam animam, in quantum ab ea percipitur in intellectu ut quoddam signum spiritualis mundationis'.

64 *ST* 3.62.4, ad 1 (2825a).

65 Cf. *ST* 3.56.1, ad 2 (2787b): 'Licet autem virtus principalis agentis non determinetur ad hoc instrumentum determinate, tamen, ex quo per hoc instrumentum operatur, instrumentum illud est causa efficiens'.

66 *ST* 3.48.6, ad 3 (2739b): 'passio Christi, secundum quod comparatur ad divinitatem eius, agit per modum efficientiae'.

67 *ST* 3.48.

68 *ST* 3.1.2, resp. (2416b): 'Sunt autem aliae plurimae utilitates quae consecutae sunt, supra apprehensionem sensus humani'.

69 Adolf von Harnack, *Lehrbuch der Dogmengeschichte,* vol. 3 (4th edition; Tübingen: Mohr, 1932), p. 540.

Chapter 6

An Accomplishment of the Moral Part of Aquinas's *Summa theologiae*

Mark Johnson

Introduction

The Dominican moralist Thomas Deman (1899–1955) once noted that the *Secunda pars*, or moral part, of St Thomas Aquinas's *Summa theologiae* constituted an 'entirely new plan' for treating of morals, a treatment resulting in the single largest portion of his monumental presentation of sacred doctrine, left unfinished at his death in 1274.[1] Seen against the backdrop of the authors and works Deman was comparing Thomas to – Augustine, Abelard, Allan of Lille, Hugh of St-Victor, Peter Lombard, the *Summa fratris Alexandri*, St Bonaventure, and St Albert – his claim for novelty still rings true. But it turns out that Deman only told half the story, for Thomas's accomplishment in writing the *Secunda pars* is also to be seen against the backdrop of Dominican authors and works that constituted the immediate context in which he wrote his work, a context closely linked to the aims of his order.[2] So, while students of Thomas's *Secunda pars* tend to focus on this or that section or doctrine of the work – say, action theory, the virtues, or natural law[3] – here I want to set in relief Thomas's accomplishment in writing the *Secunda pars* as a structured whole. Before addressing the *Secunda pars* head-on, I will first place his writing into its Dominican literary context generally. Thereafter I shall examine the *Secunda pars* as a moral treatise in its pre-existing genre, emphasizing its advances, and then conclude with a suggestion as to how seeing it in this contextual light might direct our future reading of the *pars moralis* of Thomas's masterwork.

Thomas's Dominican Context

In making his profession to the Dominican Order Thomas gave his life over to an apostolate that was explicitly pastoral.[4] Recognized by Pope Honorius III in January of 1217 as an Order of Preachers-in-General, the Order expanded church-wide the apostolate St Dominic and his small band of men had been exercising in the diocese of Toulouse for about a decade, taking a step further the Fourth Lateran Council's constitution *Inter cetera*, which had called for diocesan-bound groups of preachers.

In 1221 the Dominicans were further commissioned to be Confessors-in-General, which put into full swing the same Council's constitution *Omnis utriusque sexus*, which had required annual confession for all Christians. The young Order of the Preachers quickly set about obtaining the education necessary to meet their mandate. Immediately after their recognition in 1217, in fact, Dominic enrolled some of his brethren at the Cathedral school in Toulouse, and eventually sent others to establish Dominican priories, with their attendant schools (*studia*), at the university centres of Paris (summer, 1217), Bologna (1218), Palencia (1220), Montpellier (1221), and Oxford (1221).[5] But the study Dominic had in mind for his *fratres* was not ordered to the speculative advancement of their own minds. 'All our study', the prologue to the Order's first constitutions urged, 'should principally and with ardent highest effort intend to this: that we may be useful to the souls of our neighbors'.[6] While it is not certain that Dominic intended his friars to penetrate into the universities as regent masters,[7] it was at least clear that having them study in the university setting would result in well-trained friars and – he may have hoped, and would be proven correct if he had – quality vocations.[8]

An effect of Dominic's wisdom in seeking educated friars was the outpouring of literature within the Order suited to its apostolate, an outpouring that would become quite large indeed.[9] Given the Order's concentration upon preaching and then the hearing of confessions, it is no surprise that shortly after their dispersal to the centres of learning Dominicans began to produce works ordered to both. Biblical study was naturally a top priority, so one finds authors such as Hugh of St-Cher producing his *Postillae* on the Bible, as well as other aids to biblical study.[10] Guerric of St-Quentin wrote postills on the Bible,[11] but we also have from him, and from Hugh, a number of disputed questions.[12] Yet what is interesting about the questions of these two Dominican Parisian masters is how they reveal their authors' concern with pastoral affairs – the lion's share of their questions address questions of morals, elements of basic Christian belief, or disputes that concerned the Dominicans in particular (e.g., manual labour, age of ordination, etc.).

Outside the more rarefied air of the Universities, but often still university-trained, Dominicans also began to produce aids to the hearing of confessions, penitential literature that marks the earliest literary activity of the Order. Non-Dominican penitential literature had already been in circulation for some time, of course. Shortly before Lateran IV in 1215, for instance, Robert of Flamborough wrote his *Liber poenitentialis* at St Victor, and shortly afterwards Thomas Chobham produced his *Summa confessorum* in England.[13] Both of these works continue the move away from penitential canons to a more encompassing account of penance,[14] an account much in accord with the Council's aspirations for more regular confession, and 'discrete and cautious' confessors.[15]

But Dominican authors chose to go their own way. Within maybe five years of the Order's mandate to be Confessors-in-general, Dominicans had written three, maybe four, significant penitential manuals.[16] Possibly at Paris in the mid-1220s a Dominican wrote a *Summa penitentie fratrum predicatorum*, which leads the confessor step-by-step through the hearing of confessions.[17] In 1221, Paul of Hungary wrote a *Summa de penitentia*,[18] perhaps at the instruction of St Dominic, and possibly for distribution to the brethren attending the General Chapter meeting there that year.[19] And the German Konrad Höxter, also a canonist, produced a similar work, the *Summula magistri Conradi* around 1224, though the attribution to Conrad is not certain.[20] But far and away the single most important contribution came from Barcelona, where Raymond of Peñafort, yet another Bologna-trained canonist, wrote his wildly successful *Summa de paenitentia* (often called *Summa de casibus* or *Summa de casibus paenitentiae*) first in 1224, along with a second recension completed in Rome in 1234.[21] The work – often circulating with his later *Summa de matrimonio* (c. 1235–1236), which had effectively replaced Tancred of Bologna's earlier work of the same name by incorporating Gregory IX's matrimonial Decretals of 1234[22] – became the de facto standard within the Order, and won for Raymond the enduring esteem of his confrères.[23]

Other works in addition to these four were soon to appear. Before or while Thomas d'Aquino was a fledgling Dominican novice and student, Hugh of St Cher had written his *Speculum ecclesiae* (c. 1240),[24] William of Rennes (c. 1241) had added a popular apparatus and questions to Raymond's *Summa de casibus*,[25] and Vincent of Beauvais had begun his encyclopedic *Speculum maius* (1244–1259).[26] Possibly at St Jacques in Paris, and maybe even while Thomas was a young Dominican there, a compilation of moral teaching now known as the *Flos summarum* was produced.[27] And as Thomas became a Dominican teacher himself other Dominicans were busy tending to the educational needs of their confrères. James of Voragine (c. 1263–1267) wrote a *Legenda aurea*, a history of the saints that proved to be an ample source of *exempla* for sermons,[28] Hugh Ripelin of Strasbourg (c. 1265–1267) his *Compendium theologicae veritatis*,[29] Simon of Hinton (c. 1260–1262) his *Summa iuniroum*,[30] and Aag of Denmark (c. 1261–1266) his *Rotulus pugillaris*.[31] Sermons from many of these authors survive as well.[32]

Chief among this second 'wave' of Dominican pastoral literature is the immensely popular *Summa de vitiis et virtutibus* (c. 1249/50) of the famous preacher, William of Peraldus, which survives in as many as 500 manuscripts, numerous editions, and Flemish, French, and Italian translations.[33] The work was composed in two stages, *de vitiis* first (ca. 1236), and the *de virtutibus* second (ca. 1249/50) – the antithesis of Thomas's later practice.[34] It shows sure orientation towards the *cura animarum*, but with something of an intellectually informing bent; it is at one and the same time an ordered presentation of then-common understandings of the vices and virtues (buttressed by a healthy array of authorities ranging from the Fathers to philosophers like Aristotle, Cicero, and Seneca, to contemporaries like Anselm and Bernard) and a source-book of pithy descriptions and quotations ripe for use in preaching; all under the exhortatory influence of a call to detest vice and commend virtue. Peraldus's *Summa de vitiis et virtutibus* helped 'round out' Raymond of Peñafort's *Summa de casibus* speculatively.

The *Secunda pars* in its Genre

It was in this context of Dominican education and writing that Thomas took up his teaching duties when he returned to his home Roman province in 1259, after his first regency at the University of Paris.[35] We know that Thomas was at least aware of both the pastoral and literary tradition of the Order, because of his participation in a special committee, meeting with the Order's general chapter at Valenciennes (near Paris), in the summer of 1259, most likely at the personal request of Humbert of Romans, then Master General of the Order. This committee, comprised of the Order's best-regarded theologians (Albert the Great, Thomas, Florent of Hesdin, Peter of Tarentaise, and Bonhomme of Brittany), forged what is often called a *ratio studiorum*, the text of which was incorporated into the *acta* of that chapter. What is of interest here is that the committee mandated that Dominican students use Raymond of Peñafort's *Summa de casibus* for instruction, or, in default of that, some other such manual.[36]

One is tempted to think that Thomas, if he did side with the recommendations of the committee, did so with some reservation, or perhaps that, later in his life, he would look back upon his participation with some rue. For much had changed since those earlier days of the Order, which saw the production of so much well-intentioned pastoral literature; deeper theological reflection, perhaps coupled with and urged on by the reading of Aristotle, may well have convinced Thomas that more needed to be done than had been done up to that point.

What might Thomas have found wanting in previous literature? Quite a bit, if one examines earlier Dominican attempts through the lens of the corrective *Secunda pars* of his *Summa theologiae*. Let me address some structural issues arising from four sources of Dominican pastoral teaching, to which Thomas might have had access (though my suspicion is that Thomas consulted only Raymond's *Summa de casibus* frequently and directly).

Dating from the earliest days of the Order (circa 1220) the Dominican manual, *Cum ad sacerdotem*, is a run-of-the-mill confessor's manual. Like much penitential material of its time, its tripartite structure is indebted to the penitential rite itself, as exercised in the early thirteenth century.[37] First the penitent is received, and the confessor gathers the information necessary to assess the penitent's status, customs, etc. Thereafter the confessor gently interrogates the penitent about his sins, an interrogation that the *Cum ad sacerdotem* accomplishes by inquiring how the penitent might have sinned through the seven capital sins (pride, envy, wrath, sloth, avarice, gluttony, and lust), or against the Ten Commandments (a novel strategy in literature of this period), or, just to be complete, how the penitent might have sinned through the five senses. Finally the confessor assigns a penance, and absolves the penitent. *Cum ad sacerdotem*, in the end, is a tool for the confessor in action; its brevity makes it easily memorized – at times the text even contains Latin verse, aimed precisely at memorization – and, being simple and uncluttered with references, it is easily mastered by the simplest of confessors.

Paul of Hungary's *Summa de penitentia* is longer and more sophisticated than *Cum ad sacerdotem*. At a glance it would appear to be a twofold work, whose first part is a fairly traditional confessional manual, like the *Cum ad sacerdotem*, and whose second part is an account of the virtues and vices. The confessional section is punctuated by regular, precise references to canon law (in particular to the section of Gratian's *Decretum* known as *De penitentia*), and to Augustine and Gregory. Its presentation of virtues and vices likewise explicitly draws upon the tradition. But the apparent unity of the work is belied by the manuscript tradition, which breaks down into two distinct traditions, one which ends decisively with the end of the confessional section, and the other which includes both the confessional section, then the discussion of virtues and vices.[38] This encourages one to think that a presentation of the virtues and vices was something of an afterthought for Paul, who originally seems to have thought the work to be sufficiently complete to disseminate it as a confessor's manual solely.[39] And the eventual discussion of virtues and vices in the more complete version of the work – actually, importantly, the discussion of the vices and *then* on the virtues – shows no signs of real intellectual incorporation with the subject matter of the first part of the treatise. In short, it is not clear how the rubrics in the first half connect with the discussion of virtue and vice in the second half, or how our understanding of virtue and vice make it possible to conceive of the moral deficiency that sin is.

Writing in the early 1260s the then-former Master General, Humbert of Romans, recommended that certain texts concerning morals be at hand in the libraries of all Dominican priories, and took care to mention two texts in particular: Raymond of Peñafort's *Summa de paenitentia* (usually called the *Summa de casibus*) and William of Peraldus's *Summa de vitiis et virtutibus*.[40] Raymond's *Summa* (1224/34), as its nicknames imply, is a casuistic tool for confessors *in foro paenitentiali*, and helps confessors navigate through the treacherous waters of assessing moral culpability and dispensing adequate penance.[41] The principle of order for Raymond is not the movement of the penitential rite, as it was for the *Cum ad sacerdotem*, but it does share with the *Cum ad sacerdotem* and with Paul of Hungary's *Summa de penitentia* the focus upon sin (*crimen*) as the source of order for consideration of moral matter relative to confession. Divided into three parts that deal with 'crimes committed directly against God', 'crimes committed against neighbor', and 'God's ministers', one can see that Raymond's *summa* may have served as a handy *vademecum* for Dominican confessors, but, while instructing now and then on canon law, it could not do as a text for teachers, preachers, and confessors concerned with the total moral formation of Christians. In fairness, the work's context as a work explicitly associated with confession explains this emphasis upon sin, but the presence of accounts of the virtues in other works like Paul of Hungary's *Summa de penitentia* encourage one to think that much more was possible.

Begun in 1236 just as Raymond finished, William of Peraldus's *Summa de vitiis et virtutibus* did help to 'round out' Raymond's contribution speculatively, eventually emphasizing virtues and vices, and not letting a direct link with confession dictate the order of procedure. Yet the advance of being separated from confession seems to have been only partial, for like Paul of Hungary's *Summa de penitentia*, the work was written in two stages, with the treatment of the vices first (1236), and the treatment of the virtues second (1249/50). The old order had not been completely abandoned, so it seems.[42] And despite its unusual length (359 octavo folios in the Venice edition), learned use of authorities (ranging from the Fathers to philosophers like Aristotle, Cicero, and Seneca, to contemporaries like Anselm), intelligible ordering (vices according to traditional seven capital vices plus an added vice 'of the tongue'; virtues according to the three theological and four cardinal virtues; then the Gifts and Beatitudes), and even presentations of vice and virtue *in communi*,[43] Peraldus's *Summa* was still very much dependent upon the pre-existent forms current in his day.

To turn finally to the moral part of the *Summa theologiae*. Leonard Boyle once told me that Thomas's moral theology, as found in the *Secunda pars*, was the first such account of the Christian moral life based on the *order of being*, and not on some other order of presentation, such as the seven capital vices, the Ten Commandments, or the structures of confession, or the exigencies of canon law. As earnest as Dominican pastoral literature was in serving the needs of confession, the manifold schemes employed did not make room for what Thomas would come to regard as essential to a presentation of the totality of the moral life: an ordered account of the 'how' and the 'why' of the moral life. How does moral action take place? Why should we heed the law and frequent the sacraments (i.e., Raymond), and avoid vice, seek virtue, and cherish the Gifts and Beatitudes (i.e., Peraldus)? Most importantly, what is the purpose of it all? The goal of the *Secunda pars* was to answer those questions, by discovering some unifying notion that would encompass the moral life based rather upon the nature of the reality under consideration – the human person – than upon some preexistent order, traditionally handed on because of its link to, say, confession. Thomas's challenge was to do for a treatment of morals what he sought to do with the larger structure of the *Summa theologiae*, where he placed God as the subject of sacred doctrine, and made the formality of God to be the ordering principle of the three parts of the *Summa*.[44] In the moral part he would incorporate the best of his predecessors' literary efforts in an intelligible, unified way,[45] and thus, he hoped, provide an enduring, pedagogically sound foundation for the pastoral instruction of the Preachers.

Now in choosing to design and write a general *Summa theologiae* Thomas was not wholly on his own. There were many such *summae* that attempted to cover the entirety of the Christian religion in a complete way. His treatment of God in the *Prima pars*, as well as his treatment of Christ in the *Tertia pars*, could find remote structural antecedents in Peter Lombard's *Libri sententiarum*, and in any number of *scripta* based directly or indirectly upon Lombard, ranging from William of Auxerre's *Summa aurea* and the *Summa fratris Alexandri* to Albert's, Bonaventure's, and even his own *scriptum*. And he also had his earlier, though somewhat unsuccessful, attempt at a systematic presentation of the entirety of Christian teaching in his *Summa contra gentiles*.[46]

But when it came to designing the *Summa theologiae*'s treatment of the moral life, he was left in something of a lurch. Inherited philosophical accounts of morals by definition had no place reserved for Christian moral topics,[47] and their dialectical nature paled in comparison to the certitude offered by Christian religious instruction.[48] On the other hand, theological accounts of the moral life arising from Lombard were awkward; there is no real moral treatise in the *Libri sententiarum*, so theologians' moral speculations centred upon Lombard's *litterae* concerning original sin (Bk. 2, dd. 25-44) and the presence of the theological virtues in Christ (Bk. 3, dd. 23-40). And of course the pastoral literature of his own Order zigzagged along.

So Thomas went his own way. At the crucial moment of initiation, in the prologue to this moral part, he explains that the subject under consideration here is 'the image of God'.[49] The phrase is carefully chosen, and not only because Thomas is here recalling the authoritative terminology of St John Damascene,[50] who had won his favor by describing the image of God in terms decidedly intellectual and volitional. The phrase is chosen also because, in addition to the theological flexibility its description gives Thomas, it provides him with a perfect tool for linking the consideration of human morals with the rest of the theological enterprise. Sacred theology (*sacra doctrina*) is about God as its determining characteristic, its subject, its formal notion (*ratio formalis obiecti*), and Thomas works to ensure the unity of the discipline by insisting that all the many and various things considered by the theologian are considered only insofar as they have some relationship to God, either coming from God as their cause, or ordered to God as to their end.[51] But the *Secunda pars* of the *Summa*, which concerns human moral action, is far and away the largest portion of that work, which seems to belie Thomas's claim that theology is about God, or even that it is first and foremost a speculative, and not a practical, enterprise.[52] Yet that he persists in these claims is not only because the tradition, through received writers such as Damascene, has provided him with the resources for doing so, but also because of the way in which he fundamentally construes theological anthropology, the human being's constitution and purpose. For the human person is an image of a certain exemplar, and the exemplar is God; but God's exemplarity is viewed here precisely as an exemplarity of intellect, free choice, and the power fully to act on one's own,[53] which is just what Damascene was saying. The phrase 'image of God' is not just a title, or a moniker; it is really a description, a 'content-rich' description. And so by beginning his discussion of human moral agency with a tacit reminder that the image is only intelligible in relation to its exemplar, Thomas roots his consideration of human action in the one science, the one discipline, of theology, and at the same time announces what will be, as it were, the proximate portal of entry into moral theology; we are to study the human person, precisely under the heading of being, like God, a self-starter, a self-director, through intellect and will.[54]

Early and modern Thomists alike have picked up, in varying ways, on the richness of the Prologue to the *Secunda pars*. Beginning with an early Thomist such as Herveus Natalis (d. 1323),[55] continuing through a commentator such as Conrad Köllin (1476–1536),[56] to more recent authors such as Thomas Deman,[57] Santiago Ramírez,[58] Marie-Dominique Chenu,[59] and William Wallace,[60] a consensus has developed among these Thomists according to which what we call 'moral theology' is in reality an integral part of sacred theology, distinct as to its proximate subject matter, yet homogeneous with the rest of theology in virtue of the formality, the rubric, under which it considers the human being.

I treat of these scholastic niceties to bring out that Thomas was trying hard to develop an approach, a point of departure, for considering human action, multiple and contingent as it is, all under the sacred canopy of Christian revelation. The phrase 'moral theology' (*theologia moralis*) carries with it two distinct burdens. First, we need to arrive at an account of our sacred, Christian teaching that unifies the impressive array of items the theologian might consider – something Thomas was doing with the *Summa theologiae* generally. Thus a competent, all-encompassing description of 'theology' alone is a difficult task. Next we need to discuss the knowability of things in the domain described by the term 'moral', another difficulty in its own right, for the domain of morals comes into existence, as Thomas noted early on in his career, precisely at the moment one can spot the existence of freedom.[61] Yet the indeterminacy of the human will, the seat of human freedom, and the contingency of the matter with which the moral life is concerned, pose problems for intellective disciplines, which prefer to speak abstractly, in terms of necessity, and not in the particular, and about contingency. Is it possible to have an apodictically certain discipline of a subject matter that is, by constitution, changeable?

The answer to this question is 'yes', but only for a portion of the domain of morals under consideration, namely that portion of the domain that can be considered in a largely universal way; this sort of answer is like the answer Aristotle gave in constructing his natural philosophy, to safeguard the claim that there can be genuine knowledge of the world of constitutionally changing things. Applied to moral theology, this would be, by and large, what is considered in the *Prima secundae*, where Thomas considers moral material from the side of the human person's operative powers (the will, the emotions, the habits that serve as principles of action, the intellect operating through law, and, finally, the 'essence of the soul', as the seat of sanctifying grace). For the human being has a nature that allows for such a generalized discussion of its component, operative parts. In the *Secunda secundae* Thomas gets 'closer to the ground', as it were, and begins to consider sub-domains with which the human person is concerned (God through the theological virtues, then the domains with which the cardinal virtues are concerned, then the states of life), these all being things that one might, or might not, be actively involved with in one's life. And of course, the closer one gets to the chosen, individual act – the singular operable, in Thomistic language – the farther away one gets from certitude, for the many and varied contingent circumstances of the particular act are refractory to the intellect's need to know things in a universal way. In fact, the closest one gets to certitude in moral judgement about particulars is the somewhat abstract account of the 'vague individual' (*individuum vaguum*), where one strips away the particularizing circumstances of the singular act: 'a person in such and such a situation, with this, but not with that, should do this'.[62]

To return to the notion of the image of God, which serves as the foundation Thomas uses for providing a context in which to construe his moral theology. As Conrad Köllin points out,[63] Thomas explains the notion of 'the image of God' in terms of the perfect and the imperfect. In question 93, article 4, of the *Prima pars*, he asks whether the image of God is found in every human being. The answer is 'yes', but Thomas gets to the root of the issue; we human beings are said to be in the image of God because of our intellectual nature, and we are more in the image of God the more we become like God through knowing and loving God directly (*quantum ad hoc quod Deus seipsum intelligit et amat*).[64] And this can happen, Thomas continues, in three ways: first, in accordance with the simple fact that by having a mind each person has the aptitude to know and love God, and this, of course, is found in each human person; second, in accordance with the fact that some person is actually or habitually knowing and loving God incompletely; and third, in accordance with the person who is actually knowing and loving God perfectly. The first type of image, Thomas continues, is found in all humans. The second is found in the 'just'. And the third, importantly, is found in the blessed in heaven alone.

This is a crucial doctrine, for it provides Thomas's reader with the full rationale he employs at the outset of the moral part of the *Summa*, in establishing the nature of human happiness or beatitude.[65] Drawing upon the 'function' or *ergon* argument of Book 1 of Aristotle's *Nicomachean Ethics*, and buttressed by his notion of the image of God, Thomas builds upon the claim that the good for the human person must be assessed in accordance with the distinctive character of the human being. A knife might be an effective paperweight, but it is not a good knife on that account; a good knife is one that cuts, in virtue of the form of 'sharpness' that it possesses. The human's distinctive character, says Thomas, is reason.[66] Given this, the ultimate, superordinating goal of the human person is to be able to see God face to face, as has been promised to us, and thereby to be like God, by being as perfect an image of God as is possible for the intellectual creature.[67]

This important moment – I am tempted to call it a discovery – lets Thomas break free from previous orders in constructing an account of the moral life. The structure of the *Secunda pars* derives entirely from this account of the 'image of God, destined for beatitude'. Choosing to divide the second part into two distinct parts (the first a more universal, common consideration of moral principles, and the second a more particular consideration), Thomas proceeds in the *Prima secundae* from the notion of beatitude to its acquisition, which must be accomplished through human action (meaning both the production of imperfect happiness through our effort and the acquisition of perfect beatitude through the performance of meritorious deeds through grace, for which God rewards us with eternal life).[68] These human actions occur because of the will, which is the locus of all moral assessment, and so the order of treatment in the *Prima secundae* depends upon the proximity or remotion of a thing's relation to the will. The powers of the soul more closely impinge upon the will, so they are considered first, along with their distinctive actions (joy, anger, etc.), then the habits of the powers – the virtues and vices – are considered in a general way, with law (found in the intellect) and then grace (found in the essence of the soul, which is not immediately operative) rounding out this consideration of morals *in communi*.

The *Secunda secundae* commences the more particular consideration of the moral life, and might appear to be a standard *summa de virtutibus et vitiis* (it was sometimes copied as though it were). Yet even here Thomas intends to keep things orderly, by insisting that the intelligibility of the moral matter in the *Secunda secundae* must be seen in light of virtue, since it is the virtues that dispose us to act in a way befitting and fulfilling our human, rational nature. Even more, the virtues are the principles for understanding all the other moral matter treated even in this more particular portion of the *Summa*; the moral precepts we inherit from our Christian tradition, the Gifts of the Holy Spirit, the manifold vices to which we can be subject, can all only be understood in relation to the virtues. And so Thomas structures the lion's share of the *Secunda secundae* around the three theological virtues of faith, hope, and charity, followed by the four cardinal virtues, of prudence, justice, fortitude, and temperance; everything considered falls somehow under these seven topics. The consideration of the states of life – an analog to the third part of Raymond's *Summa de casibus* – closes the volume, and with it, the treatment of morals – though one cannot but think that the treatment of Christ in the *Tertia pars* is, in some genuine way, an extension of the moral part of the *Summa*, with Christ being the *exemplum* of moral life *par excellence*.

A Suggestion

The task of any teacher is difficult, especially when the subject matter to be covered is important, dense, and has been well-trodden. Although there are many discrete areas of moral matter in which Thomas is justly praised, we may forget that organizing his teaching notes, as it were, into an intelligible course, is an accomplishment in itself. And when there was little order beforehand, the principle of selection he employs can say as much about his own outlook on things as it does about the other orders he abandoned. In light of this, shouldn't we focus in a special way in our study of Thomas's moral teaching upon his stated principle of order – the image of God, seeking beatitude with God – and constantly retrace our steps, while we tarry elsewhere in the *Secunda pars,* back to the *de beatitudine* (I-II, qq. 1-5), so as to let the work's structure, as much as its content, teach us? Such would be the admonition of this memorial volume's honoree.

Notes

1   Thomas Deman, *Aux origines de la théologie morale* (Montreal: Institute d'etudes médiévales, 1951), p. 103: 'La matière morale est considérable et il importe avant tout de l'organiser. Saint Thomas nous met en présence d'un plan entièrement nouveau, où la distinction augustinienne du *frui* et de l'*uti* reçoit enfin sa consécration'. For more on Thomas's life and work, see Jean-Pierre Torrell's *Saint Thomas Aquinas: The Person and His Work*, trans. Robert Royal (Washington: Catholic University of America Press, 1996), and James A. Weisheipl, *Friar Thomas d'Aquino: His Life, Thought, and Work*, 2nd ed. (Washington, DC: Catholic University of America Press, 1983). Also very informative is

Simon Tugwell's 'The Life and Works of Thomas Aquinas', in *Albert and Thomas: Selected Readings* (Mahwah, NJ: The Paulist Press, 1988), pp. 201-351.

2   Readers who know L.E. Boyle's *The Setting of the* Summa theologiae *of St Thomas*, (Toronto: Pontifical Institute of Mediaeval Studies, 1982), will note my debt to him. Boyle makes the case that Thomas's intended immediate audience for the *Summa theologiae* was Dominican, a case that is circumstantial, but strong. In a paper entitled 'The *Summa theologiae* as Pedagogy', forthcoming in the proceedings for Fordham University's conference, *Education in the Middle Ages*, I have the temerity to refine Boyle's claim in a way which, I believe, strengthens the Dominican orientation of the *Summa*.

3   Some recent, representative studies are: Ralph M. McInerny, *Aquinas on Human Action: A Theory of Practice* (Washington, DC: Catholic University of America Press, 1992); Jean Porter, *The Recovery of Virtue: The Relevance of Aquinas for Christian Ethics* (Louisville: Westminster Press, 1990); idem, *Natural and Divine law: Reclaiming the Tradition for Christian Ethics* (Grand Rapids: W.B. Eerdmans Publishing, 1999); Anthony Lisska, *Aquinas's Theory of Natural Law: An Analytic Reconstruction* (Oxford: Clarendon Press, 1996); Daniel Mark Nelson, *The Priority of Prudence: Virtue and Natural Law in Thomas Aquinas and the Implications for Modern Ethics* (University Park, PA: Pennsylvania State University Press, 1992); Daniel Westberg, *Right Practical Reason: Aristotle, Action, and Prudence in Aquinas* (Oxford: Clarendon Press, 1994); Pamela M. Hall, *Narrative and the Natural Law* (Notre Dame: University of Notre Dame Press, 1994). Without copious bibliographical citation one can also refer to the works of Alasdair MacIntyre, and Germain Grisez, Joseph Boyle, and John Finnis.

4   Much of what follows in this section is based upon: Boyle, *The Setting*, 1-4; idem, 'Notes on the Education of the *Fratres communes* in the Dominican Order in the Thirteenth Century', in *Pastoral Care, Clerical Education, and Canon Law, 1200–1400*, (London: Variorum Reprints, 1981), section vi, pp. 249-67. For a handy account of the origins of the Dominican order, see Simon Tugwell's 'Introduction', in *Early Dominicans: Selected Writings*, ed. S. Tugwell (Mahwah, NJ: The Paulist Press, 1982), pp. 1-47. More comprehensive treatments are the standards provided by M.-H. Vicaire, *Dominique et ses Prêcheurs*, 2nd ed. (Fribourg: Editions universitaires, 1977); idem, *Histoire de saint Dominique*, 2nd ed. in 2 vols. (Paris: Editions du Cerf, 1982); and W. Hinnebusch, *The History of the Dominican Order: Origins and Growth to 1500*, 2 vols. (New York: Alba House, 1966-1973).

5   See Hinnebusch, *The History*, 2:5.

6   See *Constitutiones antiquae ordinis fratrum praedicatorum*, prologus, in A.H. Thomas, *De oudste Constituties van de Dominicanen: Voorgeschiedenis, Tekst, Bronnen, Onstaan en Ontwikkeling (1215–1237)* (Leuven: Bureel van de R.H.E., 1965), p. 311: '...studium nostrum ad hoc principaliter ardenterque summo opere debeat intendere ut proximorum animabus possimus utiles esse'. In commenting upon this passage the Order's fifth Master General (1254–63), Humbert of Romans, noted (*Opera de vita regulari*, ed. J.J Berthier [Turin: Marietti, 1951], 2:41) 'Notandum est autem quod studium non est finis Ordinis, sed summe neccesarium est ad fines praedictos, scilicet ad praedicationes, et animarum salutem operandam, quia sine studio neutrum possemus...'.

7   The assumed intimate link between Dominican houses of study (*studia*) and the universities has been challenged recently by M. Michèle Mulchahey, 'The Dominican *Studium* System and the Universities of Europe in the Thirteenth Century: A Relationship Redefined', in *Manuels, programmes de cours et techniques d'enseignment dans les universites médiévales* (Louvain-la-Neuve: Institut d'etudes médiévales de l'Université catholique de Louvain, 1994), pp. 277-324. For a thorough account of the Order's early educational aims

and policies, see her '*First the Bow is Bent in Study*'... *Dominican Education Before 1350* (Toronto: Pontifical Institute of Mediaeval Studies, 1998), pp. 3-71.

8   See Hinnebusch, *The History*, 1:312-17; 2:5.

9   Just how sizable Dominican pastoral literature grew to be can be seen in Thomas Kaeppeli's *Scriptores Ordinis Praedicatorum Medii Aevi*, 4 vols. (Rome: Ad Sanctae Sabinae, 1970–1993), which lists the manuscripts and editions of all Dominican writers from 1221–1500, from letters A-Z (vol. 1, A-F; vol. 2, G-I; vol. 3, I-S; vol. 4, T-Z [with *corrigenda* and *addenda* to vols. 1-3]). Saints Albert and Thomas are not included because the critical editions of their writings are already underway in Cologne and Grottaferrata.

10   Though Hugh was a master at Paris from 1229–1233, his main activity as a Dominican was administrative (prior provincial of the French province, and prior of the Convent at Paris) before he was made a cardinal. He produced a *scriptum* on the *Sentences* that survives in about 35 MSS, but his biblical works enjoy greater representation: *Postillae in bibliam*, *Correctorium bibliae*, and the immensely popular *Tractatus super missam* (*Speculum ecclesiae*). In addition the Dominicans under Hugh compiled a concordance to the Bible, which was begun in the early 1230s (see R.H. Rouse and M.A. Rouse, 'The Verbal Concordance to the Scriptures', *Archivum Fratrum Praedicatorum* 44 [1974] 5-30). See Kaeppeli, *Scriptores*, 2:269-281; 4:124-6.

11   Guerric joined the Dominicans in Paris in 1225, after first having been a teacher of medicine and a master of arts there. He was a regent master in theology from 1233–1242. See Kaeppeli, *Scriptores*, 2:61-71; 4:96.

12   See P. Glorieux, 'Les 572 Questions du manuscrit de Douai 434', *Recherches de théologie ancienne et médiévale* 10 (1938) 123-52; 225-67. Glorieux (p. 257) assigns to Hugh qq. 234, 261, 263-4, 268, 269-71, and 285, while Kaeppeli (*Scriptores* 2:271) adds to Glorieux's list qq. 26-8, 31, 35-6, 118, 129, 285, 290, 427-33, and 470-81, on the basis of Damien Van den Eynde, 'Nouvelles questions de Hugues de Saint-Cher', in *Mélanges Joseph de Ghellinck, S.J.* (Gembloux: J. Duculot, 1951), 2:815-35. For Guerric see B.-G. Guyot, 'Questiones Guerrici, Alexandri, et aliorum magistrorum parisiensium (Praha, Univ. IV.D.13)', *Archivum Fratrum Praedicatorum* 32 (1962) 5-125. Guyot (p. 120) attributes about 70 questions to Guerric.

13   See Robert of Flamborough, *Liber poenitentialis: A Critical Edition with Introduction and Notes*, ed. J.J. Francis Firth (Toronto: PIMS, 1971), and *Thomae de Chobham Summa confessorum*, ed. F. Broomfield (Louvain/Paris: Nauwelaerts, 1968).

14   The stereotype that penitential material up to the thirteenth century was marred by an almost 'mechanical' character – this sin automatically gets that penance – has been effectively mitigated by Pierre J. Payer, 'The Humanism of the Penitentials and the Continuity of the Penitential Tradition', *Mediaeval Studies* 46 (1984) 340-54, and his more recent 'The Origins and Development of the Later *canones penitentiales*', *Mediaeval Studies* 61 (1999) 81-105. For more on the penitential literature available around the time of Lateran IV in 1215, see: J. Goering, *William de montibus (c. 1140–1213) The Schools and the Literature of Pastoral Care* (Toronto: Pontifical Institute of Mediaeval Studies, 1992), pp. 30-99; Marshall Crossnoe, 'Education and the Care of Souls: Pope Gregory IX, the Order of St. Victor, and the University of Paris in 1237', *Mediaeval Studies* 61 (1999) 137-72; L.E. Boyle, 'The Inter-conciliar Period (1179–1215) and the Beginnings of Pastoral Manuals,' in *Miscellanea Rolando Bandinelli Papa Alessandro III*, ed. F. Liotta (Siena: Sede dell'Accadmia, 1986), pp. 45-56. Boyle coined the term 'pastoralia' to cover 'any and every aid to the *cura animarum*'. See also his 'The Fourth Lateran Council and Manuals of Popular Theology', in *The Popular Literature of Medieval England*, ed. T.J. Hefferman (Knoxville: University of Tennessee Press, 1985), pp. 30-43, at 38-43.

15 See Lateran Council IV, canon 21, in *Conciliorum oecumenicorum decreta*, 3rd ed., ed. J. Alberigo et al. (Bologna: Istituto per le scienze religiose, 1973), p. 245: 'Sacerdos autem sit discretus et cautus, ut more periti medici superinfundat vinum et oleum vulneribus sauciati, diligenter inquirens et peccatoris circumstantias et peccati, per quas prudenter intelligat, quale illi consilium debeat exhibere et cuiusmodi remedium adhibere, diversis experimentis utendo ad sanandum aegrotum'.

16 For a chronological listing of Dominican authors from the Order's earliest days, based upon the date of the author's death or date of last-known activity, see Kaeppeli, *Scriptores*, 4:551-78, esp. 551-3.

17 See J. Goering and P.J. Payer, 'The '*Summa penitentie fratrum predicatorum*': A Thirteenth-Century Confessional Formulary', *Mediaeval Studies* 55 (1993) 1-50.

18 See Paul of Hungary, *Incipiunt rationes penitentie composite a fratribus predicatorum*, in *Bibliotheca Casinesis siu codicum manuscriptorum qui in tabulario Casinesi asservantur*, vol. 4, part 2 (Monte Cassino, 1880), pp. 191-215. See Kaeppeli, *Scriptores*, 3:205-7; 4:219. This edition, however, needs correction, and I am currently preparing a working edition, based upon Dublin, Trinity College MS Lat. 326.

19 For more on Paul and his *Summa*, see: Heinrich Weisweiler, 'Handschriftliches zur *Summa de penitentia* des Magister Paulus von Sankt Nikolaus', *Scholastik* 5 (1930) 248-60; Pierre Mandonnet, 'La '*Summa de poenitentia magistri Pauli prebyteri s. Nicolai*' (Magister Paulus de Hungaria, OP, 1220–21)', study no. 2, in idem, *Saint Dominique: L'idée, l'homme et l'œuvre*, ed. M.-H. Vicaire (Paris: Desclée de Brouwer et Cie, 1937), 249-69 (originally published in *Aus der Geisteswelt des Mittelalters: Studien und Texte Martin Grabmann zur Vollendung des 60. Lebensjahres von Freunden und Schülern gewidmet* [Münster: Aschendorff, 1935] 1:525-44).

20 See J.-P. Renard, *Trois sommes de pénitence de la première moitié du xiiie siècle: La '*Summula Magistri Conradi*'. Les sommes '*Quia non pigris*' et '*Decime dande sunt*'*, in 2 vols. (Louvain-la-Neuve: Université catholique de Louvain, 1989), 2:1-133. Renard notes (1:73-9), however, and Kaeppeli agrees (*Scriptores*, 4:62-3), that the work's precise authorship remains in question, even if the work was readily appropriated by Order, and shows sure signs of Domincan provenance.

21 The MSS of Raymond's *Summa* are so numerous that Kaeppeli (*Scriptores*, 3: 285-6; 4:248) simply refers to the critical edition of the work, *Summa de paenitentia*, Universa Bibliotheca Iuris I-B, ed. X. Ochoa and A. Diez (Rome: Commentarium pro religiosis, 1976). More about the place and context of the work is in the editors' introduction, ibid., pp. lxxxix-xcii. See also Kaeppeli, *Scriptores*, 3:283-7; 4:248.

22 See *Summa de matrimonio*, Universa Bibliotheca Iuris I-C, ed. X. Ochoa and A. Diez (Rome: Commentarium pro religiosis, 1978), cols. 901-98, and the editors' comments, pp. cxv-cxxvii, where they go to some length to show that the *Summa de matrimonio* was a work distinct from the *Summa de penitentia*. From Raymond's opening comments I wonder whether, if he had to do it all over again, he would have included a treatment on marriage in his original *Summa de penitentia* – a treatment he likely omitted at first because he had thought Tancred's *Summa* sufficient to the purpose in the original recension of 1224. See *Summa de matrimonio*, prooemium, col. 901: 'Quoniam frequenter in foro paenitentiali dubitationes circa matrimonium, immo etiam interdum quasi perplexitates occurrunt, ad honorem Dei et animarum profectum, post "Summulam de Paenitentia" specialem de matrimonio subieci tractatum…'.

23 At Raymond's retirement from the Order's Master Generalship (1238–1240), ordained Dominicans were instructed by the General Chapter meeting then at Bologna to offer three masses in suffrage for him upon his death, a practice usually accorded to Masters General

who died while in office. See *Acta capitulorum generalium ordinis praedicatorum*, ed. B.M. Reichert, in *Monumenta Ordinis Fratrum Praedicatorum Historica* 3 (Rome: Propaganda Fidei, 1989), 1:18 (Bologna, 1240) 'Pro fratre Raymundo quondam magistro ordinis, fiat post mortem sicut pro magistro ordinis...'; ibid., 1:88 (Florence, 1257) 'Ista sunt suffragia. Pro domino papa, etc. Sciant fratres quod capitulum generale olim concessit fratri Raymundo de Penaforti quod fiat pro eo sicut pro magistro ordinis post mortem suam...'; ibid., 1:182 (Bologna, 1275) 'Ista sunt suffragia ... Pro fratre Raymundo de Penaforti defuncto quilibet sacerdos iii missas...'.

24 For Hugh, see above, note 10. According to Kaeppeli, *(Scriptores,* 2:276-9, no. 1990; 4:125), *Tractatus super missam sive Speculum ecclesiae*, dating from the 1240s, survives in more than 140 MSS. The confessional formulary *Confessio debet* was regularly attributed to Hugh. See P. Michaud-Quentin, 'Deux formulares pour la confession du milieu du xiiie siècle', *Recherches de théologie ancienne et médiévale* 31 (1964) 43-62, at 48-52.

25 See Kaeppeli, *Scriptores,* 2:156-9, nos. 1637-8; 4:107-108.

26 The work was forever a 'work-in-progress'. See: Kaeppeli, *Scriptores,* 4:435-58, nos. 3981-8; S. Lusignan, *Préface au Speculum maius de Vincent de Beauvais: réfraction et diffraction*, (Montréal: Bellarmin, 1979), esp. 115-29; J.B. Voorbij, *Het 'Seculum Historiale' van Vincent van Beauvais: Een Studie van zijn Ontstaansgeschiedenis*, (Utrecht: J.B. Voorbij, 1991), 389-94. The *Speculum maius* during Vincent's lifetime (1190–1264) contained three parts: a *Speculum naturale, historiale,* and *doctrinale.* After Vincent's death a *Speculum morale* was added, with material taken from earlier versions of the *Speculum naturale,* as well from other sources (e.g., Thomas's own *Secunda pars,* where lenghty passages on, e.g., natural law, were lifted right out of the treatment of law in the *Prima secundae*).

27 Following Pierre Mandonnet, Boyle ('Notes on the Education', p. 253) had taken the *Summa penitentie fratrum predicatorum* mentioned above (note 17) to be this work. The *Flos summarum*, is known to exist in three MSS (Paris BN Lat. 16433 and 16434, and Troyes, Archive de l'Aube 23[I]), and could be the product of Dominicans in Paris (BN Lat. 16433 attributes it to 'quibusdam fratribus sancti Iacobi'), but it dates from mid-century. This *Flos summarum* is a standard *summa de virtutibus et vitiis*, with its section on the virtues being the the work of Richard of St Laurent, and the section on the vices being the first part of William of Peraldus's *Summa de vitiis et virtutibus* (see below, p. 87). For students of Thomas's moral teaching, despite the derivative character of this work (because ordered towards teaching?), this text could be quite important, since it would be, if indeed a product of St Jacques in Paris, an important witness to the sort of moral teaching he would have received there, in the late 1240s. See Renard, *Trois sommes* 1:115, note 240.

28 Kaeppeli, *Scriptores,* 2:350-9, no. 2154; 4:139-40. The work has finally received a long-overdue critical edition, by Giovanni Maggioni, *Iacopa da Varazze: Legenda aurea*, 2 vols. (Tavarnuzze: SISMEL/Edizioni del Galluzzo, 1998). See also his *Ricerche sulla composizione e sulla trasmissione della 'Legenda aurea'* (Spoleto: Centro italiano di studi sull'alto Medioevo, 1995).

29 Kaeppeli, *Scriptores,* 2:261-9, no. 1982; 4:123-24.

30 Kaeppeli, *Scriptores,* 3:346, no. 3600. See also A. Dondaine, 'La Somme de Simon de Hinton,' *Recherches de théologie ancienne et médiévale* 9 (1937) 5-22, 205-18, and Susan Michele Carroll-Clark, *The Practical Summa* Ad instuctionem iuniorum *of Simon of Hinton, OP: Text and Context,* unpublished dissertation, University of Toronto, 1999, which contains a working edition of Simon's *Summa.* Some biblical postills also survive (Kaeppeli, ibid., nos. 3597-9).

31 Kaeppeli, *Scriptores*, 1:135, no. 341. Angelus Walz introduced, then edited the work in his 'Des Aage von Dänemark "Rotulus Pugillaris" im Licthe der alten dominikanischen Konventstheologie', *Classica et medievalia* 15 (1954) 198-252, and 'Des Aage von Dänemark "Rotulus Pugillaris"', *Classica et medievalia* 16 (1955) 136-94.

32 See Kaeppeli, *Scriptores*, 2:280, no. 1991 (Hugh of St-Cher); 2:359-67, nos. 2155-7 (James de Voragine); 3:286, no. 3411 (Raymond of Peñafort); 3:347, no. 3601 (Simon of Hinton).

33 See Kaeppeli, *Scriptores*, 2:133-42, no. 1622; 4:105-106. For more on Peraldus see A. Dondaine, 'Guillaume Peyraut: Vie et oeuvres', *Archivum Fratrum Praedicatorum* 18 (1948) 162-236, esp. 184-97; Siegfried Wenzel, 'The Continuing Life of William Peraldus's *Summa vitiorum*', in *Ad Litteram: Authoritative Texts and Their Medieval Readers* (Notre Dame: University of Notre Dame Press, 1992), pp. 135-63; Mark D. Jordan, 'Aquinas on Aristotle's *Ethics*', ibid., pp. 229-45, esp. pp. 241-2. Peraldus's ability as a preacher was well-recognized, since many of his sermons for ferials and feasts survive. See Kaeppeli, *Scriptores*, 2:143-7, no. 1623; 4:106. Wenzel is leading a team that includes Joseph Goering, Kent Emery, and Richard Newhauser in producing a working edition of the *Summa de vitiis*.

34 The categorization of the moral life into sets of virtues and vices was not simply suited to the needs of the classroom, but was also a useful preaching device, particularly as regarded the vices. See Siegfried Wenzel, 'Vices, Virtues, and Popular Preaching', *Medieval and Renaissance Studies* 6 (1976) 28-54.

35 For more on these years in Thomas's life – about which there is much uncertainty – see Torrell, *Saint Thomas Aquinas*, pp. 96-101.

36 See *Acta capitulorum generalium ordinis praedicatorum*, ed. B.M. Reichert (Rome: Propaganda Fidei, 1989), 1:99-100. For a lengthy discussion of this event, see Mulchahey, '*First the Bow is Bent in Study*', pp. 222-36.

37 See the account provided by Goering and Payer, '*Cum ad sacerdotem*', pp. 12-22.

38 See Weisweiler, 'Handschriftliches zur *Summa de penitentia*', pp. 250-52. My transcription of the beginning of the work, (Trinity College, Dublin, MS Lat. 25, fol. 1r) is: 'Quoniam circa confessiones animarum pericula sunt, et difficultates emergunt, ideo ad honorem dei sanctique Nicho<lae> ac fratrum utilitatem et deo confitentium salutem tractatum breuem de confessione compilaui sub certis titulis singula que circa confessionem requiruntur, et incidunt concludentes ut facilius lector que uelit ualeat inuenire. Cuius tractatus rubrice sunt hee: Quo tempore inceperit confessio. Quare fit instituta. Cui sit facienda. Quo sit confitendum. Que precipue in confessione requirantur. Que sunt necessaria ad ueram confessionem. De aloqutione sacerdotis et introductione ad confitendum. De circumstantiis quas peccator tenetur confiteri. Utrum circumstantie aggrauent peccatum. De interogatoribus a sacerdote faciendis. De generibus abusionum. De officio et debito sacerdotis erga penitentes. Quis peccata dimittat et per que mortalia siue uenalia dimittantur. De modo penitentie pro quolibet <[peccato]. Que debent confiteri in impositione penitentie. Quod sunt casus in quibus teneamur peccatum semel confessum interim confiteri. Quid ualeant remissiones que fiunt hospitalrioum et templariorum et in pontibus et dedicatione ecclesiarum et festis locorum. De noturna pollutione. De cohitu coniugali. De gradibus peccatorum. De dilatione penitentie. De impedimentiis confessionis. De desperatione uenie. De principalibus uitiis uel peccatis. De cardinalibus uirtutibus'. Note how the mention of vices and virtues is at the tail-end of the treatise. Many MSS of the work end at the rubric 'De desperatione uenie'.

39 The Cassino edition of Paul (cited above, note 18) at columns 195a-b, represents an earlier tradition of the work than does the Dublin MS, and in his presentation of the questions the priest should ask in confession, Paul mentions that he does want to get around to the

discussion of the vices and virtues: '...in fine tamen totius huius tractatus si potero et tempus habuero tractabo de istis vitiis principalibus, ponendo descriptiones que ex ipsis procedunt, et de virtutibus cardinalibus. Tamen ad presens tradam doctrinam beati gregorii...'.

40 See Humbert of Romans, *Instructiones de officiis* in *Opera de vita regulari*, ed. J.J. Berthier (Turin: Marietti, 1951), 2: 265: 'Item, ad ipsum [librarium] pertinet providere quod ... est biblia glossata in toto vel in parte, biblia sine glossis, summae de casibus et Gaufredi et De vitiis et virtutibus...'.

41 See Raymond's prologue in *Summa de paenitentia*, prooemium, no. 1, p. 277: 'Praesentem summulam ex diversis auctoritatibus et maiorum meorum dictis diligenti studio compilavi, ut, si quando fratres Ordinis nostri vel alii circa iudicium animarum in foro paenitentiali forsitan dubitaverint, per ipsius exercitium, tam in consiliis quam in iudiciis, quaestiones multas et casus varios ac difficiles et perplexos valeant enodare.' For more on Raymond's role see Angelus Walz's standard, 'S. Raymundi de Penyafort auctoritas in re paenitentiali', *Angelicum* 12 (1936) 346-96, esp. 362-73.

42 The text I use is Guillemus de Peraldus, *Summa aurea de virtutibus et vitiis* (Venice: Paganinus de Paganinis, 1497). The editor – perhaps under the influence of Thomas's later manner of presenting virtues and vices – placed the *de virtutibus* first and the *de vitiis* second, and accordingly rewrote the work's title! But the title should be, of course, *Summa de vitiis et virtutibus*, and the material should be in reverse order.

43 *Pace* Deman, who commented that distinct accounts of virtues *in communi* and *in speciali* originated with Thomas. See *Aux origines de la théologie morale*, p. 105: 'Après la primauté de la béatitude, nul trait n'est plus remarquable dans la *IIa Pars* que sa division en étude générale et en étude spéciale. Aucun auteur précédant (i.e., before Thomas) ne nous annonça rien de pariel'.

44 For more on the intellectual structure of sacred doctrine, see my 'God's Knowledge in Our Frail Mind: The Thomistic Model of Theology', *Angelicum* 76 (1999) 25-46, and Thomas's texts cited there.

45 Not, however, without some tacit correction, as when Thomas in the prologue to the *Secunda secundae* insists that virtues and vices are to be diversified by their relative objects, thus negating much of Peraldus's procedure and the whole idea of using the seven capital vices scheme, since the *Summa de vitiis et virtutibus* often diversifies virtues and vices according to accidental differences, such as external occasions of sin (see *Summa de vitiis et virtutibus*, ff. 293rb-306vb, passim), and Thomas's own teaching (*ST* 1-2.71.1) commits him to the view that vices are to be seen as privations of virtues, in light of common objects or *materia circa quam*. Thomas also uses Raymond, though primarily as a textual source, as Fr. Boyle noted (*The Setting*, p. 7, note. 16). In addition to the passages noted by Fr. Boyle, I have found other borrowings in Thomas's treatment in the *Secunda secundae* on scandal and usury.

46 Thomas originally intended that the first three books of the *Summa contra gentiles* be ordered on the basis that arguments found in them concern 'what faith professes and reason investigates', while the substance of book 4 concerns 'the manifestation of [divine] truth that exceeds reason' (*Summa contra gentiles*, book 1, cap. 9, in *Sancti Thomae Aquinatis Liber de Veritate Catholicae Fidei contra Errores Infidelium*, ed. C. Pera and P. Marc [Turin: Marietti, 1961], vol. 2, p. 12, nos. 55-8). Yet the goal of completeness in his presentation of the moral life in book 3 required him to discuss the beatific vision (caps. 51-63), miracles (caps. 101-7), mortal sin and damnation (caps. 143-5), and divine grace and predestination (caps. 147-53). In the course of writing the work, I suspect, Thomas realized that the division of 'what reason can know' and 'what reason cannot know' does not serve

well as ordering principles for the sweep of God's knowledge. The *Summa theologiae* makes no such use of these notions as ordering principles. For more on the intent and structure of the *Summa contra gentiles*, see Mark Jordan, 'The Protreptic Structure of the *Summa contra gentiles*', *The Thomist* 50 (1986) 173-209; Rene-Antoine Gauthier, *Saint Thomas d'Aquin, Somme contre les Gentiles: Introduction* (Paris: Editions Universitaires, 1993), and Thomas S. Hibbs, *Dialectic and Narrative in Aquinas: An Interpretation of the Summa Contra Gentiles* (Notre Dame, IN: University of Notre Dame Press, 1995).

47   In his *Sententia libri ethicorum*, ed. Leonine (Rome: Ad Sanctae Sabinae, 1969), Thomas regularly reminds readers of the limitations of Aristotle's account of the moral life – the Philosopher was, after all, a pagan. Mostly this seems to stem from Aristotle's not knowing that full human happiness could only be had in the next life. See ibid., bk 1., lect. 9 (p. 32, ll. 162-5), lect. 15 (p. 54, ll. 52-4), and bk. 3, lect. 18 (p. 178, ll. 103-8). Still, Thomas will distance himself from Aristotle's account, when he notes that the ancients would dissolve marriages for reasons of sterility (bk. 8, lect. 12 [p. 488, ll. 285-8]), or when he insists, contrary to Aristotle, that lifelong virginity is *not* an extreme relative to the virtuous mean of temperance (bk. 2., lect. 2, [p. 81, ll. 124-31])! One is reminded of Domingo Báñez's alarm at Aristotle's advocating the exposure of deformed infants in the *Politics* 7.16, 1335b20-26. See Domingo Báñez, *Scholastica commentaria in primam partem Summae Theologiae S. Thomas Aquinatis*, ed. Luis Urbano (Madrid: Editorial F.E.D.A., 1934), p. 16: 'Et 7 *Politicorum* asseruit homines, qui nascuntur orbati aliquo membro vel aliqua ratione monstrousos, interficiendos esse. Docuit etiam ibidem abortum esse procurandum saltem ante foetus animationem'.

48   The contrast between the tentative, almost halting, account of happiness in the *Nicomachean Ethics* and Thomas's account *de beatitudine* at the outset of the *Prima secundae* is telling. The faith – in the form of 1 John 3:2, often cited by Thomas ('...cum apparuerit, similes ei erimus, et videbimus eum sicuti ipse est') – simply provides the *content* of human happiness that the dialectical *form* of Aristotle's investigation could only hint at. And from this identification of 'complete human happiness' with the Christian God all else flows: divine law, grace, the theological virtues, the Gifts, the beatitudes, the counsels, the states of life, the sacraments, etc. In virtue of his baptism Thomas simply had more to go on.

49   *ST* 1-2, prologue, in *Sancti Thomae de Aquino Summa theologiae*, ed. Ottawa (Ottawa: Collège Dominicain, 1941), vol. 2, col. 710a4-15: 'Quia, sicut Damascenus dicit, homo factus ad imaginem Dei dicitur, secundum quod per imaginem significatur intellectuale et arbitrio liberum et per se potestativum, postquam praedictum est de exemplari, scilicet de Deo, et de his quae processerunt ex divina potestate secundum eius voluntatem; restat ut consideremus de eius imagine, idest de homine, secundum quod et ipse est suorum operum principium, quasi liberum arbitrium habens et suorum operum potestatem'. All references to the *Summa theologiae* are from this edition, and will be given in standard form, followed by the Ottawa edition column and line numbers.

50   See St John Damascene, *De fide orthodoxa*, lib. 2, cap. 26, in E.M. Buytaert, ed., *De fide orthodoxa. Versions of Burgundio and Cerbanus* (St Bonaventure, NY: Franciscan Institute, 1955), p. 113: '[Deus] ex terra quidem corpus plasmans, animam autem rationalem et intelligibilem per familiarem insufflationem, dans ei [homini] quod utique divinam imaginem dicimus. Nam quod quidem "secundum imaginem", intellectuale significat et arbitrio liberum'. The manuscript tradition of the *De fide orthodoxa* that Thomas cites has the extra and crucial 'et per se potestativum', but Buytaert does not follow it, despite its heavy representation in the MSS he based his edition on. See ed. cit., p.

113, *apparatus criticus* for l. 24. For Thomas's understanding of Damascene's intentions, see *ST* 1.93.9 c. (582b47-583a4).

51 See *ST* 1.1.3 and 1.1.7. Note that the second objected difficulty in each article raises concerns precisely because theology deals with the 'morals of men' (*de moribus hominum* [3b30; 6b45-46]). It is for a similar reason that Thomas can insist upon the formal unity of the virtue of charity, even though, materially speaking, the act of charity concerns things other than God; see *Summa theologiae*, 2-2.1.1c. (1401b40-1402a7); ibid., 2-2.4.6 ad 1.

52 See *ST* 1.1.4c.: '...Magis tamen [sacra doctrina] est speculativa quam practica, quia principalius agit de rebus divinis quam de actibus humanis; de quibus agit secundum quod per eos ordinatur homo ad perfectam Dei cognitionem, in qua aeterna beatitudo consistit' (4b14-19). Of course, as is well-known, the Franciscan tradition tended to the other view, that theology is more practical than speculative, a view that even St Albert tended towards.

53 See *ST* 1.93.2c., where Thomas insists that it is in light of a thing's specific difference that it is said to be in the *image* of another thing; hence humans are said to be in God's image because 'they know and understand' (*inquantum sapiunt vel intelligunt* [573b41-2]). See also the full text of Thomas's prologue to the *Prima secundae*, cited above (note 49) and *ST* 1-2.71.2. Angels also, because they have intellects – because they *are* intellects – are capable of morality. See *ST* 1, qq. 59-60, 62-3.

54 Hence the importance of the phrasing '*secundum quod et ipse* [homo] est suorum operum principium', in the Prologue's '...restat ut consideremus de eius [Dei] imagine, idest de homine, secundum quod et ipse est suorum operum principium, quasi liberum arbitrium habens et suorum operum potestatem' (my emphasis). See also *Summa contra gentiles*, 2.76 no. 1579.

55 See Engelbert Krebs, *Theologie und Wissenschaft nach der Lehre der Hochscholastik. An der Hand der bisher ungedruckten* Defensa doctrinae d. Thomae *des Hervaeus Natalis*, Beitrage zür Geschichte der Philosophie und Theologie des Mittelalters, Band 11, Heft 3-4 (Aschendorff: Munster i. Westfahlen, 1912), p. 110: 'Practicum morale, prout pertinet ad theologiam, habet considerari secundum attributionem ad obiectum speculabile. Et ex hoc sequitur ulterius quod ad unum scientiam pertinet speculabile et practicum morale speculabile theologiae, quia una est ratio considerandi alterum, scilicet speculabile est ratio considerandi practicum. In parte autem theologiae, quae est practica, quae considerat actum virtuosum ut est ad honorem Dei ... potissimum est dilectio Dei, non qua diligitur ut commodum nostrum sed qua diligitur secundum se amore amicitiae'.

56 See Köllin's comments on the Prologue in his under-read commentary on the *Prima secundae*, *Scholastica commentaria in Primam secundae Angelici doctoris Sancti Thomae Aquinatis* (Venice: Robert Meiettum, 1602), fol. 1, cols. a-b. Köllin promised, and according to tradition finished, a commentary on the first part of the *ST*, but it unfortunately has been lost. See the entry for Köllin in *Scriptores ordinis praedicatorum*, t. 2, ed. J. Quétif and J. Èchard (Paris: Ballard-Simart, 1721), fol. 100a-b. Köllin's commentary on the *Prima pars* would have been the only one not significantly influenced by Cajetan. Köllin defends the unity of the moral part of the *Summa theologiae* with the *Prima pars* thus: '...scientia huius partis [secundae] non est alia in genere, vel specie, quam scientia primae partis: constat enim quoniam scientiae non secantur secundum species rerum ut res sunt: sed secundum species scibilium, quod quandoque circa primam partem huius summae Deo duce prolixius explanabimus; quare cum actus humani, vel homo, ut operativus actionum ad Deum adducentium, vel retrahentium, esto plurimum in ratione entis different, vel magis sint diversa; tamen considerantur hic sub una ratione considerandi formali, sicut in prima parte omnia tractata et considerata sunt' (ibid., col. b).

57 See Thomas Deman, *Aux origines de la théologie morale* (Montreal: Institute d'etudes médiévales, 1951), pp. 104-5.

58 Santiago Ramírez, 'De ipsa introductione in theologiam moralem', in *De hominis beatitudine*, (Madrid: C.S.I.C, 1972), vol. 1, pp. 49-120, at pp. 60-97.

59 M.-D. Chenu, *St. Thomas d'Aquin et la théologie* (Paris: J. Vrin, 1959), p. 156.

60 See William A. Wallace, *The Role of Demonstration in Moral Theology: A Study of Methodology in St. Thomas Aquinas* (Washington, DC: The Thomist Press, 1962), pp. 143ff. In his presentation here Wallace is dependent upon Ramírez, *De hominis beatitudine*, pp. 49-98, who analyzes minutely the component parts of the definition of moral theology.

61 See *In II Sent.*, d. 24, q. 3, a. 2: 'Nullus motus ponitur in genere moris, nisi habita comparatione ad voluntatem ... et ideo ibi incipit genus moris ubi primo dominium voluntatis invenitur'.

62 This all is the theme of Wallace's book, *The Role of Demonstration*, cited above, note 60.

63 See Köllin, *Scholastica commentaria,* fol. 1, col. a.

64 *ST* 1.93.4 c.

65 Father Louis-Jean Batallion of the Leonine Commission has graciously given me advanced access to Thomas's sermons, and in two sermons devoted to the Feast of All Saints, Thomas presents at length the religious side of beatitude, though the doctrine contained there fits quite well with the more philosophical presentation one sees at the outset of the *Prima secundae*, qq. 1-5.

66 See *ST* 1-2.1.2, and ibid., q. 3. See also *ST* 1-2.71.2c.: 'sed considerandum est quod natura uniuscuiusque rei potissime est forma secundum quam res speciem sortitur. Homo autem in specie constituitur per animam rationalem. Et ideo id quod est contra ordinem rationis, proprie est contra naturam hominis inquantum est homo; quod autem est secundum rationem, est secundum naturam hominis inquantum est homo. Bonum autem hominis est secundum rationem esse, et malum hominis est praeter rationem esse, ut Dionysius dicit, iv cap. *de div. nom.*' Thomas seems to think that in this he is somewhat differing from Aristotle, who describes the bad person as one who is harmful, whereas Thomas wants to insist that acting against reason is what makes someone bad. See *ST* 1-2.18.9 ad 2: 'philosophus dicit illum esse malum proprie, qui est aliis hominibus nocivus. Et secundum hoc, dicit prodigum non esse malum, quia nulli alteri nocet nisi sibi ipsi. Et similiter de omnibus aliis qui non sunt proximis nocivi. Nos autem hic dicimus malum communiter omne quod est rationi rectae repugnans'. The *nos* would seem to be either Thomas himself, or 'we Christians'.

67 Thomas loves to quote 1 John 3:2: 'When God appears, we will become like God, and we shall see God just as God is.' See *ST* 1-2.3.8.

68 See *ST* 1-2, q. 6, prol.

Chapter 7

The Metaphysics of Higher Cognitive States in Thomas Aquinas

Pamela J. Reeve

This essay examines the metaphysical relationship between the separation of the soul and the inception of higher cognitive states in the writings of Thomas Aquinas. It begins with an account of his psychological theory followed by a discussion of general metaphysical principles concerning the relationship between immateriality and cognitivity. Texts are then examined that refer to phenomena that Thomas explains in light of the above principles. Spiritual dreams and rapture are treated in some detail. A concluding section indicates how Thomas's philosophical understanding of the conditions of the possibility of higher cognitive modalities may contribute to a debate in the contemporary study of mysticism.[1]

Philosophical Psychology

Because the extraordinary can properly be understood only against the background of the ordinary, I shall begin with a summary account of the main features of Thomas's philosophical psychology, based mainly on the *Prima pars* of his *Summa theologiae*. For Thomas, the human soul is a subsistent, incorporeal being that exists through itself (*per se subsistens*), not in accidental dependence on something else, even the body that it informs. Because the soul exists in itself, it is also capable of operating through itself. This follows from the principle that a subsistent being is also capable of a subsistent (*per se*) operation: 'a thing operates according as it is' (*eo modo aliquid operatur, quo est*).[2] In the human soul, this subsistent operation encompasses the intellectual function or understanding as well as the rational appetite or will. As a *per se* operation of an immaterial being, the understanding is an operation in which, metaphysically, 'the body does not share' (*non communicat corpus*). Understanding is not exercised through a material organ as seeing requires the eye, although it does make use of supporting functions, such as perception, imagination, and memory, which have an organic basis. This independence of the intellect from materiality is important when considering the state of the soul after death. If the soul did not have any cognitive operation that it could exercise through itself, independently of the body, then even if it did survive death, it would be completely disabled and incapable of knowing anything.

Yet, the fact that it is capable of a *per se* operation does not mean that the intellect functions purely through itself when the soul is united to the body as its form. The human soul is created *as* the life-giving principle of a physical body. Human nature as a species includes 'soul, flesh, and bones'.[3] Because of its metaphysical status as an embodied form, the intellective soul, although *capable* of a *per se* operation, naturally functions in and through the physical body when united to it in the present life.

In the anthropology of Aquinas, the intellective soul is fundamentally conditioned by its having been created as the form of a material body. The disposition to be united to a body is something belonging to the soul 'according to itself' (*secundum se*). As part of the very *esse* of the human soul, it remains even in separation as 'an aptitude and natural inclination for union to the body'.[4]

The disposition of the soul to be united to and function through a body has certain cognitive consequences. The most significant of these is the natural tendency of the human mind to understand by turning to phantasms or imaginal forms. In its embodied state, human intelligence is in a state of potency and its activation requires forms derived from sense perception. With respect to this need, Thomas compares the intellect to the sense of sight: 'Phantasms are related to the intellect as colour is to sight'.[5] While the activation of visual perception in the act of seeing is brought about through the reception of colour – a sensible form – the activation of the knowing power requires an intelligible form, abstracted from imaginal forms, which in turn derive from sense. The actualization of both sensitive and cognitive powers, therefore, involves a prior reception from an external source.

The natural tendency of the human intellect to advert to imaginal forms in the process of understanding arises from the very *esse* of the soul as an embodied form. The 'proper object' of the soul – the object that its cognitive operations are naturally proportioned to know – is 'a quiddity or nature existing in corporeal matter' or, otherwise expressed, 'the nature of a sensible thing'.[6] In its essential orientation to knowing material things, therefore, the human mind may be thought as having a certain natural extroversion. Of course, what is known primarily is a quiddity or nature – a universal, not the particular individuals themselves. Nevertheless, such universals are derived from the prior observation of material things. From an Aristotelian-Thomistic perspective, our understanding of natural species is based on sense perception, not a Platonic participation in immaterial eidetic forms (see the articles in *Summa theologiae* 1.84).

The process by which the embodied human intellect is brought from a state of potentially knowing to actually knowing depends on the intellect being able to turn to imaginal forms derived from sense perception. Having adopted an Aristotelian psychology, Thomas is philosophically committed to this view. While he admits that the intellect can, on the basis of such understanding, rise to a 'kind of knowledge' of invisible things, for example, God and separate substances, this knowledge is analogous and inferential, not a direct cognition of these things as they exist in themselves (*secundum seipsas*).[7] The highest form of the latter kind of knowledge is the visionary participation in God, in which the intellect sees God through the divine essence itself (*per essentiam*). The soul attains this intellective vision by the elevation of its cognitive operation into deiformity through receiving the light of glory. It is not that something new is known, as the intellect is also capable of an imperfect knowledge of God through reason and faith. It is, rather, a radically different *kind* of knowing that involves a modification in the actual cognitive operation of the mind.

Immateriality and Cognitivity

Thomas largely adopts the psychological theory of Aristotle as the most accurate philosophical conception of the normal mode of human understanding in the present life. Yet, he also has to deal with certain cognitive states mentioned in Scripture that apparently go beyond the normal mode, such as prophecy, spiritual dreams, the rapture of Moses and Paul, and the beatific vision itself. The knowledge attained in these states presupposes some kind of modification in human cognitive operation and reception. In explaining this Aquinas adverts to the metaphysical basis of human cognitive operations in the *esse* of the soul as an embodied form. He accounts for the possibility of modified operation and reception in terms of the partial separation of the soul from its naturally embodied state. This should not be understood, however, as implying that such separation is *all* that is necessary. For example, the inception of the beatific vision requires more than the complete separation of the soul at death. In addition the soul must receive the light of glory, which is a grace. Nevertheless, in the Thomistic account, complete separation is a necessary disposing factor for that inception, although transient elevation to the *visio Dei* is possible even before death, as will be seen below.

The present task is to articulate the general principles of the above modification. Aquinas often states these in texts dealing with particular phenomena. A convenient point of entry is an article in the *Prima pars* that treats the question whether anyone in the present life can see God *per essentiam*. In addressing this question, Thomas's immediate concern is with the cognitive limitations that arise from the embodied state of the soul. As discussed above, the embodied soul has a connatural mode of cognitive operation that involves turning to imaginal forms derived from sense. Underlying this connatural operation is the metaphysical link between the nature of something and its cognitive possibilities as expressed in the axiom 'the mode of knowledge follows the mode of the nature of the knower' (*modus cognitionis sequitur modum naturae rei cognoscentis*).[8] But God cannot be seen directly through any kind of intermediate imaginal or intelligible form, only by God raising the intellect to deiformity. The conclusion follows that the soul cannot see God in its present mortal life in which it naturally knows through such intermediate forms.

Nevertheless, Aquinas must be able to address two scriptural accounts of apparent elevations to seeing God before death: the record in Exodus 33:11 of God speaking to Moses face to face and that in 2 Corinthians 12:1-4 of Paul's being rapt into paradise. Before examining more closely Thomas's treatment of rapture itself, it will be of value to consider the metaphysical basis of this and other phenomena that involve some kind of enhanced cognitive operation or higher spiritual reception.

This metaphysical foundation involves an intimate link between being and knowing and, more specifically, between immateriality and cognitivity. Thomas discusses this relationship in an article on divine knowledge in the *Prima pars*. The nature of a being that is capable of cognitive operations has 'a greater amplitude and extension' than one whose nature lacks such operations because it is 'more contracted and limited'.[9] The greater amplitude and extension of the first nature correlates with the fact that *qua* cognitive, it is capable not only of its own form but of receiving the forms of other things as well. What determines the extent of this receptivity, however, is the extent of the immateriality of an existing form or nature since 'contraction of form is through matter'.[10] Thus, the more immaterial something is, the more open or receptive it is to the forms of other things. In this way, the basis of cognitivity is immateriality: 'the immateriality of a thing is the reason why it is cognitive'.[11]

This group of related concepts – that a cognitive nature has more 'amplitude and extension' than one that is non-cognitive, that this extension relates to the cognitive reception of forms, and that the metaphysical basis of cognitivity is immateriality, recalls an earlier determination on infinity (*ST* 1.7.2). Examining this earlier point will make more explicit the conceptual link between metaphysics and cognitivity, or being and knowing.

While acknowledging that only God is 'absolutely infinite' (*infinitum simpliciter*), Aquinas argues that things other than God may be considered infinite in a certain respect or relatively infinite (*infinitum secundum quid*).[12] This determination of relative infinity applies in a different way to things composed of matter and form and to separated forms, that is, angelic substances. Something such as a piece of wood is materially infinite because it is capable of receiving many different accidental modifications. It has the potential of being shaped into a infinite number of different forms while remaining the same piece of wood. But, with respect to its wooden nature, which is received in matter, it is formally finite – the nature or form 'is limited through the matter in which it is received'.[13] Even the relative material infinity in such a thing is only a potential since all possible shapes could never simultaneously be actualized, only one at a time.

But, not all created forms are received in matter. Angels may be considered as subsisting forms that exist in complete separation from matter. They also have a certain relative infinity, but unlike material things, this applies to their form and derives from the fact that such forms 'are neither terminated nor contracted through any matter'.[14] The angelic form itself, therefore, has a certain infinity. This infinity is not an *ontological* openness to other forms, since the angelic *esse* is contracted and limited by the angelic species or nature. Rather, it is an intellectual openness with respect to the reception of intelligible forms.

Thomas's response to an argument in the above article explicitly applies the notion of formal infinity to the issue of cognition. The argument proposes that every created intellectual substance is infinite in its essence because such substances have an infinite power – an ability to apprehend a universal that is capable of extending to an infinite number of singulars. Thomas concedes that in a way (*quodammodo*) the intellect does have such a power of extending itself to an infinity of things, adding that this 'derives from the fact that the intellect is not a form in matter'.[15] This is true both of angels and of the human soul, although not to the same degree. Angels naturally exist and act 'totally separated' from matter, while 'in the intellective soul joined to the body' it is only the 'intellective power, which is not the act of any organ' that is able to function in separation from matter.[16] In both cases, however, the formal infinity of the intellect – its openness to intelligible forms other than itself – follows from its separation from matter.

In addition, the *degree* of immateriality or separation from matter has a determining effect on the nature of the cognitive mode of which something is capable: '... the mode of cognition is according to the mode of immateriality. Thus it is stated in II *De anima* that plants do not know because of their materiality'.[17]

This proportional relationship between cognitivity and immateriality is also found within human nature in the higher cognitivity of the intellect relative to the senses. Again, the reason for this difference is the greater ontological distance of the intellect from matter: 'Sense is cognitive because it is receptive of species without their matter and the intellect is still more cognitive because it is more "separated from matter and unmixed", as stated in III *De anima*'.[18]

On the basis of this proportion between the immateriality of something and its cognitivity Thomas concludes that God is to the highest degree cognitive (*in summo cognitionis*) because God is to the greatest degree immaterial (*in summo immaterialitatis*).[19]

The above reasoning presents the metaphysical basis for Thomas's view that the withdrawal of the soul from its engagement with the senses and imaginal forms derived from sense allows it to realize a higher mode of cognitive operation or reception whether naturally or assisted by grace. It remains to examine texts where Aquinas treats specific phenomena that involve the above withdrawal.

Separation of the Soul at Death

The nature of the modified cognitive operation that ensues when the soul is withdrawn from the body is discussed in some detail in a text in the *Summa contra gentiles* where Thomas treats the immortality of the soul. The separation of the soul from the body at death only makes impossible those activities that depend on the body, such as sense and imagination. A version of the metaphysics elaborated above is cited as the basis for the view that the soul understands in a different way after death: 'The soul understands in a different way when separated from the body than when united to it, as also it exists in a different way [after death]: for everything acts according as it is'.[20] Thus, a change in the mode of being of the soul, specifically its separation from the body, results in an altered cognitive operation.

After death, the soul exercises its proper operation not in conjunction with the body but 'through itself' (*per seipsam*) in a manner similar to the angels. Although the soul must be *capable* of such an operation even when united to the body, it only emerges upon separation. Otherwise, it seems that the embodied condition so affects the intellective soul that it spontaneously exercises its cognitive capacities through the body. Yet, the capacity for a *per se* operation is crucial to Thomas's argument for survival.

A further aspect of the cognitive mode that is exercised by the soul in separation from the body involves enhanced receptivity. In addition to understanding in a quasi-angelic manner after death, the soul also is more open to receiving the influences of separate substances: 'Also, from [these substances], as from superior beings, [the soul] will be able to receive their influence more fully so as to achieve a more perfect understanding'.[21] In support of this Thomas refers to certain experiences before death that suggest that the soul knows more perfectly and is more receptive to spiritual influences when less engaged with bodily life:

> An indication of this [more perfect understanding with separation] is apparent even in the young. For the soul, when restrained from being occupied with its own body, is rendered more apt for understanding certain higher things. Hence the virtue of temperance, which withdraws the soul from bodily pleasures, especially makes human beings apt for understanding. In addition, while human beings are asleep and their bodily senses are not being used and there is no impeding disturbance of the humours or vapours, they perceive, from the impression of superior beings, certain things concerning the future that exceed the mode of human reasoning. And this happens to a much greater degree in those who have fainted or are in ecstasy, to the extent that there is a greater withdrawal (*retractio*) from the bodily senses.[22]

Having cited these examples from human life prior to death, Thomas then offers a metaphysical explanation as to why this greater receptivity and more perfect understanding should occur when the soul is less engaged with bodily life. In the following passage, he refers to the well-known image from proposition 2 of the *Liber de causis* that the soul exists at the horizon of time and eternity. But, in the present context, where he is considering the separation of the soul from the body, Thomas incorporates the image into a conception of an ascending movement in which the soul attains to higher and more spiritual cognitive modes with that separation:

> Nor does this [the above phenomenon] happen without cause. For, since the human soul ... is [situated] at the boundary of bodies and incorporeal substances, as though existing at the horizon of eternity and time, in receding from the lowest it approaches the highest. Consequently, when it is completely separated from the body, it will be perfectly likened to the separate substances with respect to its mode of understanding and will receive their influence abundantly.[23]

It should be noted that in the later treatment of the separated soul in the *Prima pars*, Thomas is more conservative in his estimation of the quality of cognition realized by the soul after death. With respect to the knowledge of natural things, he argues that it is imperfect, general, and confused in comparison with angelic knowledge.[24]

The above passages provide support for the view that Thomas conceives of altered (and often higher) cognitive modalities as being conditional on the partial or complete separation of the soul from the body. In his treatment of spiritual dreams and rapture, to be examined below, Thomas also uses the immateriality-cognitivity link to understand the possibility of a cognitive operation and reception that in some way exceeds the normal mode of human understanding described in his psychology.

Spiritual Dreams

A number of texts suggest that Thomas saw dreams as an aspect of human life in which there is a particular openness to the reception of divine influence – either directly from God or through the mediation of angels. As with the apparent rapture of Moses and Paul, Thomas has to consider the possibility of such reception in view of certain scriptural references, for example, to the dreams of Joseph in Matthew 1:20, 2:13, and 2:19.

Unlike his teacher, Albert the Great, Aquinas does not comment directly on Aristotle's treatises on sleep, dreams, and divination, although he refers to the *De somno et vigilia* as early as the *Scriptum*.[25] For Thomas, the issue of dreams often arises in the context of his treatment of prophecy and divination. Dreams were considered a medium of divine revelation in both Christian and non-Christian writings in antiquity, although Aristotle explicitly rejects this idea.[26] In his attempt to harmonize these divergent sources, Aquinas proposes that dreams have both natural and supernatural causes.

In view of the discussion up to this point, it is not surprising to find that Thomas holds that the influence of separate substances may cause revelatory dreams and that the human soul is more disposed to receive such influences when free from the concerns of corporeal life – in this case, when asleep:

> In a dream, when the exterior senses are bound, the interior powers, as though at rest from the commotion of the exterior senses, are more able to perceive the interior impressions produced in the understanding or imagination by divine or angelic enlightenment or by the power of celestial bodies or some other such things.[27]

Although, as above, many of the texts that mention higher spiritual reception in dreams occur in treatments of prophecy, Thomas's formulation of the conditions of such reception appear to indicate a general disposition that would be found in the dream state of all people. One text in particular, in Thomas's literal commentary on Job, suggests the possibility of a more general phenomenon of spiritual reception in dreams. The scripture text is Job 33:15-18 where Elihu, a friend of Job, proposes that God speaks to the soul and imparts instruction in dreams. Elihu explains that:

> God speaks but once – through a dream in a vision in the night – and does not repeat the same thing a second time. It is when human beings become drowsy and lie asleep in their beds that God opens their ears and teaches them by instructing them with knowledge, turning them away from the things they have done and freeing them from pride. [Thus

God] rescues their souls from corruption and [preserves] their lives from passing unto death [literally, 'from passing over onto the sword'].[28]

In his interpretation, Thomas repeats his view regarding the greater receptivity of the soul to divine influence during dreams, which he sees implied by the words of Elihu:

> ... he posits a divine operation with respect to someone who is asleep. This is seen first of all in the fact that when the exterior senses have been rendered immobile by deep sleep and when the person is resting quietly in bed, there is given by God [*datur divinitus*] a certain faculty for perceiving divine instruction in that the person's soul is not occupied with exterior things: hence he adds 'then God opens human ears'.[29]

The binding of the senses during sleep is referred to by Aristotle in his psychological treatise, *De somno et vigilia*.[30] Thomas makes use of this idea in a manner not anticipated by Aristotle when he incorporates it into an explanation of the psycho-physiological conditions of higher forms of reception during sleep. When the senses are suspended from their normal engagement with external things, it is as though a certain natural interiority is constituted that allows the reception of impressions from higher spiritual beings, including God. In the Job passage Thomas proposes, in addition, that a specific capacity for 'perceiving divine instruction' is 'divinely given' to the sleeper.

Rapture

One spiritual phenomenon where the immateriality-cognitivity link is especially prominent is rapture. Thomas treats this more systematically than he does dreams, usually grouping it with questions on prophecy as, for example, in the *De veritate* and the *Secunda secundae* of the *Summa theologiae*. While it might be thought that this association with prophecy indicates that Thomas considers rapture to be a charismatic grace, he also acknowledges that it is 'the highest grade of contemplation in the present life'.[31] In principle, therefore, this would be a graced spiritual elevation that anyone following the contemplative life could attain.

Rapture, in which the human soul is raised to a vision of the divine essence even before death, presents a challenge to Thomistic psychology, which holds that the mode of knowing connatural to human existence involves understanding by way of sensible things. It is impossible, of course, for God to be seen *per essentiam* through any kind of mediating image or intelligible species. Although human life is created with a natural desire to know the first cause of all things, the embodied condition of the human soul and its natural disposition to know by way of images derived from sense, makes the vision of God naturally impossible in the present life.

A major supporting text from scripture for this view is the declaration of God to Moses in Exodus 33:20 that no one shall see God and live. At the same time, Thomas has to propose an interpretation of the apparent elevation to seeing God before death that occurred with Moses and Paul. These instances require an interpretation that, on the one hand, maintains the impossibility of the *visio Dei* in the present life while, on the other, allowing it under certain conditions. These conditions pertain to the higher cognitive states that become possible with the withdrawal of the soul from its active engagement with the body. This withdrawal occurs most definitively, of course, with complete separation of the soul from the body at death, at which time the mind is no longer able to turn to imaginal forms. Prior to that, there needs to be a process of withdrawal that produces an equivalent state – a kind of suspension of normal cognitive operations in which the soul is inhibited from its natural tendency to engage in sensory, imaginal, and discursive activity.

In an article in the *Secunda secundae* that examines whether the contemplative life can attain the vision of the divine essence, Aquinas associates the above suspension with a state of life that, even before death, admits the possibility of elevation to seeing God. He discriminates between two ways of being in this life – actually (*secundum actum*) insofar as someone 'makes use of the bodily senses' and potentially (*potentialiter*) insofar as the soul remains conjoined to the body as its form, but 'makes no use of the senses or even the imagination as happens in rapture'.[32] In an earlier article on rapture, where Thomas considers the extent to which Paul's soul was separated from his body, he comments on the necessity for the soul to be withdrawn from actually making use of the senses and imaginal forms.[33] This cognitive requirement derives from the metaphysical status of the soul as an embodied form, which produces in it a natural tendency (arising from the *esse* of the soul itself) to engage in cognitive acts using the senses and imagination. Understandably, therefore, Thomas considers the withdrawal from or suspension of these activities to involve a kind of dying to embodied life.

An earlier pair of articles on rapture in the *De veritate* presents what might be called the metaphysics of rapture with respect to the necessity of some degree of separation between the soul and the body, at least with respect to the exercise of certain functions.[34] Again, the required separation not only is from the use of the bodily senses but also from the more interior imaginal forms derived from sense.

One of the main reasons Thomas gives for the need of the higher intellectual function to be withdrawn from these objects, forms, and activities concerns the materiality involved in sense and imagination. Because the vision of God involves an elevation and participation of the intellect in the 'most intensely intelligible object' (*vehementissimum intelligibile*), it needs to be as free as possible to operate in a purely immaterial way. According to the metaphysics of intelligibility, 'every intelligible thing is either in itself free from matter or is abstracted from matter by the action of the intellect'.[35] Thomas concludes from this that 'the freer (*purior*) the intellect is from contact with material things, the more perfect it is,' in its intellectual function. But, this perfection has certain natural limits. The fact that the human intellect, in its normal mode of operation, needs to abstract intelligible species from imaginal forms derived from sense indicates that it is cognitively less efficacious (*est minoris efficaciae*) than the angelic intellect, which spontaneously intuits purely intelligible, immaterial forms. For the human intellect to be raised to that 'most intense act' (*actus vehementissimus*) of the intellective vision of God, who is immaterial and intelligible in the highest degree, there needs to be a withdrawal from activities that hinder the realization of the natural perfection of its immaterial *per se* operation.[36] The intellect always remains capable of such an operation even though normally, in its fully embodied state, it naturally understands by way of imagination and sense.

At certain points, the language used by Thomas in addressing this need for a higher degree of immateriality in the intellective function, if it is to be raised to the vision of God, has an almost Manichaean tone. He writes, for example, that 'the purity of the intellect, in a certain way, is contaminated (*inquinatur*) by sensible operations'.[37] What is 'contaminated' is the concentrated immaterial purity of the intellect in its *per se* operation. This impairment arises from the need to divide attention between intellective and sensitive operations, which results in each operation being hindered by the attention given to the other (*impediunt se invicem intellectivae et sensitivae operationes*). In addition, there is a certain admixture of the intellect with sensible operations that occurs in the reception of intelligible species from imaginal forms derived from sense. The latter impairment arises from the deflection of the intellectual power that occurs in its engagement with forms derived from lower powers.

Since the union itself of the soul with the body does not involve any specific intentional operation of its *cognitive* powers, that union itself does not directly hinder the purity of intellectual operation. Complete separation of the soul, therefore, is not required for the elevation of the intellect to the vision of God. In support of the last point, Thomas refers to the metaphysical principle of cognitivity examined earlier in the present essay: '...the intellective powers do not proceed from the essence of the soul insofar as it is united to the body, but rather according as it remains free from the body, inasmuch as it is not totally subject to it'.[38] The human intellect thus has a certain inherent metaphysical freedom and transcendence of the corporeal body and the external sensible world. But it also has an inherent disposition to function as an embodied form, which causes the intellectual operation, though metaphysically separate, to be exercised in conjunction with the body and to engage cognitively with imaginal forms derived from sense.

The limiting effect of materiality on cognitive operations is suggested by Thomas's use of the verb *contraho* and its adjectival relative *contractus*. Possible English renderings in addition to the literal 'contraction' include 'shortening', 'diminishing by drawing together', 'narrowing', 'abridging', 'lessening', 'limiting', and 'restricting'. Since the angelic intellect exists as a purely spiritual self-subsistent form, it is free from the restricting effect of matter on its cognitive operations. Although the human intellective soul also is a self-subsistent, purely spiritual form, its embodied condition has a distinctly limiting effect on its cognitive operations. The withdrawal from the active engagement in bodily life is therefore also, correlatively, a withdrawal from the limiting, diminishing effects of matter. It is, simultaneously, a spiritual retreat into the inherent immateriality of the *per se* operation of the intellective soul whereby it is metaphysically disposed to higher modes of cognitive operation and reception.

Whether and to what extent Thomas considers grace to be necessary for the withdrawal of the soul from its engagement in bodily life is a further issue. For present purposes, it has been shown that he considers such a withdrawal to be a natural necessity from the perspective of the metaphysics of cognitivity. In order to function on a higher, more purely spiritual, level of reception or operation, the soul needs to withdraw or be withdrawn from its normal extroverted engagement in understanding by way of sense perception and the imaginal forms derived from sense.

Aquinas and the Contemporary Study of Mysticism

Thomas presents a comprehensive understanding of the foundations of human spiritual consciousness that integrates being and knowing and shows the intimate relationship between the two. Although his Aristotelian psychology is no longer used in the philosophical explanation of how we know, the idea of a link between being and knowing has a relevance to human spiritual aspirations that gives it more than merely historical interest. Indeed, Aldous Huxley sees this link as a key axiom in a 'perennial philosophy' that is 'immemorial and universal': 'Knowledge is a function of being. When there is a change in the being of the knower, there is a corresponding change in the nature and amount of knowing'.[39] Although we know, as Aquinas did not, that the human species and indeed all natural species are not static but continually evolving forms, there is no reason to think that the above axiom should hold at one time in human history and not at others. Similarly, there is no reason to think that it might hold for the members of one culture or religious tradition and not others, although its conceptual and linguistic expression inevitably will take different forms.

There is presently considerable debate in the philosophy of mysticism over the issue of cross-culturally invariant mystical experiences. Some scholars, such as Steven Katz, argue that mystical experience is wholly shaped by factors specific to the culture, religious training, and expectations of the mystic.[40] Others maintain that at least some mystical experiences transcend conceptual and linguistic determination. Such experiences, therefore, may be common to the members of different religions and cultures. One proponent of this view is Robert Forman, the editor of two collections of articles that argue for a cross-culturally invariant mystical experience called the 'pure consciousness event'.[41] In his more recent volume, *The Innate Capacity*, Forman argues that to the extent someone describes the mystical process in terms of a forgetting, or laying aside of sensory input, images, and thoughts, and of entering into a state of bare, non-intentional awareness or pure consciousness, this implies the experience of a state of consciousness that is not shaped or conditioned by culture-specific factors.[42] Phenomenological descriptions of such a state thus could refer to something common to the experience of the members of different religious traditions even though this experience would inevitably be expressed in different terms.

Forman argues that the capacity for this experience of pure consciousness is innate in human nature itself and thus is not relative to time, place, culture or religion. One example that he finds in the Christian mystical tradition is the *gezuchet* experience described by Meister Eckhart.[43] While the constructivist approach taken by scholars such as Katz insists that such an experience must be irreducibly different from others owing to diversity of culture and religious training, Forman maintains that the experience in question is based on 'a fundamental human psycho-physiological structure' that 'transcends cultures and eras'.[44] To the extent that the process of entering into the experience involves withdrawing from or letting go of one's normal engagement with sensing, feeling, imagining, and thinking, it is in agreement with the cognitive modification conceived by Aquinas that occurs, for example, in rapture.

Before indicating the potential contribution Aquinas might have to this debate, a critical point should be raised concerning Forman's concept of an 'innate' capacity for mystical experience. He writes that mystics such as the author of the Buddhist *Lotus Sutra*, Patañjali, and Eckhart 'suggest that mysticism results from relinquishing [the] constructive, linguistic process' that shapes our ordinary experiences. The individual thereby comes to 'something that is innate within the human being'.[45] This is something 'originating in or inherent in the constitution of the person rather than derived from culture or experience' and is experienced as the result of 'an uncovering or revealing of something innate and internal'.[46] Through a process of removing or dropping those aspects of human experience that involve 'language, learning, personality, or culture acquisition', the mystic

> thereby reveals something intrinsic about his or her own fundamental nature – his or her inherent Buddha Nature, *purusa*, or *atman*. Meditation removes or deconstructs something, revealing only the most basic 'equipment' of being human.[47]

One problem with this view or with the way it is expressed, is that it implies a certain confusion between transcendence and immanence in mystical experience. From a Thomistic perspective, although there is, in rapture, a withdrawal from sense and created images, concepts, and constructs, the term of this process is a participation in something absolutely transcendent, namely God. The above understanding of this process, however, suggests that nothing is experienced beyond what is innate and therefore intrinsic to human nature. This seems to confuse the undoubted interiority of mystical experience with the transcendence of what is actually experienced. This cannot be something intrinsic to human nature, however universal. Human nature has evolved over millions of years. But, the 'object' of most mystical experience, and certainly that described by Thomas, is something eternal that transcends time, process, and the limitations of a particular species. While the concept of an innate capacity may be of value in the attempt to find a ground for cultural invariance in mystical experience, it is essential that the transcendent dimension of that experience be properly discriminated.

The present essay shows that Aquinas conceives of a withdrawal from sense and imaginal forms and, indeed, from any created forms, to be necessary for the elevation of the soul to higher modes of spiritual reception and to the vision of God itself. While Thomas would no doubt consider the religious possibility of such an elevation in specifically Christian terms, it is also true that he sees the withdrawal of the soul from its normal cognitive modalities as being necessary on anthropological and even metaphysical grounds. In other words, while he may have considered the actual occurrence of such an elevation to require the grace and sacramental means mediated by Christianity, his understanding of the metaphysics of cognition, in terms of which a withdrawal from sense and imagination was considered a necessity, is applicable to all human beings. It is, then, the invariant structure of human nature itself, which includes 'soul, flesh, and bones' that makes such a withdrawal necessary for the realization of higher forms of cognitive operation or reception.[48]

The approach taken in the contemporary study of mysticism often involves the study of phenomenological descriptions of mystical experience. While Thomas himself did not leave any written accounts of his personal religious experience, he does present a philosophical conception of the conditions of the possibility of elevated cognitive operation and reception. Insofar as these conditions go beyond factors that are specific to time, place, culture, and religion, their philosophical elaboration may provide a valuable contribution to current debates in the study of mysticism.

Notes

1 The present essay is based on material from my doctoral thesis, Pamela J. Reeve, 'The Noetic Dimension of the Return to God in Thomas Aquinas', unpublished PhD diss. (University of Toronto, 1994).

2 *ST* 1.75.2. For the *ST*, I cite the Ottawa edition (published by the Institute of Medieval Studies, Ottawa, in 5 vols., 1941–1945). Translations from the writings of Aquinas are my own, although I have consulted the following English versions: *Basic Writings of Saint Thomas Aquinas*, vol. 1, ed. Anton C. Pegis (New York: Random House, 1945); *The Disputed Questions on Truth*, vol. 2, trans. James V. McGlynn (Chicago: Regnery, 1953); *On the Truth of the Catholic Faith*, book 2, trans. James F. Anderson (Garden City, NY: Doubleday/Image Books, 1956).

3 *ST* 1.75.4.

4 *ST* 1.76.1 ad 6: '[A]nima humana manet in suo esse cum fuerit a corpore separata, habens aptitudinem et inclinationem naturalem ad corporis unionem'.

5 *ST* 1.75.2 ad 3: '[P]hantasma comparatur ad intellectum sicut color ad visum'.

6 *ST* 1.84.7: 'Intellectus autem humani, qui est coniunctus corpori, proprium obiectum est quidditas sive natura in materia corporali existens'; *ST* 1.84.8: '[P]roprium obiectum intellectui nostro proportionatum est natura rei sensibilis'.

7 *ST* 1.84.7: '[P]er huiusmodi naturas visibilium rerum etiam in invisibilium rerum aliqualem cognitionem ascendit'. See also *ST* 1.88.1 ad 1.

8 *ST* 1.12.11.

9 *ST* 1.14.1: '[N]atura rei non cognoscentis est magis coarctata et limitata; natura autem rerum cognoscentium habet maiorem amplitudinem et extensionem'.

10 *ST* 1.14.1: 'Coarctatio formae est per materiam'.

11 *ST* 1.14.1: '[I]mmaterialitas alicuius rei est ratio quod sit cognoscitiva'.

12 *ST* 1.7.2.

13 *ST* 1.50.2 ad 4: 'Creaturae materiales habent infinitatem ex parte materiae, sed finitatem ex parte formae quae limitatur per materiam in qua recipitur'.

14 *ST* 1.7.2: '[H]uiusmodi formae non terminantur neque contrahuntur per aliquam materiam'.

15 *ST* 1.7.2 ad 2: '[V]irtus intellectus extendit se quodammodo ad infinita, procedit ex hoc quod intellectus est forma non in materia'.

16 *ST* 1.7.2 ad 2: '[Virtus intellectus] vel totaliter separata, sicut substantiae angelorum; vel ad minus potentia intellectiva, quae non est actus alicuius organi, in anima intellectiva corpori coniuncta'.

17 *ST* 1.14.1: '[S]ecundum modum immaterialitatis est modus cognitionis. Unde in II *De An.* dicitur quod plantae non cognoscunt propter suam materialitatem'.

18 *ST* 1.14.1: 'Sensus autem cognoscitivus est, quia receptivus est specierum sine materia; et intellectus adhuc magis cognoscitivus, quia magis "separatus est a materia et immixtus", ut dicitur in III *De An*'.

19 *ST* 1.14.1: 'Unde cum Deus sit in summo immaterialitatis ... sequitur quod ipse sit in summo cognitionis'.

20 *SCG* 2.81.12 (ed. Leonine): '[A]lio modo intelligit anima separata a corpore et corpori unita, sicut et alio modo est: unumquodque enim secundum hoc agit secundum quod est'.

21 *SCG* 2.81.12: '[Anima separata] intelligit per seipsam, ad modum substantiarum quae sunt totaliter secundum esse a corporibus separatae.... A quibus etiam, tanquam a superioribus, uberius influentiam recipere poterit ad perfectius intelligendum'.

22 *SCG* 2.81.12: 'Cuius signum etiam in iuvenibus apparet. Nam anima, quando impeditur ab occupatione circa corpus proprium, redditur habilior ad intelligendum aliqua altiora: unde et virtus temperantiae, quae a corporeis delectationibus retrahit animam, praecipue facit homines ad intelligendum aptos. Homines etiam dormientes, quando corporeis sensibus non utuntur, nec est aliqua perturbatio humorum aut fumositatum impediens, percipiunt de futuris, ex superiorum impressione, aliqua quae modum rationcinationis humanae excedunt. Et hoc multo magis accidit in syncopizantibus et exstasim passis: quanto magis fit retractio a corporeis sensibus'.

23 *SCG* 2.81.12-13: 'Nec immerito hoc accidit. Quia cum anima humana ... sit in confinio corporum et incorporearum substantiarum, quasi in horizonte existens aeternitatis et temporis, recedens ab infimo, appropinquat ad summum. Unde et, quando totaliter erit a corpore separata, perfecte assimilabitur substantiis separatis quantum ad modum intelligendi, et abunde influentiam eorum recipiet'.

24 *ST* 1.89.3.

25 *Scriptum super sententias*, 2.7.2.2 arg 6.

26 Aristotle presents three arguments against the view that prophetic dreams are sent by God in the *De divinatione per somnum* (462b19, 463b12, 464a21), proposing that their occasional predictive success may be explained by purely natural causes. But see also *De philosophia*, fragment 10.

27 Thomas Aquinas, *Quaestiones disputatae de veritate*, Leonine Edition, 22 (Rome: Bibliotecha Apostolica Vaticana, 1982), 12.3 ad 2: 'In somno ligatis exterioribus sensibus interiores vires quasi quietatae ab exteriorum sensuum tumultibus magis percipere possunt interiores impressiones factas in intellectu vel in imaginatione ex illustratione divina vel angelica, vel ex virtute caelestium corporum aut etiam quorumcumque'.

28 Thomas Aquinas, *Expositio super Iob ad litteram*, Leonine Edition, 26 (Rome: Bibliotheca Apostolica Vaticana, 1965), 33, 175-176 (Job 33:15-18): 'Semel loquitur Deus et secundo

id ipsum non repetit, per somnium in visione nocturna. Quando irruit sopor super homines et dormiunt in lectulo, tunc aperit aures virorum et erudiens eos instruit disciplinam, ut avertat hominem ab his quae fecit et liberet eum de superbia. Eruens animam eius de corruptione et vitam illius ut non transeat in gladium'.

29 Ibid.: '[P]onit operationem divinam circa dormientem, quae quidem attenditur primo quantum ad hoc quod, immobilitatis exterioribus sensibus per soporem et homine in lectulo quiescente, datur divinitus homini facultas quaedam percipiendi divinam instructionem eo quod eius anima circa exteriora non occupatur, unde subdit 'tunc aperit aures virorum'.

30 *De somno et vigilia* 454b10, 454b26, 455b10, 458a29.

31 *ST* 2-2.180.5: '[S]upremus gradus contemplationis praesentis vitae est qualem habuit Paulus in raptu, secundum quem fuit medio modo se habens inter statum praesentis vitae et futurae'. That this rapture may occur in the 'present life' is qualified by the additional specification that the state in which it is realized is somehow between the present and the future life.

32 *ST* 2-2.180.5: '[I]n hac vita potest esse aliquis dupliciter. Uno modo secundum actum, inquantum scilicet actualiter utitur sensibus corporis.... Alio modo potest esse aliquis in hac vita potentialiter, et non secundum actum, inquantum anima eius est corpori mortali coniuncta ut forma, ita tamen ut non utatur corporis sensibus, aut etiam imaginatione, sicut accidit in raptu'.

33 *ST* 2-2.175.5.

34 *Quaestiones de veritate* 13.3-4.

35 Ibid., 13.3: '[O]mne intelligibile vel est in se a materia immune vel est actione intellectus a materia abstractum, et ideo quanto intellectus purior est a materialium quasi contactu tanto perfectior est'.

36 Ibid., 13.3 ad 5.

37 Ibid., 13.4: '[E]x sensibilibus operationibus quodam modo intellectus puritas inquinatur'.

38 Ibid.: '[V]ires intellectivae non procedunt ex essentia animae ex illa parte qua est corpori unita, sed magis secundum hoc quod remanet a corpore libera utpote ei non totaliter subiugata'.

39 Aldous Huxley, *The Perennial Philosophy* (New York: Harper & Row, 1944; New York: Harper Colophon Books, 1970), p. vii.

40 Steven T. Katz, 'Language, Epistemology, and Mysticism', in *Mysticism and Philosophical Analysis*, ed. Steven T. Katz (New York: Oxford University Press, 1978).

41 I have not been able to consult Robert Forman's latest book, *Mysticism, Mind, Consciousness* (State University of New York Press, 1999), which was released just as the present essay was being completed.

42 Robert Forman, *The Innate Capacity: Mysticism, Psychology, and Philosophy*. New York: Oxford University Press, 1998), pp. 3-41.

43 Robert Forman, 'Eckhart, *Gezücken*, and the Ground of the Soul', in *The Problem of Pure Consciousness*, ed. Robert K.C. Forman (New York: Oxford University Press, 1990).

44 Forman, *The Innate Capacity*, p. 27.

45 Ibid., p. 11.

46 Ibid., pp. 11, 13.

47 Ibid., pp. 11-12.

48 *ST* 1.75.4.

Chapter 8

Thomas Aquinas on the Assent of Faith

Carl N. Still

It might be expected that Thomas Aquinas's thought about faith is well understood. It is laid out in three discussions in his major works and has been studied extensively over the past 30 years.[1] Yet its interpretation remains a matter of dispute, with no clear consensus in sight. On a 'naturalistic' reading, Aquinas thinks that there are arguments of sufficient credibility not only to prove that God exists, but to move one intellectually to embrace Christian faith. According to 'voluntarist' interpretations, Aquinas makes it clear that potential believers, lacking sufficient evidence, must will their assent to the Christian mysteries. Recently, John Jenkins has challenged both of these interpretations and shown that each comes up short in capturing Aquinas's views on faith.[2] The account Jenkins provides aims to be comprehensive by incorporating the roles of the intellect and will noted by others, while also taking the bold step of making grace integral to coming to faith. If Jenkins is correct, he may well have provided the complete and accurate interpretation of Aquinas's thought on faith needed before it can be properly evaluated.

It is my contention that while Jenkins has shed considerable light on this complex topic, his account does not render Aquinas's position on faith entirely coherent. The crux of the matter is what Aquinas calls the 'interior act' or 'assent' of faith. How does this assent take place? As we shall see, Aquinas teaches that it requires the co-operation of human intellect and will with divine grace. Jenkins has insisted on the role of the gifts of the Holy Spirit in bringing about assent. While agreeing on the importance of the gifts in the life of faith, I argue that the role he suggests for the gifts generates certain difficulties of interpretation that require further attention. If seen in proper relation to faith, however, the gifts may provide a strong motive for believing the Christian faith, as they promise that faith need not remain entirely beyond a faithful believer's knowledge in the present life.

According to Christian tradition, faith is one of the three theological virtues, along with hope and love, which are called 'theological' because they come from God. Aquinas gives an extended analysis of faith in the *Scriptum on the Sentences* book 3, distinctions 23-25, *De veritate* question 14, and *Summa theologiae* part 2-2, questions 1-16. I shall focus on the discussion in the *Summa*, the so-called Treatise on Faith, because it is the last and the richest of the discussions and prominently links faith to the gifts of understanding and knowledge.[3] From the outset in question 1, Aquinas makes it clear that faith is formally about God: while Christians *qua* Christians believe many things, all that they believe is 'ordered in some way to God'.[4] Yet while faith is about God, it exists in human believers, who therefore grasp God not in his perfect simplicity but by means of propositions composed of terms: namely, complex, truth-bearing statements such as are found in the Christian creeds. This does not mean that believers believe in statements rather than God, since 'the act of the believer does not reach its end in a statement, but in the thing: we do not form statements except so that we may have apprehension of things through them'.[5]

Though he accepts as adequate the biblical definition of faith as 'the substance of things hoped for and the evidence of things not seen' (Hebrews 11:1), Aquinas himself characterizes faith as 'an assent of the intellect to what is believed'.[6] This raises the question of how this assent is generated. Assent can be generated by a cognitive object's moving the intellect, as happens when we assent to first principles because they are self-evident, and when we assent to conclusions known through premises. But this is not the case in faith, whose objects are not evident to us. Hence,

> in a second way, the understanding assents to something, not because it is sufficiently moved by the proper object, but by a choice of the will tending to one alternative rather than another. And if this occurs with doubt and hesitation about the other alternative, there is opinion. If it occurs with certainty and without any such hesitation, there is faith.[7]

Aquinas thus points to the epistemology of faith while dealing with the object of faith. The person in the state of faith (*fides*) is in an epistemic condition that is stronger than opinion (*opinio*), since in faith assent is firm, yet weaker than knowledge (*scientia*), since the object of faith is not subject to demonstration. Thus believers themselves do not know the truth of what they believe on faith, nor are there any demonstrative reasonings to prove the things of faith[8]; at best there are 'persuasions for showing that what is proposed in faith is not impossible'.[9] Aquinas's believer recognizes that the things of faith are to be believed, either 'because of the evidence of signs or because of something else of this kind'.[10] Unbelievers fail to see that the objects of faith are believable. Yet however well the object of faith might be articulated in the statements of the creeds, what motivates the believer's assent?

This brings us to the inward act of faith, addressed in question 2. Aquinas accepts Augustine's formula that to believe is 'think with assent' (*cum assensione cogitare*), which implies that the intellect is inquiring, and so not yet perfected by vision of its object.[11] Falling between knowledge and opinion, faith is different from all other acts of understanding that are about the true and the false.[12] While it lacks the demonstrative quality of natural reason, faith 'has some inquiry into the things by which a man is led to believe, namely that they are said by God and confirmed by miracles'.[13] As we have seen, however, the believer's intellect is determined to one alternative not by reasoning, but through the will. Thus, the assent in Augustine's definition refers to 'an act of the intellect so far as it is determined to one alternative by the will'.[14] Faith is thus a willing assent to a number of truth-bearing statements, which are held to be as certainly true as any item of our knowledge. So why is the willed assent to these statements as firm as the assent to things which are known?

Aquinas's answer is that the statements of faith are believed firmly because they are taken to be said by God, who is the 'first truth' (*prima veritas*). Where we speak most naturally of 'believing in God', Aquinas follows Augustine's proposal that the verb *credere* (to believe) can be related in three distinct ways to its object: (1) *credere Deo* (believing God as giving authoritative testimony), (2) *credere Deum* (believing things about God), and (3) *credere in Deum* (believing for the sake of attaining God).[15] Because believing involves both intellect and will, the object of faith can be specially related to the intellect or to the will. If the object of faith is related to the intellect and considered 'materially', the act of faith is believing about God (*credere Deum*), since 'nothing is proposed to us for believing except as it pertains to God'.[16] The object can also considered 'formally', in which case faith's act is believing God (*credere Deo*), since 'the formal object of faith is the first truth, in which man inheres so that through it he might assent to what is believed'.[17] And, finally, if the object is considered according to the intellect's being moved by the will, the act of faith is believing for the sake of God (*credere in Deum*), since the will is related to the first truth as the end it ultimately seeks.[18] All this follows from the scholastic principle that the act of a power is determined according to the ordering of the power to its object. Considered from these three distinct angles, God is at once the cause of faith, the subject matter (or object) of faith, and the goal of faith. In sum, the object of faith is the first truth mediated through the truth-bearing statements enunciated in the creeds, and believing is an act of the intellect, moved to assent by the will, which desires the first truth as its perfecting end.

This analysis implies that believing about God (*credere Deum*) is based on believing God (*credere Deo*), which itself responds to believing for the sake of attaining God (*credere in Deum*). Aquinas does not spell these relations out explicitly. However, in explaining how some who are not among the faithful also believe about God, he responds:

> It should be said that believing about God (*credere Deum*) does not belong to unbelievers under the same rationale by which an act of faith is taken. For they do not believe God to be under those conditions which faith determines. And therefore they do not believe truly about God (*vere Deum credunt*), because as the Philosopher says in *Metaphysics* 9, in simple things a defect of apprehension just by itself makes for not grasping them entirely.[19]

In this way, Aquinas distinguishes between faithful and unfaithful (in Aquinas's terms, heretical) believing about God. The distinguishing mark seems not to be only what is believed about God, but rather how the beliefs are determined. The 'conditions which faith determines' for believing refer surely to *credere Deo*: the faithful believer believes about God because he *believes God*, that is, submits himself to what God has revealed about himself. Later in the Treatise, Aquinas says that 'one rightly has Christian faith who by his will assents to Christ (*assentit Christo*) in those things that truly belong to his teaching'.[20] The unfaithful believer, by contrast, 'holds the things that are of faith in some way other than by faith'.[21] Such a person might be thought of as detaching his believing about God from his believing God; that is, the heretic 'intends to assent to Christ' but 'does not choose the things that are truly handed down by Christ, but the things that his own mind suggests to him'.[22] The unfaithful believer might be anyone who has beliefs about God that are not based on divine revelation, whether he be a pagan (believing about God independently of revelation) or a heretic (believing about God only what appeals to his own judgement).

If believing about God is dependent on believing God to meet the conditions required by faith, what moves the faithful believer in believing God? In the genesis of faith, as we have seen, both believing about God and believing God seem to depend on believing for the sake of God (*credere in Deum*), since the will desires God as the final goal and moves the intellect to believe God. Aquinas teaches that the will moves the intellect to assent not only because the will is attracted to the good things promised to the believer, but also because God moves the will by grace. In addressing the question of whether faith is infused into the believer by God, Aquinas replies that the cause of the believer's assent to the articles of faith

> can be considered in two ways. In one way, as an outward inducement, such as a miracle seen or a human persuasion inducing one to faith. Neither of which is a sufficient cause. Among those seeing one and the same miracle, and those hearing the same preaching, some believe and some do not believe. And so another inward cause must be recognized, which moves man inwardly to assent to the things that are of faith. This cause the Pelagians put as nothing more than man's free choice.... But this is false. Since man, in assenting to the things that are of faith, is raised above his nature, this must happen in him by a supernatural principle moving inwardly, which is God. And so as regards assent, which is the principal act of faith, faith is from God moving inwardly by grace.[23]

The action of grace prepares one's will to embrace what is beyond its own natural capability, but it does not override the will's power to choose. In this way, the assent of faith is both graced and voluntary, and consequently meritorious as well.

> [O]ur acts are meritorious so far as they proceed from free decision moved by God in grace.... So every human act that comes under free decision can be meritorious, if it is related to God. Believing itself is an act of the intellect assenting to divine truth by command of the will, moved by God in grace, and so it lies under free decision as ordered to God. So the act of faith can be meritorious.[24]

The necessary role of grace raises a host of questions about the possibility of some people being excluded from assent apart from their will. Aquinas does not delve into these questions, except to acknowledge that not all are given the grace needed to assent. One cannot assent to the articles of faith without grace any more than one can love God or neighbour without it, but one is still bound to believe in order to attain salvation. To the objection that belief is not in our natural power, Aquinas replies that 'this help is given mercifully to whomever it is given. To whom it is not given, it is justly denied in punishment for preceding sin, especially original sin, as Augustine says'.[25]

In the first two questions of the *Secunda secundae*, then, Aquinas gives a detailed account of what is believed on faith (the 'object' of faith) and how it is believed (the 'act' of faith). The object of faith is God, the 'first truth', presented in the propositional articles of the Creed and materially in all the facts contained in Scripture. The assent of faith is prepared intellectually by considerations ranging from signs and miracles to rational arguments for the reality of God, and clinched volitionally by grace inwardly moving the potential believer to truths beyond his natural grasp. Believing God to speak truthfully, the believer then believes those things about God proposed by the church,[26] with a view to attaining to the fruition of the good things promised to the believer by Christ.

This is a remarkably coherent view about faith, yet apart from describing how one might come to believe, it does not say much about why anyone ought to believe. Both these points could use some further development. If Aquinas's account is meant to be descriptive only, a richer account is needed of the way in which grace induces one to assent, without binding the believer's will. If the account is meant to be at all prescriptive, Aquinas must explain why one should believe the Christian faith, given that there is not sufficient evidence to confirm it prior to assent. I shall begin with the second question by noting two objections to faith that Aquinas himself considers, before returning to the complexities of the descriptive account.

Lest we think that the criticism of faith was unthought of by Aquinas in his serene reflection on the nature and genesis of Christian belief, Aquinas considers two such objections in principle to Christian belief in the Treatise on Faith. In question 2, article 9 he considers the objection that believing cannot be meritorious because the believer either has a sufficient cause moving him to believe, or does not. If he does, believing is not meritorious because it is not voluntary, but compelled. If, on the other hand, 'he does not have something sufficient inducing him to believe, believing is frivolous'.[27] In reply Aquinas parses carefully the distinctions laid out earlier in question 2: the believer does have sufficient inducement to believe, namely, 'the authority of divine teaching confirmed by miracles' and also 'an inward impulse towards God, who invites him'. Since these sufficiently move the will, the person of faith 'does not believe lightly (*leviter*)', even if he lacks evidence sufficient for knowledge.[28] As before, if one had sufficient intellectual reason for assenting to the articles of faith, faith and the concomitant act of the will would not be necessary. The meritoriousness of faith comes from the willingness of the believer to believe God without compelling evidence offered from the outset. The evidentialist demand for proof before believing thus belies the very nature of faith. Aquinas does not, however, cast the believer in the role of a fideist who demands no inducements to believe or, more extreme yet, believes in the teeth of all the apparent evidence. Aquinas's believer has both outward and inward inducements that play a role in assent.

Even if belief is not frivolous, it still involves accepting something that exceeds all natural human cognition.[29] How can such an epistemic risk be conducive to salvation? In the context of that question another objection urges that it is dangerous for a man to assent to things when he cannot judge whether what is proposed is true or false.... But a man cannot make such a judgment about the things that are of faith, since a man cannot trace them back to first principles, by which we judge all things. Therefore it is dangerous to give faith to such things.[30]

If this objection holds, it would be reasonable to think that salvation must not depend on accepting things about which one cannot judge. Aquinas's reply takes us to the heart of his position when he writes:

> Just as man assents to principles by the natural light of understanding, so a man with the virtuous habit of faith judges rightly about things appropriate to that virtue. Likewise, by the light of faith divinely infused in him, man assents to what things are of faith, but not to their contraries. So there is nothing dangerous or of damnation for those who are illuminated by Jesus Christ in faith.[31]

Is this answer satisfying? At first glance it seems to present two related problems. First, the analogy to natural understanding of first principles is not exact, since first principles are *per se nota* once their terms are understood, and as such compel one's assent. But for reasons by now clear, that cannot be true in the case of the articles of faith. Instead, the articles of faith become as first principles to those who assent to them, and so enable the believer to judge in their light. Second, it seems to propound a circular argument: those who have the habit of faith will know how to judge correctly about what is to be believed on faith, and so will not fall into grievous error or, worse yet, damnation. The way out of this bind is provided by the 'light of faith' (*lumen fidei*). Aquinas invokes this phrase in only two other instances in the Treatise on Faith, and in both cases says that the light of faith makes one recognize what is to be believed.[32] Here the context is that of taking on belief as a student first believes his teacher, so that he later comes to understand what the teacher knows. Aquinas seems to be saying that the light of faith, given by God, is the cause of the assent of faith; once one has faith, one will of course be able to judge appropriately about what to believe. If we recall that God moves the will by grace to assent to some truths beyond a believer's intellectual competence, that movement may be thought of as corresponding to the light of faith divinely infused. And since God would not, Aquinas insists, move a person to believe false things under the guise of faith,[33] the light of faith would explain how the potential believer succeeds in believing the right things about God; or, in other words, how believing God is realized in believing the Christian faith.

Aquinas's replies to the two objections that faith is either frivolous or dangerous reveal how little concerned he is with providing reasons that would justify faith. Indeed, he ultimately closes the door to this approach when he says, 'A man ought to believe the things that are of faith not because of human reason, but because of divine authority'.[34] The attempt to give an intellectual justification of faith cannot succeed on Aquinas's terms because the believer's intellect – the locus of assent – must be moved by the will, which in turn requires grace. Neither a naturalist nor a voluntarist explanation offers the final word on the cause of assent, since neither the intellect nor the will is ultimate in this analysis.[35] Because Aquinas insists that God is the first cause of the believer's faith, the role of grace in assent becomes paramount. After showing up the limitations of interpretations that omit grace, Jenkins offers a reading of the *Summa* account of faith that relies on the gifts of the Holy Spirit to produce faith. He offers the following summary of his position:

> Faith must begin with a hearing of the Gospel, the essentials of which are contained in the Creed, which is proclaimed as divinely revealed. This requires no infused light. Subsequently, by virtue of the infused light of faith and with the theological virtue along with the Gift of Understanding, the prospective believer, by a non-discursive intuition, understands the articles of faith as propositions to be believed on divine authority and to which he should adhere in spite of considerations to the contrary. Finally, through a second operation of the infused light and with the theological virtue along with the Gift of Scientia, one immediately (i.e., not as the result of discursive reasoning) assents to the articles as divinely revealed. Unlike assent to principles naturally known, this assent requires a deliberate act of the will co-operating with grace, and so it is voluntary and meritorious.[36]

This interpretation has three elements that we have seen previously: the articles of faith (expressed in the Creed), the light of faith, and the will moved by grace. The new element that Jenkins adds is the gifts of understanding and knowledge, which he finds necessary to assist the theological virtues in order that one be able to assent firmly to the articles of faith.

Does Aquinas think that these gifts play an essential role in bringing the potential believer to faith? The evidence appears mixed. In the seven questions in the *Summa* devoted to the virtue of faith, there is only one mention of the gifts. In question 4, article 8 Aquinas asks whether faith is more certain than knowledge, understanding, and wisdom, which are acquired intellectual virtues but also gifts of the Holy Spirit. If considered as gifts, Aquinas says that 'they are compared to faith as to a principle that they presuppose',[37] and so faith is more certain. If the gifts presuppose faith, it is perplexing to think that they could be required to produce it. On the other hand, in question 8, article 4 Aquinas holds that 'by the gift of understanding [the Holy Spirit] illuminates the mind of man that it apprehend a certain supernatural truth, to which the right will must tend'.[38] On Jenkins' view, the gift of understanding is needed to help one apprehend that the articles of faith are to be believed, a recognition which is preliminary to judging by the gift of knowledge that they are true. In the following article, however, Aquinas disjoins faith and understanding by showing their different relations to sanctifying grace (*gratia gratum faciens*):

> Faith implies only assent to the things that are proposed. But understanding implies some perception of the truth, which cannot be about the end except in him who has the grace that makes one pleasing.... And so there is no similar reasoning about understanding and faith.[39]

There can be faith without sanctifying grace, as it can be 'unformed' by charity and yet still a virtue, but the gift of understanding is in all who have sanctifying grace and only in them. If faith and the gifts are not co-terminous, how then can the assent of faith require that the gifts be operative?

In question 9, however, Aquinas asserts a relation between the assent of faith and gifts of understanding and knowledge. In the course of explaining how knowledge (*scientia*) can be a gift, he says that,

> in order that the human intellect completely assent to the truths of faith, two things are required. One of which is that it healthily grasp the things that are proposed, which belongs to the gift of understanding.... The other is that it have certain and right judgment about them, namely, discerning what is to be believed from what is not to be believed. And for this the gift of knowledge is necessary.[40]

This passage provides the best evidence for Jenkins' interpretation, but also raises some vexing questions. If the gifts are required for the assent of faith, why are they never mentioned in question 2, which treats exhaustively of the interior act of faith? Worse yet, this position seems to embrace a contradiction. On the one hand, the gifts presuppose faith, since supernatural apprehension is founded in us by faith.[41] On the other hand, the gifts must already be operative in a person before he can assent to faith. Jenkins does not address these difficulties.

There are, however, a number of hints that this apparent impasse is not inescapable. As Aquinas distinguishes gifted understanding into complete and incomplete, so the operative term *perfecte* ('completely' in the passage above) suggests that there may be some such distinction with respect to assent. In addressing the priority of faith to understanding or vice versa, Aquinas points out that some understanding must precede assent, although a greater understanding will arise from assent.

> [F]aith cannot universally precede understanding; for man cannot assent to some proposed things through believing unless he understands them somewhat. But the completion of understanding follows upon the faith that is a virtue, to which completion of the understanding there follows a certainty of faith.[42]

It is possible, though far from evident, that gifted understanding is effective prior to faith in enabling a potential believer to understand the doctrines sufficiently well to grasp them, and operative after assent in providing a more complete understanding of the things believed. What is striking about Aquinas's reply is that the more complete understanding provided by the gift secures the certainty of faith. We have already seen, however, that the faithful believer's assent is certain at the time of belief. Whence then the new certainty?

An answer to this question, I suggest, is to be sought by returning to question 4, article 8, which considers the certainty of faith. There Aquinas determined that faith is more certain than wisdom, knowledge, and understanding as intellectual virtues, since it is caused by divine truth, while they arise from human reason. On the part of the subject, however, faith is less certain than the intellectual virtues, since the things of faith are above human understanding and so appear less fully to our minds. Since this shortfall in certainty arises from a disposition in the subject, it can be overcome in the event that our minds are rendered more amenable to apprehending divine things. Thus Aquinas writes that 'the completeness of understanding and knowledge exceeds the apprehension of faith as regards greater manifestness', but not 'as regards a more certain inhering' in the truth.[43] The initial assent of faith is not made more certain, as if under the influence of the gift one could finally assent fully, without any lingering doubts. But the believer's mind can be purified so that the realities of faith appear to it more clearly, or manifestly. Aquinas does not think that the central mysteries of Christian faith such as the Trinity and Incarnation can be completely understood by anyone in the present life, but only enough to know that nothing in the world truly contradicts them. When it comes to certain other things 'ordered to faith', which include the sacred facts of Scripture, he allows that they can be understood completely by a believer whose mind is raised to a new level of knowing by the gift of understanding.[44]

The bearing of the gifts of the Spirit on the life of faith has considerable importance for Aquinas's theological spirituality, which has seen a revival of interest in recent years.[45] By calling attention to passages where Aquinas connects the gifts to the assent of faith, Jenkins has shifted the ground in our understanding of how Aquinas conceives of that assent. Whether a new consensus will form around this interpretation remains to be seen. As I have aimed to show, the divine contribution to the believer's act of faith is something of a two-edged sword: it begets new problems of interpretation that remain unresolved in Jenkins' account. On the other hand, the gifts' influence on faith suggests an approach to one of the most troubling aspects of the epistemology of faith, namely, how the assent of faith can be certain although the things of faith remain beyond the believer's grasp. Provided that the potential believer is willing to assent, the gifts of understanding and knowledge can so strengthen the believer's intellect that the realities of faith are confirmed and, with the gift of wisdom, experienced.[46] Whether these possibilities might have some bearing on one's willingness to assent is a question worth pondering.[47]

Notes

1 Among the many philosophical studies, see Timothy C. Potts, 'Aquinas on Belief and Faith', in *Inquiries into Medieval Philosophy: A Collection in Honor of Francis P. Clarke*, ed. James F. Ross (Westport, CT: Greenwood, 1971), pp. 3-22; Terence Penelhum, 'The Analysis of Faith in St Thomas Aquinas', *Religious Studies* 13/2 (1977) 133-54; James F. Ross, 'Aquinas on Belief and Knowledge', in *Essays Honoring Allan B. Wolter*, ed. William A. Frank and Girard J. Etzkorn (St Bonaventure, NY: The Franciscan Institute, 1985), pp. 245-69; Eleonore Stump, 'Aquinas on Faith and Goodness', in *Being and Goodness: The Concept of the Good in Metaphysics and Philosophical Theology*, ed. Scott Macdonald (Ithaca: Cornell University Press, 1991), pp. 179-207. More recently, Alvin Plantinga has presented an 'Aquinas/Calvin model' for theistic belief in *Warranted Christian Belief* (New York/Oxford: Oxford University Press, 2000), esp. ch. 6, though I do not consider that interpretation here.

2   John I. Jenkins, *Knowledge and Faith in Thomas Aquinas* (Cambridge: Cambridge University Press, 1997), ch. 6 (pp. 161-210).

3   It is generally acknowledged that there is no significant change of doctrine in the three treatments. For a comparative analysis of the discussions, see Tad W. Guzie, 'The Act of Faith according to St. Thomas: A Study in Theological Methodology', *The Thomist* 29 (1965) 239-80. In *Knowledge and Faith in Thomas Aquinas*, Jenkins also discusses all three accounts (187-97), but gives priority to the *Summa* account.

4   *ST* 2-2.1.1: 'Sic igitur in fide, si consideremus formalem rationem obiecti, nihil est aliud quam veritas prima, non enim fides de qua loquimur assentit alicui nisi quia est a Deo revelatum; unde ipsi veritati divinae innititur tanquam medio. Si vero consideremus materialiter ea quibus fides assentit, non solum est ipse Deus, sed etiam multa alia. Quae tamen sub assensu fidei non cadunt nisi secundum quod habent aliquem ordinem ad Deum...'.
    For the Treatise on Faith in the *ST*, I have used Mark D. Jordan's translation, *On Faith: Summa Theologiae 2-2, qq. 1-16 of St. Thomas Aquinas* (Notre Dame: University of Notre Dame Press, 1990), with occasional modifications.

5   *ST* 2-2.1.2 ad 2: 'Actus autem credentis non terminatur ad enuntiabile, sed ad rem, non enim formamus enuntiabilia nisi ut per ea de rebus cognitionem habeamus, sicut in scientia, ita et in fide'.

6   *ST* 2-2.1.4: '[F]ides importat assensum intellectus ad id quod creditur.' Aquinas discusses the biblical definition in *ST* 2-2.4.1 and offers his own definition of faith: 'fides est habitus mentis, qua inchoatur vita aeterna in nobis, faciens intellectum assentire non apparentibus'.

7   *ST* 2-2.1.4: 'Alio modo intellectus assentit alicui non quia sufficienter moveatur ab obiecto proprio, sed per quandam electionem voluntarie declinans in unam partem magis quam in aliam. Et si quidem hoc fit cum dubitatione et formidine alterius partis, erit opinio, si autem fit cum certitudine absque tali formidine, erit fides'.

8   See *ST* 2-2.2.10.

9   *ST* 2-2.1.5 ad 2: '[R]ationes quae inducuntur a sanctis ad probandum ea quae sunt fidei non sunt demonstrativae, sed persuasiones quaedam manifestantes non esse impossibile quod in fide proponitur'.

10 *ST* 2-2.1.4 ad 2: '[E]a quae subsunt fidei dupliciter considerari possunt. Uno modo, in speciali, et sic non possunt esse simul visa et credita, sicut dictum est. Alio modo, in generali, scilicet sub communi ratione credibilis. Et sic sunt visa ab eo qui credit, non enim crederet nisi videret ea esse credenda, vel propter evidentiam signorum vel propter aliquid huiusmodi'.

11 For the source in Augustine, see *De praedestinatione sanctorum* ch. 2, sect. 5 (PL 44.963). The phrase 'cum assensione cogitare' is discussed by T.C. O'Brien in 'Belief: Faith's Act', Appendix 4 to his translation of *ST* 2-2.1-7 in the Blackfriars translation of *Summa theologiae*, vol. 31 (New York: McGraw-Hill, 1974), pp. 205-15; and by R. Bellemare in '*Credere*: Note sur la définition thomiste', *Revue de l'Université d'Ottawa* 30 (1960) 37*-47*.

12 *ST* 2-2.2.1.

13 *ST* 2-2.2.1 ad 1: '[F]ides non habet inquisitionem rationis naturalis demonstrantis id quod creditur. Habet tamen inquisitionem quandam eorum per quae inducitur homo ad credendum, puta quia sunt dicta a Deo et miraculis confirmata'.

14 *ST* 2-2.2.1 ad 3: '[I]ntellectus credentis determinatur ad unum non per rationem, sed per voluntatem. Et ideo assensus hic accipitur pro actu intellectus secundum quod a voluntate determinatur ad unum'.

15 *ST* 2-2.2.2. I have followed (with slight emendations) the translations for these terms in Jordan, *On Faith*, pp. 68-71. For the translation rationale, see n. 14 (69-70). For the source in Augustine, see *Sermones ad populum* 144.2 (PL 38.788) and *In Joannis Evangelium* 29.6 on 7:17 (PL 35.1631).

16 *ST* 2-2.2.2c: 'Et sic ponitur actus fidei credere Deum, quia, sicut supra dictum est, nihil proponitur nobis ad credendum nisi secundum quod ad Deum pertinet'.

17 *ST* 2-2.2.2c: 'Et sic ponitur actus fidei credere Deo, quia, sicut supra dictum est, formale obiectum fidei est veritas prima, cui inhaeret homo ut propter eam creditis assentiat'.

18 *ST* 2-2.2.2c. and ad 4.

19 *ST* 2-2.2.2 ad 3: '[D]icendum quod credere Deum non convenit infidelibus sub ea ratione qua ponitur actus fidei. Non enim credunt Deum esse sub his conditionibus quas fides determinat. Et ideo nec vere Deum credunt, quia, ut philosophus dicit, IX Metaphys., in simplicibus defectus cognitionis est solum in non attingendo totaliter'. For the reference to Aristotle, see *Metaphysics* 9.10 (1051b23-27).

20 *ST* 2-2.11.1: '[Q]ui recte fidem Christianam habet sua voluntate assentit Christo in his quae vere ad eius doctrinam pertinere'. Though Aquinas has varied the terminology here, *assentire Christo* is clearly parallel to *credere Deo*.

21 *ST* 2-2.5.3: 'Unde quicumque non inhaeret, sicut infallibili et divinae regulae, doctrinae Ecclesiae, quae procedit ex veritate prima in Scripturis sacris manifestata, ille non habet habitum fidei, sed ea quae sunt fidei alio modo tenet quam per fidem'.

22 *ST* 2-2.11.1: 'A rectitudine igitur fidei Christianae dupliciter aliquis potest deviare. Uno modo, quia ipsi Christo non vult assentire, et hic habet quasi malam voluntatem circa ipsum finem. Et hoc pertinet ad speciem infidelitatis Paganorum et Iudaeorum. Alio modo, per hoc quod intendit quidem Christo assentire, sed deficit in eligendo ea quibus Christo assentiat, quia non eligit ea quae sunt vere a Christo tradita, sed ea quae sibi propria mens suggerit'. Cf. 2-2.5.3c. and ad 1.

23 *ST* 2-2.6.1c.: 'Quantum vero ad secundum, scilicet ad assensum hominis in ea quae sunt fidei, potest considerari duplex causa. Una quidem exterius inducens, sicut miraculum visum, vel persuasio hominis inducentis ad fidem. Quorum neutrum est sufficiens causa, videntium enim unum et idem miraculum, et audientium eandem praedicationem, quidam credunt et quidam non credunt. Et ideo oportet ponere aliam causam interiorem, quae movet hominem interius ad assentiendum his quae sunt fidei. Hanc autem causam Pelagiani ponebant solum liberum arbitrium hominis.... Sed hoc est falsum. Quia cum homo, assentiendo his quae sunt fidei, elevetur supra naturam suam, oportet quod hoc insit ei ex supernaturali principio interius movente, quod est Deus. Et ideo fides quantum ad assensum, qui est principalis actus fidei, est a Deo interius movente per gratiam'.

24 *ST* 2-2.2.9: '[A]ctus nostri sunt meritorii inquantum procedunt ex libero arbitrio moto a Deo per gratiam. Unde omnis actus humanus qui subiicitur libero arbitrio, si sit relatus in Deum, potest meritorius esse. Ipsum autem credere est actus intellectus assentientis veritati divinae ex imperio voluntatis a Deo motae per gratiam, et sic subiacet libero arbitrio in ordine ad Deum. Unde actus fidei potest esse meritorius'. See also *ST* 1-2.114.3-4 on how the willed cooperation with divine grace yields a meritorious act.

25 *ST* 2-2.2.5 ad 1: 'Quod quidem auxilium quibuscumque divinitus datur, misericorditer datur; quibus autem non datur, ex iustitia non datur, in poenam praecedentis peccati, saltem originalis peccati; ut Augustinus dicit, in libro de Cor. et gratia'. Jordan (*On Faith*, p. 78, n. 46) corrects the reference from Augustine's *De correctione et gratia* to his *Epistola* 190, ch. 3, sect. 3, and to *De praedestinatione sanctorum* ch. 8.

26 Though Aquinas's general emphasis is placed on believing God, in *ST* 2-2.5.3 he refers to the church's teaching as an 'infallible rule' to which the faithful believer gives assent.

27 *ST* 2-2.2.9 arg. 3: 'Praeterea, ille qui assentit alicui rei credendo aut habet causam sufficienter inducentem ipsum ad credendum, aut non. Si habet sufficiens inductivum ad credendum, non videtur hoc ei esse meritorium, quia non est ei iam liberum credere et non credere. Si autem non habet sufficiens inductivum ad credendum, levitatis est credere, secundum illud Eccli. XIX, qui cito credit levis est corde, et sic non videtur esse meritorium. Ergo credere nullo modo est meritorium'. The reference is to Ecclesiasticus 19:4.

28 *ST* 2-2.2.9 ad 3: 'Ad tertium dicendum quod ille qui credit habet sufficiens inductivum ad credendum, inducitur enim auctoritate divinae doctrinae miraculis confirmatae, et, quod plus est, interiori instinctu Dei invitantis. Unde non leviter credit. Tamen non habet sufficiens inductivum ad sciendum. Et ideo non tollitur ratio meriti'.

29 Cf. Walter Principe, 'Affectivity and the Heart in Thomas Aquinas' Spirituality', in *Spiritualities of the Heart: Approaches to Personal Wholeness in Christian Tradition*, ed. Annice Callahan (New York/Mahwah, NJ: Paulist Press, 1990), p. 55: 'The mysteries of God so surpass the grasp of the created human mind that it cannot grasp their evidence or intelligibility and so cannot assent to them as it does to truths that are accessible to its level of being'.

30 *ST* 2-2.2.3 arg. 2: 'Praeterea, periculose homo assentit illis in quibus non potest iudicare utrum illud quod ei proponitur sit verum vel falsum.... Sed tale iudicium homo habere non potest in his quae sunt fidei, quia non potest homo ea resolvere in principia prima, per quae de omnibus iudicamus. Ergo periculosum est talibus fidem adhibere...'.

31 *ST* 2-2.2.3 ad 2: '[S]icut homo per naturale lumen intellectus assentit principiis, ita homo virtuosus per habitum virtutis habet rectum iudicium de his quae conveniunt virtuti illi. Et hoc modo etiam per lumen fidei divinitus infusum homini homo assentit his quae sunt fidei, non autem contrariis. Et ideo *nihil periculi vel damnationis inest his qui sunt in Christo Iesu*, ab ipso illuminati per fidem'. The italicized phrase is adapted from Romans 8:1: 'Nihil ergo nunc damnationis est iis qui sunt in Christo Iesu: qui non secundum carnem ambulant'.

32 See *ST* 2-2.1.4 ad 3 and 2-2.1.5 ad 1. The former suggests that the phrase *lumen fidei* may, however, be a variant of *habitus fidei*, which Aquinas uses frequently.

33 In *ST* 2-2.1.3, Aquinas denies that anything false belongs under faith inasmuch as faith is formally about the first truth. Cf. 2-2.2.4, in which the certainty of faith is attributed to the fact that God cannot lie.

34 *ST* 2-2.2.10: '[I]ta credere debet homo ea quae sunt fidei non propter rationem humanam, sed propter auctoritatem divinam. Alio modo ratio humana potest se habere ad voluntatem credentis consequenter'.

35 In *Knowledge and Faith in Thomas Aquinas*, Jenkins gives an extended critique of the naturalist interpretations offered by Penelhum and Plantinga among others (163-75) and of the voluntarist interpretations offered by Ross and Stump (175-85). On both points he seems to me to have made his case.

36 Jenkins, *Knowledge and Faith in Thomas Aquinas*, p. 196.

37 *ST* 2-2.4.8: 'Similiter etiam, si accipiantur tria praedicta secundum quod sunt dona praesentis vitae, comparantur ad fidem sicut ad principium quod praesupponunt. Unde etiam secundum hoc fides est eis certior'.

38 *ST* 2-2.8.4: '[I]ta etiam per donum intellectus illustrat mentem hominis ut cognoscat veritatem quandam supernaturalem, in quam oportet tendere voluntatem rectam'.

39 *ST* 2-2.8.5 ad 3: '[F]ides importat solum assensum ad ea quae proponuntur. Sed intellectus importat quandam perceptionem veritatis, quae non potest esse circa finem nisi in eo qui habet gratiam gratum facientem.... Et ideo non est similis ratio de intellectu et fide'. Cf. 2-

2.8.6 ad 2, which specifies how faith and the gift of understanding differ in their relation to the 'first principles of graced apprehension'.

40 *ST* 2-2.9.1: 'Et ideo ad hoc quod intellectus humanus perfecte assentiat veritati fidei duo requiruntur. Quorum unum est quod sane capiat ea quae proponuntur, quod pertinet ad donum intellectus, ut supra dictum est. Aliud autem est ut habeat certum et rectum iudicium de eis, discernendo scilicet credenda non credendis. Et ad hoc necessarium est donum scientiae'. Jenkins cites this passage (*Knowledge and Faith in Thomas Aquinas*, p. 194). Cf. 2-2.8.6, which makes much the same claim about 'the things that are proposed for believing by faith' but without mentioning the act of assent.

41 See *ST* 2-2.8.6.

42 *ST* 2-2.8.8 ad 2: '[F]ides non potest universaliter praecedere intellectum, non enim posset homo assentire credendo aliquibus propositis nisi ea aliqualiter intelligeret. Sed perfectio intellectus consequitur fidem quae est virtus, ad quam quidem intellectus perfectionem sequitur quaedam fidei certitudo'.

43 *ST* 2-2.4.8 ad 3: '[P]erfectio intellectus et scientiae excedit cognitionem fidei quantum ad maiorem manifestationem, non tamen quantum ad certiorem inhaesionem. Quia tota certitudo intellectus vel scientiae secundum quod sunt dona, procedit a certitudine fidei, sicut certitudo cognitionis conclusionum procedit ex certitudine principiorum. Secundum autem quod scientia et sapientia et intellectus sunt virtutes intellectuales, innituntur naturali lumini rationis, quod deficit a certitudine verbi Dei, cui innititur fides'.

44 *ST* 2-2.8.2. The distinction between those doctrines that fall directly under faith and those ordered to faith echoes the distinction in question 1, article 1, of the 'material object' of faith into God as first truth and the many things ordered to God as 'effects of divinity' that aid the believer in tending towards God.

45 I borrow the term 'theological spirituality' from Walter Principe, 'Toward Defining Spirituality', *Studies in Religion/Sciences Religieuses* 12 (1983) 127-41. Recent work on the gifts includes Anthony Kelly, 'The Gifts of the Spirit: Aquinas and the Modern Context', *The Thomist* 38 (1974) 193-231; Romanus Cessario, *Christian Faith and the Theological Life* (Washington, DC: Catholic University of America Press, 1996); Carl N. Still, '"Gifted Knowledge": An Exception to Thomistic Epistemology?', *The Thomist* 63 (1999) 173-90; and Bruce Marshall, 'Faith and Reason Reconsidered: Aquinas and Luther on Deciding What is True', *The Thomist* 63 (1999) 1-48, esp. 17-21, where he links faith to the gift of wisdom.

46 On how the gift of wisdom involves experience of the divine realities believed on faith, see *ST* 2-2.45.2. I hope to develop this point further in a future study.

47 I wish to express my thanks to Kevin Corrigan and James Ginther, who read earlier versions of this paper and made valuable suggestions, and to James Cutsinger and Brian Shanley for helpful advice. It is dedicated to the memory of Walter Principe, who introduced me to the important role of the gifts of the Spirit in Aquinas's thought.

Chapter 9

Capreolus on
Faith and the 'Theologal' Life

Romanus Cessario, OP

In a certain sense, the 'Thomist tradition' begins in the early fifteenth century when the French Dominican John Capreolus (c. 1380-1444) set about to 'defend' the teachings of St Thomas Aquinas. Prior to the work of this friar from Rodez, it is more appropriate to speak about the various schoolmen who followed Aquinas's teaching on certain points than of Thomists associated with a set of school doctrines.[1] After the work of Capreolus, however, theologians were able to identify themselves as Thomists. Thus, Capreolus is called the *princeps Thomistarum*, the first in a distinguished line that would soon include the better-known Thomist figures of the sixteenth century, such as Cardinal Cajetan. Thanks to recent research, we now know that most of the Renaissance Thomists first learned about Aquinas's positions through the efforts of this fifteenth-century Thomist loyalist.[2]

For reasons that are associated with the tumultuous circumstances of his period in history, Capreolus accomplished his work in the French provinces. Though only a brief sojourner at Paris, he possessed the gift of recognizing those who did not follow the positions of the Angelic Doctor. For the most part, his adversaries formed a group of theologians who argued along voluntarist, and more so nominalist, lines. A notable opponent came from the ranks of Capreolus's own religious order, the Dominican, and later bishop, Durandus of Saint-Pourçain.

Capreolus's critique of Durandus's views about the theological virtue of faith clearly illustrates the temper of Capreolus's *Defensiones Divi Thomae*, the multi-volume collection of arguments and replies that he completed in 1432. Two Dominican Fathers, Ceslaus Paban and Thomas Pègues, put out a modern printed edition of the *Defensiones* between 1900 and 1908 at Tours, and the Catholic University of America Press recently published a new English translation of the treatise on the virtues.[3] In one distinction of his *Defensiones*, Capreolus assembles the texts from Aquinas that reveal the latter's conviction that faith sanctifies the intellect, and that the certitude of faith possesses its own unique kind of scientific value. The present essay invites further study of this important figure in late-medieval scholasticism by presenting Capreolus's case for the certitude of faith.

Faith and the Theologal Life

In order to stress the distinctive ways that mind and heart figure in the Christian life, French theologians commonly distinguish between the terms *théologique* and *théologal*. The former term principally signifies speculative study and learning, whereas the latter is used to describe the actual practice of Christian faith. In the seventeenth century, the English poet and divine John Donne wrote that the 'Theologall vertues, Faith, Hope, and Charity, are infus'd from God'.[4] But until recently the English term 'theologal' has not been widely used, even though its nuance is important for a Thomist account of faith. I am happy to report that the English translation of the *Catechism of the Catholic Church* has re-introduced this crucial distinction, which had fallen into desuetude among English-speaking theologians after the seventeenth century. So now we once again have a lexical way of distinguishing between a person who knows about the Christian religion and a believer who lives the Christian mysteries.

Because he lived before the period when one undertook the work of theological investigation independent of Christian commitment, John Capreolus does not remark on the significance of the distinction between theological and theologal.[5] But the notion of the theologal life is at work in his discussion of the virtue of faith, especially as this unfolds in his debate with Durandus. I would like to propose that the theologal life – *la vie théologale* – refers to the Christian life precisely as experienced. In suggesting this, I am not taking exception to Cardinal Newman. When he argues that the intrinsic superiority of divine faith is not a matter of experience, but is above experience, Newman clearly is referring to the evidential role of experience that is a prelude to conceptualization in the development of knowledge.[6] Aquinas of course would agree that experience in this sense does not ground belief. Yet he would still consider it correct to speak about the Christian life as experienced. In fact, he describes wisdom as 'tasting' the divine goodness, and envisages the gifts of the Holy Spirit as producing a sort of experimental knowledge (*quasi experimentalis*) of God.[7]

Theologians today devote considerable reflection to the notion of experience. Some of their discussions, however, fail to note that the experience associated with the theologal life is to be distinguished from the modern understanding of experience as the horizon in which normative subjectivity operates.[8] If one follows Aquinas's view, however, the theologal life points to the prayerful interiority that develops as a result of a person's being united with God and which forms part of what the Swiss theologian Hans Urs von Balthasar calls the 'integral Christian experience'.[9] Since this interiority depends on divine grace, it represents more than a metaphysical understanding rooted in the interiority of created being.

As the first fruits of the grace of justification, the virtues of faith, hope, and charity enable the justified soul to enter into personal communion with the blessed Trinity. Aquinas, it should be remembered, argues for the existence of the theologal virtues on the basis of the requirement that each person pursue the twofold end of human life: 'one [end] is proportionate to human nature ... the other, a happiness surpassing his nature'.[10] And since human nature possesses no inherent operative capacities capable of theologal loving, hoping, and believing, these virtues are God's special gifts to his creatures. The theologal virtues are entirely distinct from the intellectual and moral virtues, even when the latter exist in the believer as infused virtues. Why? The theological virtues enable the human person directly to attain God, whereas the moral virtues only enable the believer to behave in a Godly way.

John Donne describes faith as 'theologall' because believing inaugurates the experience of the theologal life. In this assertion, the Anglican Donne, I regret to say, better represents the thought of Aquinas than does the Dominican Durandus. For the latter interprets the phrase *credere in Deum* ('to believe unto God') – which comes from a definition of Augustinian provenance – not precisely as an act of faith, but of faith and charity working together. While it is true that the movement unto God reaches perfection only in charity, Aquinas would argue that even a Christian who lacks charity – a person of dead faith – can be said to experience the beginning of this movement precisely because believing involves both intellect and will. This holds true even if, as happens in the case of the person without charity, this experience entails the contradiction of being *affectively* drawn toward an end that one does not love.

Belief: Love in the Service of Knowledge

The virtues listed by St Paul in 1 Corinthians 13:13 describe how intellect and will reach out for God. As mother of the virtues, charity ranks hierarchically first among them, but in the order of coming to be faith precedes the other two because, as Aquinas says, 'no human appetite is for anything, either by hoping or loving, unless it be apprehended by sense or mind'.[11] Faith perfects the mind. It is, of course, the intellectual character of belief that triggers the exchange between Durandus and Capreolus about the virtue's certitude. Durandus fails to grasp that belief entails both that the mind know the truth and that the will adhere to the truth. As a hybrid activity, belief puts love at the service of knowledge.

The claim of Durandus that empirical knowledge produces greater surety reflects his confusion about the role that the will plays in belief. Because Capreolus does not abstract from considerations of the will and the influence of God upon the will in explaining the act of belief, he is able to identify the kind of certitude that faith enjoys. Capreolus explains this important feature of Christian faith by comparing faith and scientific knowledge:

> Although it is easier to separate oneself from the assent of faith than from the assent of scientific knowledge, it is still the case that the assent of *faith is firmer* than the assent of scientific knowledge. For the essences of the two firmnesses are not properly speaking the same, but different, since the *firmness of adherence* of faith has its principal cause *in the will*, while the firmness of scientific knowledge is in the understanding as the evidence of the complex object, to which assent is sometimes given against the will. Therefore, the understanding of one who believes, since it is inclined to give assent to the things believed both by its own habit and by a command of the will, adheres more firmly and more

intensively – though perhaps not more rootedly (*radicatius*) – than does the understanding of one who knows scientifically. Nevertheless, just as it is impossible for one who knows scientifically to dissent from a conclusion scientifically known and demonstrated while the habit of scientific knowledge is present, so it is impossible for one who believes to dissent from an article of belief while the habit of belief is present, as is self-evident.[12]

When Capreolus allows that faith may not produce as radical an attainment of truth as science achieves in its proper domain, he undoubtedly has in mind the ultimate irreducibility of Christian mystery to causal explanation. But the apophatic feature of faith does not weaken faith's hold on the truth. For what makes faith a strong virtue is the believer's 'firm and intense' adherence to the Word of God.

Theological Faith and Certitude

Since faith is a virtue that perfects the intellect in coordination with the will, the certitude of faith depends on a person's adhering to God as First Truth Speaking.[13] Hardheaded ('Durus') Durandus refuses to recognize adherence to the word of another as grounds for constituting certitude, and so he depreciated Aquinas's account of faith as an intellectual virtue. Since Durandus became a bishop, one can only assume that he had another way to uphold the primacy of faith in the Christian life. In any event, Capreolus takes strong exception to the reductionist leanings of Durandus. He argues that since First Truth validates the certitude of faith, the virtue enjoys support both from the side of its formal object, First Truth in Being, and from the side of its motivating object, the cause on account of which assent is given, First Truth Speaking. To use his own words: 'the assent of faith is said to be firmer by reason of its cause, and by reason of the infallibility of the middle term on account of which assent is given to what is adhered to'.[14]

When Capreolus refers to the 'middle term', he actually has in mind what St Paul teaches in Romans about 'hearing' the Gospel preached: 'And how are they to believe in one of whom they have never heard?' In his reply to this rhetorical question, St Paul makes the important remark: 'So faith comes from what is heard, and what is heard comes through the word of Christ' (Rom. 10:14b;17). Durandus wants to make St Paul's words work against the certitude of faith by claiming that sight is more certain than hearing. Capreolus recognizes that there is a distinction between looking at certitude from the point of view of the subject and looking at it from point of view of the cause or middle term. And for this view he has the authority of Aquinas:

> All things being equal, seeing is more certain than hearing. But if the one from whom something is heard far excels the sight of one who sees, then hearing is more certain than seeing. An example: a person with scant learning is far surer of something he hears from an expert than he is of any insight of his own. Thus anyone is far surer of what he hears from the infallible God than of what he sees with his own fallible reason.[15]

Capreolus again stresses the 'firmness of adherence that depends on the will', which, he insists, 'is the kind of firmness present in the assent of faith'.[16]

The Church affirms that 'by divine revelation God has chosen to manifest and communicate both himself and the eternal decrees of his will for the salvation of humankind, "so as to share those divine treasures that totally surpass human understanding"'.[17] Because the person who relies on the Word of Wisdom comes to participate in the divine wisdom itself, faith is a strong virtue. Durandus had argued, however, that because the 'more wondrous [noble] object' of faith surpasses human understanding, faith is a weak virtue. Capreolus replied:

> Although a habit or act is not called more certain on the basis of the certitude of the object alone, it can nevertheless be called more certain on the basis of the certitude of the object and that of the middle term or cause, even though the certitude is imperfectly participated by the subject of the habit or act. Such is the present case. For it is not merely the object of faith that is more certain than the object of scientific knowledge: *but the First Truth on which faith rests is more certain than the natural light on which scientific knowledge rests.*[18]

In other words, Capreolus wants to insist that the virtue of faith enjoys its certitude within the larger context of the theologal life. The encounter with First Truth in the preaching Church (*auditus exterior*) and the witness of First Truth Speaking in the heart (*auditus interior*) initiates an integral Christian experience: We move from the creed, to the sacraments, the moral life, and prayer.

Adherence to the First Truth is not a leap into the dark, but a conformity of the whole person to God. So, faith, precisely as a perfection of the intelligence, creates in the believer a true experience of the divine riches, one that the gifts of understanding and knowledge perfect. Though Durandus's emphasis on experience may sound a strikingly modern note, it fails to produce a Catholic understanding. Or, perhaps, Durandus anticipates Reformation cries for greater emphasis on fiduciary faith. If this is the case, his *nihil est certius experientia* will take on a plaintiff tone in Luther's cry for a merciful God.

Notes

1   This assertion modifies only slightly the view of Frederick J. Roensch, *Early Thomistic School* (Dubuque: The Priory Press, 1964), who contended that Thomists working at the University of Paris within fifty years of Aquinas's death 'appreciated fully the basic conceptions which have come to be known historically as Thomism' (p. 57). For Capreolus's place in the broader history of Thomism, see my *Le thomisme et les thomistes* (Paris: Les Éditions du Cerf, 1999).

2   For recent information on the biography and work of Capreolus, see *Jean Capreolus et son temps (1380–1444)*, ed. R. Cessario, G. Bedouelle and K. White, Mémoire Dominicaine, numéro spécial, 1 (Paris: Les Éditions du Cerf, 1997) and the review by Jean-Pierre Torrell in *Medievalia et Humanistica* New Series, No. 25 (1998) 128-31. For a specialized study

of Capreolus's influence, see Michael Tavuzzi, *Prierias: The Life and Works of Silvestro da Prierio, 1456–1527* (Durham: Duke University Press, 1997).

3   *John Capreolus: On the Virtues*, translated with an Introduction and Notes by Kevin White and Romanus Cessario, OP (Washington, DC: The Catholic University of America Press, 2001); the 'Introduction' provides information on Capreolus's *Defensiones Theologiae Divi Thomae Aquinatis*. Translations of Capreolus in this essay are taken from the White and Cessario edition.

4   See John Donne, *Pseudo-martyr*, 190 and 210: 'This is not meant onely of Charitie, as it is a Theologall vertue'.

5   To the best of my knowledge, the distinction comes into currency only with the ascendancy of French as a theological language.

6   See 'Thesis Five' of his *Theses de Fide* in 'Cardinal Newman's *Theses de Fide* and his Proposed Introduction to the French Translation of the University Sermons', ed. Henry Tristram, *Gregorianum* 18 (1937) 219-60. For translation of and commentary on the Latin text of Newman, see Carleton P. Jones, OP, 'Three Latin Papers of John Henry Newman: A Translation with Introduction and Commentary' (PhD diss., Pontifical University of Saint Thomas, 1995), pp. 60-1.

7   See *ST* 2-2.97.2 ad 2; 1.43.5 ad 2.

8   For example, Werner Schneiders, 'Experience in the Age of Reason', in *Concilium* 113 (1979) 22: 'Experience as direct encounter with present reality, or as an experientially planned and controlled discovery of reality, would be the basis of thought and action'. For commentary, see Kenneth L. Schmitz, 'St Thomas and the Appeal to Experience', *Proceedings of The Catholic Theological Society of America* 47 (1992) 1-20.

9   See Hans Urs von Balthasar, *The Glory of the Lord* (San Francisco/New York: Ignatius/Crossroad, 1982), I, *Seeing the Form*, pp. 219-425, specifically p. 295.

10 See *ST* 1-2.5.5. Steven A. Long provides some of the best analysis of this central Thomist thesis in 'Obediential Potency, Human Knowledge, and the Natural Desire for God', *International Philosophical Quarterly* 37 (1997) 45-63; and idem, 'On the Possibility of a Purely Natural End for Man', *The Thomist* 64 (2000) 211-37.

11 See *ST* 1-2.62.4. The theological virtues form an indispensable element of the Church's theological understanding of what Christian living entails. During the Council of Trent (1545–1563), the Fathers included a reference to the theological virtues in chapter 7 of the Decree on Justification: 'Consequently, in the process of justification, together with the forgiveness of sins a person receives, through Jesus Christ into whom he is grafted, all these infused at the same time: faith, hope, and charity. For faith, unless hope is added to it and charity too, neither unites him perfectly with Christ nor makes him a living member of his body. Hence it is truly said that faith without works is dead and barren [see James 2: 17, 20], and in Christ Jesus neither circumcision is of any value nor uncircumcision, but faith "working through love"' (Gal. 5:6).: *Decrees of the Ecumenical Councils*, ed. N. P. Tanner, 2 vols. (London, 1990), vol. 2, pp. *673, *674.

12 *Defensiones* Bk III, dist. 25, q. 1, art. 3, § 3, ad 2m: 'licet facilius sit recedere ab assensu fidei quam ab assensu scientifico, cum hoc stat quod assensus fidei est firmior quam assensus scientiae: quia firmitas haec et illa non sunt proprie unius rationis, sed alterius; cum firmitas adhaesionis fidei principalem causam habeat in voluntate, firmitas vero scientiae in intellectu, scilicet evidentiam complexi, cui assentit aliquando contra voluntatem; intellectus ergo credentis, cum inclinetur ad assentiendum creditis, tum ex proprio habitu, tum ex imperio voluntatis, firmius adhaeret et intensius quam intellectus scientis, licet forte non radicatius. Verumtamen, sicut impossible est scientem, stante habitu scientiae, dissentire conclusioni scitae ac demonstratae; ita impossible est

credentem, stante habitu fidei, dissentire articulo credito, ut de se patet' (emphasis added).

13 'Virtue' signifies a class of qualities that represent stable, 'habitual' features of the personality. These are firmly rooted dispositions for properly good human activity that both constitute and describe the spiritual character of the human person.

14 *Defensiones* Bk III, dist. 25, q. 1, art. 3, § 3, ad 2m: '...assensus fidei dicitur firmior, ratione causae suae, et ratione infallibilitatis medii propter quod assentit ei cui inhaeret...'. For further commentary on the Thomist account of faith, see my *Christian Faith and the Theological Life* (Washington, DC: The Catholic University of America Press, 1996).

15 *ST* 2-2.4.8 ad 2, trans. T.C. O'Brien in Volume 31 of the *Summa Theologiae* (New York/London: McGraw-Hill Book Company/Eyre & Spottiswoode, 1974).

16 *Defensiones* Bk III, dist. 25, q. 1, art. 3, § 3, ad 2m: '...[de] firmitate adhaesionis quae dependet ex voluntate; cujusmodi est in assensu fidei'.

17 The 'Dogmatic constitution on divine revelation', *Dei Verbum*, chap. 1, no. 6, which includes a citation from the 'Dogmatic constitution on the Catholic faith', *Dei Filius*, chap. 2 of the First Vatican Council: H. Denzinger and A. Schönmetzer, *Enchiridion symbolorum* (Barcinone: Herder, 1976), n. 3005.

18 *Defensiones* Bk III, dist. 25, q. 1, art. 3, § 3, ad 3m: '...habitus, vel actus, licet non dicatur certior ex sola certitudine objecti; tamen ex certitudine objecti, et medii, vel causae suae, potest dici certior; quamvis certitudo imperfecte participetur a subjecto habitus, vel actus. Sic autem est in proposito: quia objectum fidei non solum est certius objecto scientiae...' (emphasis added).

Chapter 10

Richard Swinburne, St Thomas, and Many Gods

Lawrence Dewan, OP

Some years ago, Richard Swinburne[1] proposed a doctrine 'that necessarily if there is at least one God, then there are three and only three Gods' (234). He claimed that what he is saying, while not expressed in the 'traditional terminology', is nevertheless in fundamental agreement with the traditional Christian doctrine of the Trinity (234-37). It appears to me that more than 'terminology' is involved here. That there are not three Gods but only one God is a rather basic Christian assertion.[2] However, Swinburne provides reasons for thinking as he does, and in what follows I wish to explore these reasons, or some of them, and (hopefully) expose their weaknesses. In making the exploration, I will take as my guide St Thomas Aquinas, since he has such authority as an ecclesiastical spokesman, and also because his metaphysical approaches to God have been tested over centuries.

First, let us recall the steps in Swinburne's presentation. He tells us: 'I understand by a God a person necessarily necessary, eternal, essentially bodiless, omnipresent, creator and sustainer of any world there may be, perfectly free, omnipotent, omniscient, perfectly good, and a source of moral obligation' (225). He then proceeds to comment on the various properties (as he calls them)[3] included in his notion of a God.

After presenting his conception of a God, he goes on to ask whether there could be more than one God (230). He argues:

> [T]here can be more than one God if it is necessary that the first God brings about the existence of a second God. It is possible that there be more than one God only if it is necessary that there be more than one God. But since nothing affects how a God acts except reason, this can only be if the first God has an *overriding reason* to bring about the existence of a second God. (233, italics added)

Next, he argues that there must be a third God and that there cannot be more than three (233-34). It is at this point that he tells us what it is he regards as the 'overriding reason' that a God has for producing another God. Lastly, he argues that what he is saying, while not expressed in the 'traditional terminology', is nevertheless in fundamental agreement with the traditional Christian doctrine of the Trinity (234-37).

What is Swinburne's proposed 'overriding reason'? He says:

> So is there overriding reason for a first God to create a second or third or fourth God? I believe that there is overriding reason for a first God to create a second God and with him to create a third God, but no reason to go further. If the Christian religion has helped us, Christians and non-Christians, to see anything about what is worthwhile, it has helped us to see that love is a supreme good. Love is sharing, giving to the other what of one's own is good for him and receiving from the other what of his is good for one; and love is cooperating with another to benefit third parties. (233)[4]

And later we read:

> If God is love, he must share, and sharing with finite beings such as humans is imperfect sharing. God's love has to be manifested in a sharing with a God, and that (to keep the divine unity) means within the godhead. And that is the core of my argument. (237)

In order to criticize this argument, I propose to consider the reason why Thomas Aquinas did not accept one similar attempt. However, before I make my criticism of the particular argument, I wish to make two general observations. One concerns why, in general, Thomas Aquinas thinks we can supply *no* necessary reason for positing a trinity of persons in God. The other concerns Swinburne's conceptions of God's being 'almighty' and 'good'.

Thomas presents a certain conception of the capacity of the human mind, which requires that if it comes to know God in a *natural* way, then it must come to know him only through the things God *makes*; and this character of things as *made* is seen in the most penetrating way when man comes to consider beings *as beings*, and sees the need to posit one fontal source of beings as beings.[5] Thomas judges that the Church's doctrine of the Trinity is such that such an approach to God simply cannot encounter it, at least with any necessity. From the vantage point of the given orthodoxy, he says: the creative power of God is common to the Trinity as a whole, and thus pertains to the *unity* of the divine essence, not to the distinction of persons.[6] Swinburne does not accept this (236), noting that theologians earlier than Thomas Aquinas had other opinions. All I can see can be done in such a matter is to see how convincing Swinburne's arguments are, and how really compatible they are with what the Church has proposed for belief. In the present forum, I will simply question one of his lines of argument.

Swinburne prepares the way for his argument by spelling out some of the notions he employs concerning God. Among these, particular attention is given to God's being 'almighty' (227-28) and to his being 'perfectly good' (228-30). What strikes me is how little he says about the simplicity and perfection of the divine *being*.[7] The emphasis is rather on God as a doer, as an origin of action, or even as an action. Thus he says:

> I now introduce the notion of an almighty being as one who is pure limitless intentional power, in the following sense. He is ever acting intentionally; all his actions are intentional actions; he acts as he does because he means so to do. (227)

The action or actions of which Swinburne is speaking are frequently characterized as 'choices' (227-29). I would say it is a question to what extent 'action' can be attributed to God, and especially whether 'choice' can be attributed to him. In Thomas Aquinas' procedure, *after* discussions of simplicity and goodness, the issue of 'operations' is introduced, first with *intellection* and only subsequently with *volition* (in both cases, the question: to what extent are these really 'actions', 'operations', is appropriate). Only at this stage is it asked: Could *choice* be attributed to God; and much later: can power, might, and omnipotence be attributed to God? I would accordingly raise the question: is there not a serious mistake already in viewing 'doing' and especially 'choosing' as rather dominant in the divine being? It is, I would say, symptomatic of a grave difficulty that Swinburne can speak of God as able, metaphysically, to commit suicide, but as having such a choice ruled out because of his perfect goodness (he never does a bad thing) (229).

Again, in going on to present the almighty being as 'perfectly good', he says: 'He acts intentionally, and that means that, as with any of us, whatever he does he believes in some way good to do...' (228). I.e., the *goodness* of God is being considered from a *moral* point of view. What actions are 'open to God' (229)? To the extent that there is a calculation of what God *ought* to do, Swinburne speaks of 'essential acts' (229). Within a *framework* of such acts, there may be things *not dictated*, and these Swinburne calls 'acts of will' (229). Thus, what he is saying in his argument, that there *must* be more than one God, is that to produce another God is a *choice* a perfectly good being *must* make.

Let us come now to Thomas Aquinas. Theologians of his time made arguments not unlike Swinburne's, as can be seen from the discussion in *Summa theologiae* 1.32.1, especially obj. 2 and ad 2. For example, some argued that it would be unfitting that the infinitely good not communicate its goodness by producing something infinitely good; others argued that there can be no joyful possession of any good thing unless it be shared (quoting the non-Christian author Seneca). St Thomas accorded such arguments a certain usefulness, once one has already posited that there is within the Godhead a trinity of persons. Such reflections, however, do not provide a necessary reason for positing the existence of a trinity. In the case of infinite goodness, he points out that the infinite goodness of God is manifested even in the production of a creature, because it takes infinite power to produce from nothing. It is not necessary, if in his infinite goodness he communicate himself, that something infinite come forth from God, but simply that it receive the divine goodness in a measure befitting that creature.[8]

As for the argument from joy in sharing, Thomas says such reasoning works when perfect goodness is not found in one person: in such a situation, that person needs for the full goodness of enjoyment the good which consists in someone else sharing with oneself.[9] Clearly, Thomas is saying that the argument has not appreciated how perfect is the intrinsic goodness of a divine personal being.

To see the adequacy of Thomas's rejection of the adversary's argument, and that it truly replies also to Swinburne regarding sharing, I believe it is necessary to review Thomas's presentation of the divine will. This is especially so because a key doctrine of Thomas, in that presentation, is that it pertains to the divine will most especially that it communicate the divine goodness to others as far as this is possible. This seems to coincide remarkably well with what Swinburne is saying. In the remainder of this paper, then, I will focus on the problem of love and sharing, leaving aside the issue of *infinite* sharing as less problematic.[10]

Since the point of controversy is God's act of love, and this is an act of the will,[11] Thomas's position on the will must be considered. Once we have established the simplicity and perfection of the divine being,[12] we see that such questions as 'should "will" be attributed to God?' have a point. Such a thing as will commonly involves a variety of acts: love, desire, enjoyment, intention, choice, etc., and one might well wonder about the appropriateness of attributing all these to the simple being of the divinity, even though it encompasses in itself all perfections, and does so in a mode more sublime than such perfections have in our world.[13]

Accordingly, Thomas's technique is to present what we know of will in things other than God, and to show how will is of a nature such that it should be attributed to God *most of all*. Indeed, he has already carried this out with God and *intellect*,[14] and, linking as he does will to intellect, the task of presenting God's will is already well begun.

The first point I would stress is that, because of the divine simplicity, not only will Thomas *identify* the divine substance and the divine intellect with the divine *will*, not only will he identify *the will* (conceived as a 'power' or principle of an act of willing) with the very *act of willing*, but he will affirm that there is *only one act* of the divine will.[15] If we say (as we are going to) that God loves *himself*, that he loves his own goodness, and that he loves *creatures*, i.e., the beings he *wills* into existence, and that he *chooses* that things exist, all of these expressions refer to one single act which is identical with the divine being. If we are to find justification for our variety of descriptions of the one simple being: e.g., 'God loves himself with a love that is *natural and necessary*' and 'God *freely chooses* to create something other than himself', such variety of description must find its *raison d'etre* in the variety of notions we originally use to describe *the things in a lower mode of being*, and in the extent to which our propositions end up as speaking not merely of God alone, but also of other beings as related to God. Thus, not only is 'God wills' different from 'God knows' or 'God is', but 'God loves himself' is different from 'God chooses to create'. 'God chooses to create' includes the being of creatures, and the nature of the relation these have to the divine being.[16]

The second point I wish to make concerns the way Thomas's ascent or climb to the divine will works. We see this already in his presentation of the divine *intellect*. He starts at the lowest level, with things which by nature have no knowledge, but do have the formal perfection proper to their own nature. Then, secondly, things which *have* knowledge are seen as having formal perfections in a more 'liberated', 'freed up', or unconstrained way. Thirdly, this is truer of the higher mode of knowing than of the lower, i.e., of intellect more than of sense. In this way, a *direction-indicating structure* is presented, with God at the summit of ontological amplitude (and so at the summit of cognitional operation). More truly of him than of the soul, one can say: he is, in a way, *all things*.[17]

This movement, from the being of things as constricted, to the more ample mode of being, is presented once more in asking whether 'will' is to be attributed to God. Thomas begins with the *inclination* or *tendency* to be found in *merely natural* things, i.e. those whose nature does not involve their knowing anything. Whatever perfection is natural to them, they *tend towards* it when they do not have it and *rest in it* when they have it. He then climbs to the level of intellect, proposing a higher *mode of inclination*, with a tendency toward the intellectually apprehended good (goodness seen in the light of 'what it is to be good'). This is the most perfect way of 'being inclined'.[18] Once more, we have a kind of direction-indicating structure, pointing us towards the divine being now characterized not merely as a sublime act of intellect, but as a sublime act of will (primarily a *resting-in* the divine goodness).[19]

The will and its act are conceived as ordered towards an *object*, on the analogy with sight's order to colour, or hearing's order to sound. The object of appetite and will is the good. This might seem to put God in a position of being affected by something other than himself, and so not being entirely uncaused. Thomas rejects this difficulty by teaching that the object of the divine will is God's own goodness, which is his essence.[20] (This, of course, is not to be understood as if God's will cut out, for its object, merely some particular good, the *divine* good, a good standing as it were side by side with other, *created* good: the divine good is the entirety of what we call 'goodness', existing by priority in a higher mode. The object of God's will is 'the good'.)[21] It is not surprising, then, that Thomas requires a further query: does God will *things other than himself*? The technique here for replying is once again the direction-indicating ascent, beginning with non-cognitive natures. The natural thing not only seeks its perfection when lacking it, and reposes in its perfection once had, but *diffuses* that perfection in other things as much as possible. This diffusiveness of a thing's good is accordingly to be attributed to *will*, at the higher level of reality. And, Thomas stresses, it is *most especially* to be attributed to *divine* will. (He says this because the *radiant* or *self-diffusive* character of things is related to their coming into their *perfect* state, i.e., a thing *reproduces* when it arrives at the condition we call '*maturity*', when it has everything which pertains to its 'fullness of being'. Hence, since, claims Thomas, every *perfection* is a likeness of divine *will*, it is to divine will most of all that is to be attributed *communicating its good to others to the extent that this is possible*.)[22]

With this ascending technique, so as to present the nature of divine willing, it is little wonder that many readers get the idea that God's causal production is somewhat necessarily determined, somewhat 'automatic'. I would say we can reject this interpretation by paying attention to the way the ascent is into or towards the nature of *freedom*, and into the nature of *generosity*.

Certainly, it is this doctrine that it belongs to the very idea of will, and especially divine will, that it communicate its good to others as much as possible – it is this doctrine which makes St Thomas look like he should agree with Swinburne who says that God, being love, *must share* (and with Norman Kretzmann saying that God, being goodness, *must* be self-diffusive).[23] Let us see what Thomas says.

Already, in *Summa theologiae* 1.19.2, Thomas concludes that, though God wills *both* himself and things other than himself, he wills himself *as end* (or primary good) and others *as having an order towards that end* (or as secondarily, derivatively, good). So also, he stresses that the divine goodness itself, i.e., God himself, is the entirely primary, all-pervasive object (or characterizing principle) of God's act of willing himself and others. But it is in 1.19.3 that the issue is most directly met. Does God will *of necessity everything* that he wills? Obviously, the express point is that he wills *both* himself and others, but himself *of necessity*, others by *choice*.[24]

Thomas first distinguishes the absolutely necessary from the suppositionally necessary. Absolute necessity is seen by examining the relationship of the subject and predicate terms of a proposition. Either the predicate is contained in the intelligibility of the subject: 'man is an animal', or the subject is contained in the intelligibility of the predicate: 'number is either odd or even'. Suppositional necessity is a sort of *factuality* of a situation. While 'Socrates is seated' is not an expression of absolute necessity, still it can be called 'suppositionally necessary': i.e., *supposing* that he *is* seated, then it is necessary that he be seated *while* he is seated. (There is a necessity in the situation that, insofar as it obtains, flows into and affects those zones of the situation which, considered in themselves, are not necessary.)

Thomas then tells us that 'God wills X' is the expression of an absolute necessity, where 'X' is the divine goodness itself, i.e. God's very own being. This goodness is the *proper object* of the divine will, and so the proposition: 'the divine will wills the divine goodness' is comparable to such propositions as 'the human will wills happiness' or 'by virtue of sight, one apprehends the coloured'.

As regards 'God wills X', where 'X' is things other than God, he says this is not absolutely necessary. The reason is that he wills these inasmuch as they are ordered to the divine goodness, *as toward an end* (as towards what makes the being of the 'towards' item *worthwhile*). Furthermore (and this is crucial: and notice that we are once again *ascending* from will as we know its nature in ourselves to an application to God), as regards things ordered towards an end, *we* do not will them *of necessity* when we will the end, *unless* they are such that without them the end cannot *be*. Hence, since the divine goodness is *perfect,* and can *be* without other things, since nothing is *added* to its perfection from them, it follows that 'God wills things other than himself' is not an expression of an absolute necessity.

Thomas hastens to add that it *is* an expression of suppositional necessity. Granted that he *does* will them, he *cannot* not will them, because his will cannot be *changed*. (Thus, his willing creatures is necessary by virtue of the very necessity of his own uncreated being, even though, considering the relation of the act of the will to the precise object of willing, it is *impossible* for the act to be *anything but free choice*.[25])

Clearly, everything here depends on our keeping our attention fixed upon the *proportion* of created goodness to uncreated goodness.[26] The divine goodness is not divisible into parts, such that there would be the perfection which it would have by God being God, and the perfection which it would have *by* giving of itself to others. Rather, it is perfect *in itself,* and because it is such, it is *appropriate* that it give being and goodness to others. However, its act of giving *cannot* be conceived otherwise than as *option, choice*, because of the *level of goodness* which such an *other* must have. If the divine will were, by virtue of its own inner nature, *necessarily* to give rise to such *low-grade good*, it would *eo ipso* have ceased behaving *as will*.

Much depends on seeing that, in his ascents, Thomas is leading us from the realm of finite determinisms to their source in the higher, free mode of inclination. Once we have arrived at the heights, we still find the aspect of being, nature, and necessary willing, but only vis-à-vis a suitably proportionate object (divine suicide and even a divine death-wish are metaphysical, and not merely moral, impossibilities). The *same act of will*, seen as encompassing in its object the created mode of being, is rightly judged to be and called 'an act of choice'.[27]

God, as love, must share? If the 'must' bears on what *we* must *conclude* from observing *what love is*, as revealed in the things we more immediately know, then I think it is true. I.e., considering what love is, God, who is love, is rightly and necessarily judged to be *a being who shares*. However, if it means that, because he is love, God's sharing is something he is inwardly necessitated to do, this Thomas judges (and I would say, rightly judges) to be *impossible*. The same act of will, viewed in relation to its primary object, is rightly seen as inwardly necessitated, and viewed in relation to the secondary object is rightly seen as not inwardly necessitated.

Before concluding, there is a possible difficulty I wish to mention, to be found in Thomas's saying that the divine goodness could be, even though the creature did not have being. Someone might object: this is so from the viewpoint of being, but not from the viewpoint of goodness. I.e., it is one thing to say that God's being is such that all else depends on him, and he does not 'depend' on anything whatsoever. It is something else to say that God's creatures might not be, and he would still be rightly called 'good'. Hence, his 'goodness' seems to *depend* on the being of creatures (or on there being creatures). I believe this is sufficiently cleared up by considering Thomas's text. The being of creatures does not constitute a 'plus' for the divine goodness (as though something were *added* to God's goodness by his producing creatures): as if, by creating, he merited a badge, and by *not* creating, he would have a demerit. Rather, the divine goodness just is the divine being with its intrinsic wealth of being. The being of creatures has the character of being 'worth being, and so being worthy of being produced' by virtue of its likeness to, participating in, the divine goodness. If one says that the divine goodness cannot be goodness unless other things be, in any sense which makes their being and good *part* of the goodness of God, then the divine goodness has been robbed of its proper perfection.

To conclude, Swinburne introduces the element of choice into his conception of God at a far too primary level.[28] It should not bear upon the divine being itself, with such ideas as divine suicide. However, even as regards creatures, the zone where divine choice and the properly moral dimension obtains,[29] can we speak of *necessitating* reasons for God's action of creating? As though he were *cornered* by circumstances (thus, we say: I really have *no choice* in the matter)? No, according to Thomas. That would mean that the *goal* proposed could not be obtained unless the action were performed, whereas the goal of the divine will, the divine goodness itself, is already *fully* realized, prior to the positing of any creature. For God, the creature is strictly optional.

But what about the phrase: 'as much as possible' in the doctrine: 'It belongs to goodness and will to diffuse itself *as much as possible*'? Thomas's argument, in *Summa theologiae* 1.19.3, means that such perfection of the good and of will is *already completely given* in the existence of the divine good and will, in which *all* perfection pre-exists in a higher mode. The mode of reproduction of the divine good constituted by creatures *must* have the aspect of option, though one entirely in accord with the divine goodness.

Is reproduction *within* the divine infinite goodness a *possibility*, even though it obviously *could not be* 'by choice'?[30] It does not seem to me that the philosopher can even pronounce on such a possibility.

Notes

1   Richard Swinburne, 'Could There Be More Than One God?', *Faith and Philosophy* 5 (1988) 225–41. Further references to this article will be made in the main text, simply by giving the page number. Where it is deemed helpful, references to it will include the page, column and line in the Ottawa edition published in 1941 by the Collège dominicain d'Ottawa.

2   Perhaps the most authoritative document one might cite is the Creed '*Quicumque*' (the 'pseudo-Athanasian Creed'): 'Ita Deus Pater, Deus Filius, Deus Spiritus Sanctus; et tamen non tres Dii, sed unus Deus'. ['Thus, the Father is God, the Son is God, the Holy Spirit is God; and nevertheless there are not three Gods, but one God'.] Seemingly composed about 430–500 by an unknown author, it eventually came to have such authority in both Eastern and Western Churches, that in the Middle Ages it was treated on an equal footing with the Apostles' Creed and Nicenean Creed. Cf. H. Denzinger, and A. Schonmetzer, *Enchiridion Symbolorum*, Barcelona, 1967 (34th ed.): Herder, p. 41, #75.

3   Is there any need to question this term? In *ST* 1.30.1, Thomas Aquinas calls goodness and wisdom 'proprietates absolutae in divinis', as distinguished from such things as paternity which he calls 'proprietates relativae in Deo'. The only reason I have for preferring another word such as 'attribute' is that 'property' seems to some people to suggest something *inhering* after the manner of an accident (in the general Aristotelian sense), even though an inseparable accident: and that would compromise the divine simplicity. Cf. my 'St. Thomas, Alvin Plantinga, and the Divine Simplicity', *The Modern Schoolman* 66 (1989) 142, n. 1.

4   Notice the Swinburne conception of 'sharing', which includes mutual benefit, so that each participant must be lacking, just in itself, the good proper to the other. In this sense, can a God share anything with anything?

5   *ST* 1.32.1 and 1.44.1 and 2. Notice also, in Thomas's *Scriptum* 1.2.1.1 (M59) (whether God is one only): the second argument for divine plurality runs as follows: 'Item, sicut dicitur V *Metaph.*, text. 18, perfectum unumquodque est, quando potest producere sibi simile in natura. Sed divina essentia est perfectissima. Ergo videtur quod possit producere aliam essentiam sibi similem, ita quod sint plures divinae essentiae'. Thomas replies in the ad 2 (M61): '...hoc est de perfectione divinae essentiae, quod sibi similis et aequalis alia essentia

esse non potest. Si enim ab ipsa esset, oporteret quod esse illius esset dependens ab ipsa, et sic incideret in illam essentiam potentialitas, per quam distingueretur ab essentia divina, quae est actus purus. Non autem oportet quod quidquid est de nobilitate creaturae, sit de nobilitate Creatoris, quae ipsam improportionabiliter excedit; sicut aliquid est de nobilitate canis, ut esse furibundum, quod esset ad ignobilitatem hominis, ut dicit Dionysius', cap. iv *De div. nom.*, #25, col. 727, t.I.

Swinburne says: 'All arguments to the existence of God derive their force, in my view, from their ability to explain the orderly complexity of our world as deriving from a single source of being. To suppose that there were two or more sources of being, neither of which was dependent on the other, would deprive such arguments of their force. But how can there be an almighty being which depends on another almighty being for its existence? How can there be a necessary being which derives its existence from another? No problem, as long as the derivation is necessary...' (231). Here, one would wish to say to Swinburne that this will hardly do, if God is discovered precisely as the necessary being which is the fontal source of all necessity. And this *is* Thomas's doctrine of God. God is not merely a necessary being. Absolute necessity of being is found among creatures. God is the necessary being whose necessity has no cause (cf. *ST* 1.2.3: the 'third way'). Of course, there *is* the doctrine of the Trinity. How can one divine person proceed from another? Let us notice, at least, that 'another' is ambiguous, and in Latin might be in the masculine or feminine or neuter. In Thomas's trinitarian doctrine, one cannot say that the Son is 'another' or 'something else' (neuter: *aliud*) than the Father, though one can say he is 'someone else' (masculine: *alius*): cf. *ST* 1.31.2, esp. ad 4. Let us notice, secondly, that in Thomas's presentation, the expression 'the generative power' according to which the Father generates the Son signifies not primarily the paternity which is the divine person, but the divine *essence*, so that that by virtue of which the generator generates is *numerically identical* in the generator and in the being who is generated, unlike what happens in created things where the two are only specifically the same (*ST* 1.41.5 ad 1). Is one then really sure one is speaking about anything at all when one speaks of the Father generating the Son? Can one appeal to the difference between first substance and second substance (or, in other words, the substantial individual and the nature)? Hardly, when one considers that, because all perfections pre-exist in the divine essence, that essence can be understood under the aspect of both first substance and second substance: cf. *ST* 1.25.1 ad 3.

6   *ST* 1.32.1. This does not prevent Thomas, given the existence and nature of the Trinity, from assigning various roles to the divine Persons in the one creative act: cf. *ST* 1.45.6.

7   Indeed, what one gathers about the being of his Gods is rather disquieting. For example, each of the Gods is viewed as having the power, in the 'compatibilist' sense, to *annihilate* the other (232-3). So also, a God has the 'compatibilist' power to annihilate itself ('commit suicide', 229). The Gods are, however, just too good and reasonable to act that way: thus, their 'almightiness' in the 'absolute' sense, is limited.

8   *ST* 1.32.1 ad 2 (ed. Ottawa, 210a24-31). For the argument that it requires infinite power to make something from nothing, cf. *ST* 1.45.5 ad 3; notice that this argument is *not* based on a conception of infinite 'distance' between nothing and being: for between such extremes, distance is entirely imaginary (*ST* 1.45.2 ad 4). That it is *impossible* to *make*, i.e., to *create*, something unqualifiedly infinite (i.e., infinite as to essence, and not merely in dimensive quantity), cf. *ST* 1.7.2 ad 1. Hence, God 'cannot' do it. That the doctrine of the 'proceeding' of person from person in the Trinity cannot be treated as *an effect* proceeding from *a cause*, cf. *ST* 1.27.1 (ed. Ottawa, 181b19-27). If it were, the effect would not be truly a God. Thomas criticizes the cause-effect conception of the Trinity as, at heart, an *ad extra* conception of the process. He goes on to propose an *ad intra*

conception through a consideration of pure intellectual process. While Swinburne *says* he is remaining '*within* the Godhead', it seems to me that his conception of the process as one of 'creation' (even the sort of 'creation' he proposes, p. 232, i.e., 'division' of the divine substance) has already betrayed the very possibility of what he wishes to propose. (Notice that for Thomas the divine nature cannot be generated as happens with human nature, where part of the substance of the generator goes to the one generated: *ST* 1.41.3:259b27-37.)

9 *ST* 1.32.1 ad 2 (ed. Ottawa, 210a31-37). This is not *exactly* Swinburne's argument, since it links sharing with enjoyment rather than with love. However, it seems to me close enough to show Thomas's view of an argument such as that of Swinburne. Thomas does not simply identify love with sharing, as Swinburne seems to do. For Thomas, love is the fundamental stance of appetite vis-à-vis the good. Self-love is thus not merely possible and virtuous: it is at its maximal in God, and in created wills it is the principle and model for all the love we have for our fellow-creatures: 'love thy neighbour *as thyself*'. Cf. *ST* 1.20.1, esp. ad 3; also 1.60.3 and 4, esp. ad 2.

10 I am grateful to a Canadian Philosophical Association reader of an earlier version of this paper for calling my attention to N. Kretzmann, 'Goodness, Knowledge and Indeterminacy in the Philosophy of Thomas Aquinas', *Journal of Philosophy* supplement to vol. 80 (1983) 631-49 (to which Swinburne himself refers, at p. 239, n. 14). Kretzmann thinks that Thomas's use of the doctrine that the good is self-diffusive, together with that of God as goodness itself, commits him to a doctrine of necessary creation. Kretzmann tries to save the situation somewhat by suggesting that the creating could be a natural and necessary act of the divine will (still characterized as 'free'). I believe that what I will say to Swinburne will also serve as a reply to Kretzmann. – Regarding the doctrine of the good as self-diffusive, and its relation to final and efficient causality, cf. my 'St. Thomas and the Causality of God's Goodness', *Laval theologique et philosophique* 34 (1978) 291-304. For my criticism of Kretzmann's more recent writing on this matter, cf. my 'Review of Norman Kretzmann, *The Metaphysics of Theism*', *EIDOS* (University of Waterloo) 14 (1997) 97-121.

11 Cf. *ST* 1.20.1.

12 Cf. *ST* 1.3-13.

13 Cf. *ST* 1.4.2 and 1.13.2.

14 *ST* 1.14.1.

15 *ST* 1.19.2 ad 4.

16 Cf. *ST* 1.19.2 ad 1; also 1.19.3 ad 6.

17 *ST* 1.14.1.

18 Cf. *ST* 1.59.1 (ed. Ottawa, 358a41-51).

19 *ST* 1.19.1; cf. 1.80.1. This resting of the divine will in its own goodness, i.e., God loving and being delighted with his own goodness, is the natural and necessary act of the divine will. I.e., it is its act as, like all other things, having a nature. Nature is the primary feature of the act so taken, whereas will is its 'mode'. It is the divine act of willing (*velle*) taken as manifesting the divine act of being (*esse*): *ST* 1-2.10.1 ad 1; also 1.60.1 and 1.41.2 ad 3.

20 *ST* 1.19.1 ad 3.

21 Cf. *ST* 1.6.4 (ed. Ottawa 36a36-39).

22 *ST* 1.19.2.

23 See earlier reference.

24 I use the words 'choice' and 'option' in my presentation of Thomas's position. He seems to avoid such words as '*electio*'. He simply argues that the divine will is not *necessarily* ordered towards objects having a certain mode of being and being good. He does speak of

God as, 'in a way, free to go either way': cf. *ST* 1.41.2 ad 3: 'Sed circa alia a se, voluntas Dei se habet ad utrumque quodammodo...'. Cf. 1.19.3 obj. 4 and ad 4. In 1.19.10, precisely on the basis of 1.19.3, he attributes to God '*liberum arbitrium*'.

25 *ST* 1.19.3.

26 Concerning the use of '*proportio*' to describe the relation of the created to the uncreated, cf. *ST* 1.12.1 ad 4.

27 *ST* 1.41.2 ad 3 and 1.19.3 ad 4.

28 On the need for order in our considerations of God, who himself is altogether simple, cf. *ST* 1.13.11 and 1.44.4 ad 4.

29 Cf., e.g., *ST* 1.21.3, where it is explained how 'goodness', 'justice', 'generosity', and 'mercy' all apply to God's actions towards creatures, including the very act of creating. Cf. also my 'St. Thomas, God's Goodness, and God's Morality', *The Modern Schoolman* 70 (1992) 45-51.

30 Cf. *ST* 1.41.2.

Chapter 11

Sketches of Walter

Charles Principe, CSB

It was very kind of the editors to invite me to add a personal memorial tribute to my brother, Walter Principe. I accepted happily their invitation because of my great affection and admiration for Walter. Though I shall be consciously incomplete about many features of his character and life, I hope that those who knew Walter through his academic work and perhaps also through personal contacts will recognize him in what I do say out of my own relationship with him as brother, student, and fellow Basilian priest.

Walter and I were born the two youngest of six boys among the all-male children of our dear parents, Arthur and Louise Principe. I imagine that Walter said to himself, as I do looking back: 'Poor Mom!' But when she died at age forty-five, we were only thirteen and seven, respectively, and probably, at least in my case, too young to realize how true that was. How true also of our father, who lost not only his spouse in 1936, but, a year and a half later, his second son at age twenty-four who was studying theology in the diocesan seminary in Rochester, New York. I point out these few details merely to suggest that those family experiences had an effect upon our own outlook on life and strengthened rather than weakened the religious character of our family, leading in part (as I believe) to our own future vocations.

One aspect of Walter's character was revealed in the late 1930s. My big brothers were quite different, some a little rougher than others but all very good and faithful to their friends. Walter treated me gently but firmly, for example, even when playing scrub football on our front lawn when I was not yet a teenager and he was. He could have thoroughly trounced me immediately, of course, but he remembered that he was six years older than I and many pounds heavier. His tactic was to allow me to score some points, and then suddenly reverse the destiny of the game lest I become too arrogant or over-confident! That kind of balanced sensibility, it seems to me, remained throughout his life, appearing in various forms according to different situations. Later on in our lives as priest-teachers, he was always kind and supportive, even referring to me or quoting me when occasion arose. This did not prevent him from giving sound brotherly advice when he judged I could do better in any way! It was easy to take, however, for I always knew it came from warm brotherly love. This combination of faithful and supportive friendship, along with his insistence on always trying to do better himself and urging others to do so, comprised Walter's idealism, which became noticeably infused with Christian charity and concern for all others. In particular, he would always remain close to his family, his Basilian confreres, his former students, and his countless friends.

Walter attended high school at the Aquinas Institute, Rochester, New York, where a large community of Basilians taught alongside many sister religious and a few laypeople. He was one of the most brilliant students in the history of that school. At Aquinas, he also played the clarinet in the student band, and the clarinet or oboe in the concert band. Following graduation in 1940, Walter entered the Basilian Novitiate in Toronto. I was to follow that path in 1946, beginning many new years of fairly close proximity as Basilians even when we were not (as happened most often) members of the same local Basilian community.

Once again, Walter proved to be an outstanding student, this time at the University of Toronto. It is surprising to most that his undergraduate degree was in Political Science and Economics. Those studies, along with philosophy and theology, would not be without value in future contacts with other academics and laypeople, for they already broadened his horizons. But following his four years at St Basil's Seminary, Toronto, theology would become his specialty in teaching and research. He was ordained a priest in 1949 and was immediately designated to go on to graduate studies.

Thus it came about that Walter taught me dogmatic theology (as it was called back then) at St Basil's. He was one of several Basilians who had been sent off to Europe after World War II to do graduate work in theology, history, and the social sciences. Returning in the early 1950s, these young men reinvented the seminary courses. Walter had just returned from graduate studies at the *École pratique des hautes études* and *Le Saulchoir* under Marie-Dominique Chenu, and was thus also in contact with Yves Congar. These influences, and that of Henri de Lubac, are reflected in Walter's lifelong insistence on the importance of the history of theology. During those years he perceived for the first time, in my opinion, what it was to think in original ways as a serious theologian, while remaining faithful to the Church in the face of any rejection by certain authorities. He would develop his own approach to theological questions, especially later on, but would remain true to his role as faithful teacher in the Church.

From 1955 to 1965, Walter was Dean of the Faculty of Theology at the University of St Michael's College, Toronto. While occupied with these teaching and administrative responsibilities, he obtained in 1963 the MSD (*summa cum laude*) from the Pontifical Institute of Mediaeval Studies. The fruit of his doctoral thesis appeared in four volumes on *The Theology of the Hypostatic Union in the Early Thirteenth Century* (1963–1975).

Walter was one of the best teachers the Basilians had, and many other students of his have concurred over the years. Characteristic of his method in teaching dogma was his careful structuring of the voluminous notes he handed out: each dogma was presented according to Scripture, the Fathers of the Church, then a series of later theological teachings and opinions, with the *Summa theologiae* of Thomas Aquinas as our main text. He was already expert at asking and answering questions. Even then, doubtless applying what eminent Dominicans had taught him, Walter stressed the status of each doctrine, proceeding through all the degrees of theological authority, certitude, or probability, from *de fide* down: the theological marks or hierarchy of truths. These distinctions would always be a hallmark of his theological argumentation and the basis for what he saw as the academic freedom and responsibility of Catholic theologians. The Marquette lecture on the development of Church doctrine, along with several articles touching that subject, is to me a later and prime example of his care for absolute precision in this matter, as well as an implicit criticism of those who would multiply *de fide* dogmas without thoroughly studying their history and their theological place in the profession of faith.[1] It was clear that Walter had studied long and deeply the history of the Church's faith and chronological formulations by the Fathers, Councils, and theologians over the centuries. As I see him, Walter was a theologian, but an historical theologian who saw and accepted the unsurprising development (and even what some would call 'changes') in the way the faith was taught officially by the Church, while the Spirit never failed, as Jesus promised, to preserve the absolutely fundamental truths of that faith.

Thus, over the years, Walter began to reflect more and more the kind of original approach to doctrine he had witnessed in France and elsewhere. It would lead him to take positions that drew occasional criticism, as is expected in academia, but which could be more sensitive in the field of theology and teaching within the Catholic Church. He was encouraged, as were so many Catholic thinkers, by the spirit of *aggiornamento* flowing from the Second Vatican Council. In contrast, he was to be disappointed during his experience as a member of the Vatican's International Theological Commission (1980–1985). The absence of frank discussion about different aspects of a theological issue (especially if they involved what he considered original insights among the commission's members) and the failure to treat thoroughly all aspects of a question as presented by theologians of varying backgrounds – all this led Walter not to seek or accept further membership on the Commission.

I must return to the past to stress my growing awareness of another essential component of Walter's person as Christian theologian. In the years after I returned from teaching English in the original Basilian school at Annonay (Ardèche), France, and thesis preparation at the Sorbonne, I noticed more clearly what others had doubtless remarked much earlier. This was his deepening interest in theology as life, as inspiration for a deeper spiritual life, without which theology would remain a purely academic discipline. This theological spirituality shines through all of his published lectures and writings that were not purely academic, and also in his letters to people that I have been privileged to read. He shed new light on features of the spirituality contained in the teachings of St Thomas Aquinas, too often seen as mostly a cold, even dry, logician and theologian. Building on Thomas, Walter stressed the presence and gifts of the Holy Spirit and the indwelling of the Trinity in each believer. All this led to his being called upon to give lectures on spirituality and to facilitate retreats. These contacts were extremely important to him. It showed in his eagerness to take part in or preside at liturgical celebrations. Walter was a clear exponent of Scripture and doctrine, remaining at the same time down-to-earth in his preaching and homilies. His emphasis was not only on presentation of dogma; he was equally concerned about practical aspects of pastoral and sacramental life among God's people.

Walter was not only a medievalist. He kept abreast of the thought of our contemporary theologians. He contributed greatly not only to his specialty, Christology, but also to continuing theological reflection on such subjects as the Trinity, the Holy Spirit, and spirituality. He was able to do so owing precisely to his keen sense of the importance of history in the field of theology. The breadth of Walter's expertise, seasoned as I see it with his engaging personality, made him ideal in situations of difficult dialogue. These combined qualities were, I believe, recognized as an asset by Church authorities and theological societies, and resulted in his appointment to ecumenical and inter-religious committees, or to task forces studying the role of theologians with relation to bishops, and the Profession of Faith and Oath of Fidelity promulgated by the Vatican Congregation for the Doctrine of Faith.

There is another development I came to observe in Walter's theological reflection. Again, following the new attitude towards world religions embraced by Vatican II, Walter delved into the varied spiritualities of many Catholic, Protestant, and non-Christian faiths, as evidenced in his recorded and published lecture on the meaning and varieties of mysticism at the 1976 Conference on Mysticism at the University of Calgary; and also in his taped lectures and articles that examine the very notion and nature of spirituality.[2] This aspect of his thought interested me particularly because of my own research specialty in the French Jesuit missionaries of New France and their descriptions and appraisals of the native peoples of North America in the early contact period.

For Walter, research was never an end in itself. Walter was born to be a teacher. Besides his intellectual honesty and care for precision in his teaching, he had the reputation of being unstintingly generous in the care and time for consultation that he afforded his students and those whose theses he was directing. He was also a firm guide. He demanded of them the same preciseness he brought to his own work. Walter remained deeply attached to Thomas Aquinas. He uncovered neglected insights in Thomas, for instance in theological spirituality, even as he studied and grew in openness to positions of other theological schools, ancient and modern. In the 1980s, one of his students said to him one day: 'I think I am becoming a Thomist'. To which Walter replied: 'That is the way to freedom'.

Besides the many academics who consulted Walter, his acquaintances of all backgrounds took advantage of his desire to share his gifts of knowledge and guide them in answers to their questions. Of course, this took place often through more formal ways of communication. But how many of his friends and acquaintances could tell of Walter's openness in this way while at meals, while travelling together, or at other leisure moments. He was always ready and willing to discuss what was so close to his mind and heart: not just the exterior of his work but its meaning in his personal life of faith and that of the Church, theology, philosophy, history, and spirituality. Such occasions would happen with graceful ease at a curve away from baseball talk.

All of this, including his travels in Europe and elsewhere for lectures, research or tourism, combined with his ease in meeting people and made him a rich conversationalist. In these situations, as in his teaching and publishing, Walter possessed a special ability to integrate seemingly disparate elements of a question into an enlightening whole.

This ability was nourished by Walter's universal interests and insatiable curiosity. In any conversation, Walter might suddenly introduce echoes of his continuing general reading in many other fields, whether political science and economics, the various sciences, literature, and popular culture. He enjoyed several styles of music: classical (for him, Mozart was the greatest – I still reproach him for not expanding his taste to J.S. Bach!), musical comedies, popular songs, and jazz. It was a blessing for him and for others when he returned to his high-school clarinet skill at a doctor's recommendation. The other 'fine arts' interested him equally. He kept up with much of old and recent cinematographic output. Until occupations, time, and a first by-pass operation (1982) imposed certain restrictions, he played baseball, handball, tennis, and golf with enthusiasm. He was an example of a true Renaissance person.

In Houston, Texas, in the last two years of his life on this earth, Walter continued working to the very end, preparing the publication of an article on spirituality, which appeared at the time of his death. Far more important, he returned to his research towards a critical edition of Guerric of Saint-Quentin's *Quodlibets*. This has just appeared posthumously with editorial revision and a preface by Jonathan Black and an introduction by Jean-Pierre Torrell, OP.[3] During this same time he attended lectures on the sciences and political economy at Rice University – or so I discovered in a couple of small notebooks, his quick hand having scribbled ideas in a small, neat, flowing script, still marked by the old Palmer method taught him by the Sisters of Mercy in our parish school. I also found a lengthy prayer he jotted down not quite a year before his death, obviously written during a visit to a group of close friends, one of whom was near death. Walter here reveals a very humble sense of his limitations in this crisis, and of his need for greater union with Christ to bear fruit in his mission as he brings these friends strongly into his prayer, along with a relative of ours. But that is all drawn into the main focus of his prayer, his personal relationship with Jesus, the Father, the Spirit, no surprise for those who know how Trinitarian was his own spirituality. For me, that prayer is a kind of testament.

Notes

1 *Faith, History and Cultures: Stability and Change in Church Teachings.* The Pere Marquette Lecture in Theology, 22 (Milwaukee: Marquette University Press, 1991).
2 'Mysticism: Meaning and Varieties', in *Mystics and Scholars: The Calgary Conference on Mysticism, 1976,* ed. H. Coward and T. Penelhum, SR Supplements, 3 (Waterloo: Wilfrid Laurier University Press, 1977), pp. 1-15.
3 Guerric of Saint-Quentin, *Quaestiones de quolibet,* ed. W.H. Principe and J. Black, Studies and Texts, 143 (Toronto: PIMS, 2002).

Bibliography of the Writings of
Walter H. Principe, CSB

James K. Farge, CSB and James R. Ginther

This bibliography was originally published along with Principe's obituary in Medieval Studies *58 (1996) vii-xx. It is now reproduced here with the kind permission of the Pontifical Institute of Mediaeval Studies, with some minor emendations. This list differs from the original in that Principe's writings are listed chronologically, whereas Fr. Farge had organized them thematically.*

1962:

'Report of a Thesis Recently Defended at the Pontifical Institute of Mediaeval Studies: "The Theology of the Hypostatic Union in the Early Thirteenth Century: The Doctrines of William of Auxerre, Alexander of Hales, Hugh of Saint-Cher, and Philip the Chancellor".' *Mediaeval Studies* 24: 392-94.

1963:

The Theology of the Hypostatic Union in the Early Thirteenth Century, vol. 1: William of Auxerre's Theology of the Hypostatic Union. Studies and Texts 7. Toronto: Pontifical Institute of Mediaeval Studies. Pp. 332.

'Hugh of Saint-Cher's Stockholm "Gloss on the Sentences": An Abridgment Rather than a First Redaction.' *Mediaeval Studies* 25: 372-76.

1964:

'The Priest-Teacher: A Theological Evaluation.' *The Basilian Teacher* 8 Supplement: 61-85.

1965:

'Vocations and Contemporary Theology.' *The Basilian Teacher* 9: 499-522.

'Comment on F. Black, 'Clerical Dress.' The *Basilian Forum:* Supplement to *The Basilian Teacher* 9/5 (February): 73-75.

1966:

'Contemporary Theology of Christ.' *The Basilian Teacher* 10: 387- 404.

'The Variety of Religious Vocations.' In *Donum Dei* 11:45-62. Ottawa: Canadian Religious Conference. French translation: 'La varieté des vocations religieuses.' In *Donum Dei* (French edition) 11:41-59. Ottawa: Conference Religieuse Canadienne.

'A Communion of Freedom: Freedom, Authority and Obedience.' *The Field at Home* 42: 4-7, 28-32.

'Capital Punishment: Death Penalty Itself Should Stand Trial and Be Judged.' The *Canadian Register*, 19 February, p. 7.

1967:

The Theology of the Hypostatic Union in the Early Thirteenth Century, vol. 2: *Alexander of Hales' Theology of the Hypostatic Union*. Studies and Texts 12. Toronto: Pontifical Institute of Mediaeval Studies. Pp. 254.

Bibliographies and Bulletins in Theology. Typed, photocopied edition. Toronto: At the author's. Pp. 44.

'Bus, Cesar de, Ven.' In *New Catholic Encyclopedia* 2:908a-b. New York: McGraw-Hill.

'Celestine IV, Pope.' Ibid., 3:365a.

'Compagnie du Saint-Sacrement.' Ibid., 4:85b-86a.

'Destiny, Supernatural.' Ibid., 4:807a-808b. New York: McGraw Hill, 1967.

'Innocent V, Pope, Bl.' Ibid., 7:525a-b.

'Obediential Potency.' Ibid., 10:606a-607a.

'Orléans-Longueville, Antoinette d'.' Ibid.10:783a-b.

'Preternatural.' Ibid. 11:763b- 764b.

'Spondanus, Henri (de Sponde).' Ibid., 13:614b-615a.

'Vocation to Supernatural Life.' Ibid., 14:736b-738a.

'The Human Psychology of Christ and the Christian Life.' *The Basilian Teacher* 11: 399-408. Italian translation: 'Che cosa ha imparato Cristo dagli uomini.' *Rocca* [Assisi, Italy] 26/22 (1 dicembre, 1967): 27-30. Reprinted as 'Christ's Human Psychology and the Christian Life.' *Catholic Mind* 66, no. 1224 (June 1968): 14-21; and *Christian Unity Digest* 3/9 (September 1968): 31-33.

Vocations and Renewal of Religious Life. Conferences Given at the Canadian Religious Conference Study Days for Local Religious Directresses, St Michael's Retreat House, Lumsden, Sask., 12-15 August 1966, and St Joseph's Seminary, Edmonton, Alberta, 18-21 August 1966. Edmonton: Grey Nuns, Regional Centre, 9810 165 Street, Edmonton, Alberta. Pp. 89.

1970:

The Theology of the Hypostatic Union in the Early Thirteenth Century, vol. 3: *Hugh of Saint-Cher's Theology of the Hypostatic Union*. Studies and Texts 19. Toronto: Pontifical Institute of Mediaeval Studies. Pp. 265.

1971:

Review of Antonio Piolanti, *Il Corpo Mistico e le sue relazioni con l'Eucaristia in S. Alberto Magno*, Studi di Teologia Medievale della Pontificia Universita Lateranense 1 (Rome: Pontificia Universita Lateranense, 1969), in *The Thomist* 35: 182-83.

1972:

'Foreword.' In *Guide to Religious Studies in Canada/Guide des Sciences Religieuses au Canada*, 1972, compiled and edited by C[harles] P. Anderson, 5. Corporation for the Publication of Academic Studies in Religion in Canada. Waterloo: Wilfrid Laurier University Press.

1973:

'The Hermeneutic of Roman Catholic Dogmatic Statements.' *SR: Studies in Religion/Sciences Religieuses* 2: 157-75.

1974:

'St. Thomas on the Habitus-Theory of the Incarnation.' In *St. Thomas Aquinas, 1274-1974: Commemorative Studies*, 2 vols., edited by Armand A. Maurer et al., 1:381-418. Toronto: Pontifical Institute of Mediaeval Studies.

'St. Bonaventure's Theology of the Holy Spirit with Reference to the Expression 'Pater et Filius diligunt se Spiritu Sancto.' In *S. Bonaventura, 1274-1974* 4:243-69. Grottaferrata (Rome): Collegio S. Bonaventura.

'St. Bonaventure's Theology of the Holy Spirit as Love between Father and Son.' *The Cord* 24: 235-56.

Review of Edouard-Henri Weber, *La controverse de 1270 a l'Université de Paris et son retentissement sur la pensée de S. Thomas d'Aquin*, Bibliothèque Thomiste 40 (Paris: Vrin, 1970), in *Speculum* 49: 163-67.

1975:

The Theology of the Hypostatic Union in the Early Thirteenth Century, vol. 4: Philip the Chancellor's Theology of the Hypostatic Union. Studies and Texts 32. Toronto: Pontifical Institute of Mediaeval Studies. Pp. 234.

'St. Thomas Aquinas.' The *Basilian Annals* 5: 58-62.

1976:

'Thomas Aquinas' Principles for Interpretation of Patristic Texts.' In *Studies in Medieval Culture* 8 & 9, edited by John R. Sommerfeldt and E. Rozanne Elder, 111-21. Kalamazoo, Mich.: The Medieval Institute, Western Michigan University.

1977:

'*Quaestiones* Concerning Christ from the First Half of the Thirteenth Century: I. *Quaestiones* from the Bibliothèque Nationale, Paris.' *Mediaeval Studies* 39: 1-59.

'Odo Rigaldus, a Precursor of St. Bonaventure on the Holy Spirit as *effectus formalis* in the Mutual Love of the Father and Son.' *Mediaeval Studies* 39: 498-505.

'Mysticism: Its Meaning and Varieties.' In *Mystics and Scholars: The Calgary Conference on Mysticism* 1976, edited by Harold Coward and Terence Penelhum, 1-15. SR Supplements 3. Waterloo, Ontario: Wilfrid Laurier University Press.

'Chairman's Report/Rapport du president.' In *Humanities Research Council of Canada: Annual Report, 1976-1977/Le Conseil canadien de recherches sur les humanites: Rapport annuel, 1976-1977*; 5-7 (in both English and French sections). Ottawa: HRCC-CCRH (now Canadian Federation for the Humanities/ Federation canadienne des études humaines).

1978:

'Richard Fishacre's Use of Averroes with Respect to Motion and the Human Soul of Christ.' *Mediaeval Studies* 40: 349-60.

1979:

'Early Explicit Use of Averroes by Richard Fishacre with Respect to Motion and the Human Soul of Christ.' In *Actas del V Congreso Internacional de Filosofia Medieval*, 2 vols., edited by Salvador Gomez Nogales, 2:1127-37. Madrid: Editora Nacional.

1980:

Introduction to Patristic and Medieval Theology. Typed, photocopied text. Toronto: At the author's; 2d ed., 1982. Pp. 312; 2d ed. (slightly revised). Pp. 316.

'*Quaestiones* Concerning Christ from the First Half of the Thirteenth Century: II. *Quaestiones* from Douai MS. 434: The Need for the Incarnation; The Defects Assumed by Christ.' *Mediaeval Studies* 42: 1-40.

1981:

'*Quaestiones* Concerning Christ from the First Half of the Thirteenth Century: III. *Quaestiones* from Douai MS. 434: The Hypostatic Union.' *Mediaeval Studies* 43: 1-57.

'Augustinians.' In *Abingdon Dictionary of Living Religions*, edited by Keith Crim, Roger A. Bullard, and Larry D. Shinn, 77. Nashville, Tenn.: Abingdon Press.

'Beguines.' Ibid., 94.

'Benedictines.' Ibid., 95.

'Capuchins.' Ibid., 157.

'Carmelites.' Ibid., 157.

'Carthusians.' Ibid., 157.

'Celestines.' Ibid., 161.

'Cistercians.' Ibid., 186-87.

'Dominicans.' Ibid., 229.

'Flagellants.' Ibid., 260.

'Franciscans.' Ibid., 266.

'Jesuits.' Ibid., 379.

'Mendicant Friars.' Ibid., 476.

'Religious Orders.' Ibid., 616-18.

'Trappists.' Ibid., 765.

'Ursulines.' Ibid., 779.

1982:

'*Quaestiones* Concerning Christ from the First Half of the Thirteenth Century: IV. *Quaestiones* from Douai MS. 434: Christ as Head of the Church: The Unity of the Mystical Body.' *Mediaeval Studies* 44: 1-82.

'The Dynamism of Augustine's Terms for Describing the Highest Trinitarian Image in the Human Person.' In *Studia Patristica* 17 (Proceedings of the Eighth International Conference of Patristic Studies, Oxford, 3-8 September 1979), 3 vols., edited by Elizabeth A. Livingstone, 3:1291-99. Oxford and New York: Pergamon Press.

'Nikolaus M. Häring, S.A.C. (1909-1982).' *Mediaeval Studies* 44: vii-xvi.

Review of Jaroslav Pelikan, *The Christian Tradition: A History of the Development of*

Doctrine, vol. 3: *The Growth of Medieval Theology (600–1300)* (Chicago and London: University of Chicago Press, 1978), in *Speculum* 57: 922-26.

1983:

'Christology.' In *Dictionary of the Middle Ages,* 3:319-24. New York: Charles Scribner's Sons.

'Toward Defining Spirituality.' *SR: Studies in Religion/Sciences Religieuses* 12: 127-41.

1984:

Thomas Aquinas' Spirituality. The 1984 Gilson Lecture. The Etienne Gilson Series 7. Toronto: Pontifical Institute of Mediaeval Studies. Pp. 29.

'The Dignity and Rights of the Human Person as Saved, as Being Saved, as to Be Saved by Christ.' *Gregorianum* 65: 389-430.

'Liturgy: The Message of Easter.' *The Canadian Catholic Review* 2/4: 38/154.

'Liturgy: The Ascension.' *The Canadian Catholic Review* 2/6: 37/233-38/234.

1985:

'Mary Ward: Changing Concepts of Holiness.' In *Journey into Freedom: Mary Ward: Essays in Honour of the Fourth Centenary of Her Birth,* pp. 14-33. The Way: Supplement, no. 53.

'Bishops, Theologians, and Philosophers in Conflict at the Universities of Paris and Oxford: The Condemnations of 1270 and 1277.' The Catholic Theological Society of America: Proceedings of the Fortieth Annual Convention, San Francisco, June 5-8, 1985, 40: 114-26.

'Priest-Professor in China.' *The Canadian Catholic Review* 3, no. 4:139-43; no. 5: 175-78; no. 6: 217-22; no. 7: 259-62; no. 9: 331-35.

1986:

'Personal Reflections on the Church in China.' *Catholic New Times* (Toronto), 31 August, 8-9.

'Catholicity: A Threat or Help to Identity?' In *Identity Issues and World Religions,* Selected Papers and Other Proceedings of the Fifteenth Congress of the International Association for the History of Religions (University of Sydney, Australia, 18-23 August 1985), edited by Victor C. Hayes, 224-33. Netley S.A., Australia: Wakefield Press. A complete version with full notes and slight changes appeared in Canadian Theological Society: Papers Presented at the Annual Meeting Held at Winnipeg, June 2-4, 1986, 135-75.

'Of Change in "Authentic" Teaching.' *Canadian Theological Society Newsletter* 6/1: 3-7.

1987:

'Philosophy and Theology, Western European: Twelfth Century to Aquinas.' In *Dictionary of the Middle Ages* 9:590-606. New York: Charles Scribner's Sons.

'Relations of the Canadian Theological Society with La Societé Canadienne de Théologie: Some Recollections.' *Canadian Theological Society Newsletter* 6/2: 10-14.

'When "Authentic" Teachings Change.' *The Ecumenist* 25: 70-73.

'Catholicity, Inculturation, and Liberation Theology: Do They Mix?' *Franciscan Studies* 47: 24-43.

1988:

'The History of Theology: Fortress or Launching Pad?' In The *Sources of Theology*, edited by John P. Boyle and George Kilcourse, pp. 19-40. Current Issues in Theology 3. Catholic Theological Society of America.

'*Quaestiones* Concerning Christ from the First Half of the Thirteenth Century: V. *Quaestiones* from Douai MS. 434: Christ's Knowledge.' *Mediaeval Studies* 50: 1-45.

1989:

'The School Theologians' Views of the Papacy, 1150–1250.' In *The Religious Roles of the Papacy: Ideals and Realities, 1150–1300* (Conference hosted by the Pontifical Institute of Mediaeval Studies, 13-16 May 1985), edited by Christopher Ryan, pp. 45-116. Papers in Mediaeval Studies 8. Toronto: Pontifical Institute of Mediaeval Studies.

'Monastic, Episcopal, and Apologetic Theology of the Papacy, 1150–1250.' Ibid., pp. 117-70.

1990:

'Affectivity and the Heart in Thomas Aquinas' Spirituality.' In *Spiritualities of the Heart*, edited by Annice Callahan, 45-63. New York: Paulist Press.

'Some Examples of Augustine's Influence on Medieval Christology.' In *Collectanea Augustiniana: Melanges T. J. van Bavel*, 2 vols. (successive pagination), edited by B. Bruning, M. Lamberigts, and J. Van Houtem, pp. 955-74. Bibliotheca Ephemeridum Lovaniensium XCII / A-B. Leuven: Leuven University Press; also published as *Augustiniana* 40-41 (1990–1991).

'*De veritate humanae naturae*: Theology in Conversation with Biology, Medicine, and Philosophy of Nature.' In *Knowledge and the Sciences in Medieval*

Philosophy: Proceedings of the Eighth International Congress of Medieval Philosophy (SIEPM), vol. 3, edited by Reijo Tyorinoja, Anja Inkeri Lehtinen, and Dagfinn Follesdal, 486-94. Annals of the Finnish Society for Missiology and Ecumenics 55. Helsinki.

'Boethius.' In *Encyclopedia of Early Christianity*, edited by Everett Ferguson et al., 156-57. New York and London: Garland.

'Filioque.' Ibid., 347-50.

'The New Profession of Faith and Oath of Fidelity.' *Catholic New Times* (Toronto), 21 January, p. 8. Reprinted as 'The Oath of Fidelity.' *The Ecumenist* 28 (1989-90): 33-36.

'A Theologian Responds to the *Instruction.*' *Catholic New Times* (Toronto), 22 July, p. 3. French translation: 'Un document qui pose question.' *L'Eglise canadienne* 23 (1990): 465-68. German translation: 'Eine Theologe antwortet auf die Instruktion.' In *Streitgesprach um Theologie und Lehramt: Die Instruktion über die kirchliche Berufung des Theologen in der Diskussion*, edited by Peter Hunermann and Dietmar Wieth, 99-107. Frankfurt-am-Main: Josef Knecht, 1991.

'Changing Church Teachings.' *Grail: An Ecumenical Journal* 6: 13- 40.

'Newer Theology of the Papal and Episcopal Conferences.' In *The Role and Exercise of Authority in the Church: Roman Catholic/United Church Dialogue, 1986-1990*, edited by Donna Geemaert. Ottawa: CCCB. Pp. 9.

'Remarks on the Paper by Hallet Llewellyn, "Reflections on the Place of Authority in the Church".' Ibid., pp. 7.

(With Michael J. Buckley, Margaret Farley, John Ford, and James Provost.) *Report of the Catholic Theological Society of America Committee on the Profession of Faith and the Oath of Fidelity (April I5, 1990)*. Silver Spring, Md.: Washington Theological Union. Pp. 133.

1991:

Faith, History and Cultures: Stability and Change in Church Teachings. The Pere Marquette Lecture in Theology, 1991. Milwaukee: Marquette University Press. Pp. 63.

'The International Theological Commission.' In *Modern Catholicism: Vatican II and After*, edited by Adrian Hastings, 194-99. London: SPCK; New York: Oxford University Press.

'"The Truth of Human Nature" according to Thomas Aquinas: Theology and Science in Interaction.' In *Philosophy and the God of Abraham: Essays in Memory of James A. Weisheipl, OP*, edited by R. James Long, 161-77. Papers in Mediaeval Studies 12. Toronto: Pontifical Institute of Mediaeval Studies.

'The Unity of the Church and the Multitude of Nations.' In *Kirchen im Kontext unterschiedlicher Kulturen: Auf dem Weg ins dritte Jahrtausend*, edited by Karl Christian Felmy, Georg Kretschmar, Fairy von Lilienfeld, Trutz Rendtorff, and Claus-Jürgen Roepke, 69-90. Gottingen: Vandenhoeck & Ruprecht. [Paper given at the *Internationale Okomene-Symposion* of the Evangelischen Akademie Tutzing, Germany, 16-19 May 1990.]

'The Catholic Theological Society of America.' In *Bulletin of the European Society for Catholic Theology*, the *Europaische Gesellschaft fur katholische Theologie*, etc. 2/1 (Tubingen): 105-13.

'Was Scripture used as a Critique of Development of Dogma in Relation to the Definitions of the Immaculate Conception, Infallibility of Papal Teaching, and Mary's Assumption?' Paper given at the Lutheran-Catholic Dialogue, February 1991 (submitted to the press).

'Catholic Theology and the Retrieval of Its Intellectual Tradition: Problems and Possibilities' (Presidential Address). In *The Catholic Theological Society of America: Proceedings of the Forty-Sixth Annual Convention, Atlanta, June 12-15, 1991.* 46: 75-94.

'Homily at the Catholic Theological Society of America convention liturgy, Feast of St Anthony of Padua, Doctor of the Church.' Ibid., 219-22.

Citation for the John Courtney Murray Award of the Catholic Theological Society of America. Ibid., 207-8.

1992:

'*Quaestiones* Concerning Christ from the First Half of the Thirteenth Century: VI. *Quaestiones* from Douai MS. 434: Saving Activities of Christ.' *Mediaeval Studies* 52: 1-48.

'Theological Trends: Pluralism in Christian Spirituality.' *The Way: Contemporary Christian Spirituality* 32: 54-61.

'Aquinas' Spirituality for Christ's Faithful Living in the World.' *Spirituality Today* 44: 11-31.

'How Do Historians Determine What Is Authentic Christianity?' *Historical Papers 1992: Canadian Society of Church History* (Annual Conference, University of Prince Edward Island, June 8-9, 1992), edited by Bruce L. Guenther, 146-50.

(With Denise Callaghan, Tom Callaghan, Velma Goetting, Robert Howell, and Carole Thompson.) *Lay Association within the Congregation of St Basil: Final Report of the Committee established by the General Chapter of the Congregation of St Basil, 1989.* Toronto: Basilian Fathers. Pp. 34.

1993:

'Guerric of Saint-Quentin, OP, on the Question: Utrum Filius Dei esset incarnatus si homo non peccasset?' In *Ordo Sapientiae et Amoris: Image et message de saint Thomas d'Aquin à travers les recentes etudes historiques, hermeneutiques et doctrinales: Hommage au Professeur Jean-Pierre Torrell, OP à l'occasion de son 65 anniversaire*, edited by Carlos-Josaphat Pinto de Oliveira, OP, 509-37. Studia Friburgensia, Nouvelle Series, 78. Fribourg/Suisse: Editions Universitaires.

'Western Medieval Spirituality.' In *The New Dictionary of Catholic Spirituality*, edited by Michael Downey, 1027-39. Collegeville, Minn.: The Liturgical Press.

'Michael McMahon Sheehan, CSB, MSD (1925-1992).' *Mediaeval Studies* 53: vii-xi (with bibliography compiled by Mary C. English and James K. Farge, pp. xi-xvi).

'Spirituality, Christian.' *The New Dictionary of Catholic Spirituality*, edited by Michael Downey, 931-38. Collegeville, Minn.: The Liturgical Press.

Review of R.W. Southern, *Saint Anselm: A Portrait in a Landscape* (Cambridge and New York: Cambridge University Press, 1990; rpt. 1991), in *Theological Studies* 54: 347-50.

'Meditation: Love, not partisan rancour, keeps us on Jesus' way.' *Catholic New Times* 17/4, 21 February, p. 3.

1994:

'"Tradition" in Thomas Aquinas's Scriptural Commentaries.' In *The Quadrilog: Tradition and the Future of Ecumenism: Essays in Honor of George H. Tavard*, edited by Kenneth Hagen, 43-60. Collegeville, Minn.: The Liturgical Press.

'An Important New Study of Thomas Aquinas: Jean-Pierre Torrell's *Initiation à saint Thomas d'Aquin.*' *The Thomist* 58: 489-99.

'Broadening the Focus: Context as a Corrective Lens in Reading Historical Works in Spirituality.' *Christian Spirituality Bulletin: Journal of the Society for the Study of Christian Spirituality* 2/1: 1, 3-5.

1995:

'Loving Friendship According to Thomas Aquinas.' Chapter 6 in *The Nature and Pursuit of Love: The Philosophy of Irving Singer*, edited by David Goicoechea, 128-41. Amherst, NY: Prometheus Books.

'Catholic Theological Society of America.' In *The HarperCollins Encyclopedia of Catholicism*, edited by Richard P. McBrien, p. 287. San Francisco: HarperCollins.

'Chenu, M.-D. [Marie-Dominique].' Ibid., 303-4.

'International Theological Commission.' Ibid., 673.

'St. Thomas Aquinas.' Ibid., 83-89.

'Saulchoir, Le.' Ibid., 1164.

'Scholasticism.' Ibid., 1169.

'Summa Contra Gentiles.' Ibid., 1229-30.

'Summa Theologiae.' Ibid., 1229-30.

1996:

Review of David B. Burrell, *Freedom and Creation in Three Traditions* (Notre Dame, Ind.: University of Notre Dame Press, 1993), in *Horizons: The Journal of the College Theology Society* 23/1: 190-91.

Review of Giles Constable, *Three Studies in Medieval Religious and Social Thought* (Cambridge and New York: Cambridge University Press, 1995), in *Horizons: The Journal of the College Theology Society* 23/3, 334-336.

Writings Published Posthumously

1997

'Theologie: Westen.' In *Lexikon des Mittelalters*, 9 vols., edited by Thomas Meier and Charlotte Bretscher-Gisiger, 8: 650-55. Munich: Artemis & Winkler.

1998

'Michael Sheehan: A Personal Profile by a Friend.' In *Women, Marriage, and Family in Medieval Christendom: Essays in Memory of Michael M. Sheehan, CSB*, edited by Constance Rousseau, pp. 1-10. Studies in Medieval Culture, 37. Kalamazoo, Mich.: University of Western Michigan Press.

2002

Guerric of Saint-Quentin, *Quaestiones de quolibet*, ed. W.H. Principe and J. Black, Studies and Texts, 143. Toronto: Pontifical Institute of Mediaeval Studies. Pp. 462.

Index